ATLA Monograph Series
edited by Dr. Kenneth E. Rowe

1. Ronald L. Grimes. *The Divine Imagination: William Blake's Major Prophetic Visions.* 1972.
2. George D. Kelsey. *Social Ethics Among Southern Baptists, 1917–1969.* 1973.
3. Hilda Adam Kring. *The Harmonists: A Folk-Cultural Approach.* 1973.
4. J. Steven O'Malley. *Pilgrimage of Faith: The Legacy of the Otterbeins.* 1973.
5. Charles Edwin Jones. *Perfectionist Persuasion: The Holiness Movement and American Methodism. 1867–1936.* 1974.
6. Donald E. Byrne, Jr. *No Foot of Land: Folklore of American Methodist Itinerants.* 1975.
7. Milton C. Sernett. *Black Religion and American Evangelicalism: White Protestants, Plantation Missions, and the Flowering of Negro Christianity, 1787–1865.* 1975.
8. Eva Fleischner. *Judaism in German Christian Theology Since 1945: Christianity and Israel Considered in Terms of Mission.* 1975.
9. Walter James Lowe. *Mystery & The Unconscious: A Study in the Thought of Paul Ricoeur.* 1977.
10. Norris Magnuson. *Salvation in the Slums: Evangelical Social Work, 1865–1920.* 1977.
11. William Sherman Minor. *Creativity in Henry Nelson Wieman.* 1977.
12. Thomas Virgil Peterson. *Ham and Japheth: The Mythic World of Whites in the Antebellum South.* 1978.
13. Randall K. Burkett. *Garveyism as a Religious Movement: The Institutionalization of a Black Civil Religion.* 1978.
14. Roger G. Betsworth. *The Radical Movement of the 1960's.* 1980.
15. Alice Cowan Cochran. *Miners, Merchants, and Missionaries: The Roles of Missionaries and Pioneer Churches in the Colorado Gold Rush and Its Aftermath, 1858–1870.* 1980.

16. Irene Lawrence. *Linguistics and Theology: The Significance of Noam Chomsky for Theological Construction.* 1980.
17. Richard E. Williams. *Called and Chosen: The Story of Mother Rebecca Jackson and the Philadelphia Shakers.* 1981.
18. Arthur C. Repp, Sr. *Luther's Catechism Comes to America: Theological Effects on the Issues of the Small Catechism Prepared In or For America Prior to 1850.* 1982.
19. Lewis V. Baldwin. *"Invisible" Strands in African Methodism.* 1983.
20. David W. Gill. *The Word of God in the Ethics of Jacques Ellul.* 1984.
21. Robert Booth Fowler. *Religion and Politics in America.* 1985.
22. Page Putnam Miller. *A Claim to New Roles.* 1985.
23. C. Howard Smith. *Scandinavian Hymnody from the Reformation to the Present.* 1987.
24. Bernard T. Adeney. *Just War, Political Realism, and Faith.* 1988.
25. Paul Wesley Chilcote. *John Wesley and the Women Preachers of Early Methodism.* 1991.
26. Samuel J. Rogal. *A General Introduction of Hymnody and Congregational Song.* 1991.
27. Howard A. Barnes. *Horace Bushnell and the Virtuous Republic.* 1991.
28. Sondra A. O'Neale. *Jupiter Hammon and the Biblical Beginnings of African-American Literature.* 1993.
29. Kathleen P. Deignan. *Christ Spirit: The Eschatology of Shaker Christianity.* 1992.
30. D. Elwood Dunn. *A History of the Episcopal Church in Liberia, 1821–1980.* 1992.
31. Terrance L. Tiessen. *Irenaeus on the Salvation of the Unevangelized.* 1993.
32. James E. McGoldrick. *Crucial Questions in Baptist History.* 1993.

IRENAEUS ON THE SALVATION OF THE UNEVANGELIZED

by

Terrance L. Tiessen

ATLA Monograph Series, No. 31

The Scarecrow Press, Inc.
Metuchen, N.J., & London
1993

BT
759
.T54
1993

British Library Cataloguing-in-Publication data available

Library of Congress Cataloging-in-Publication Data

Tiessen, Terrance L., 1944-
    Irenaeus on the salvation of the unevangelized / by Terrance L.
Tiessen.
        p.   cm. -- (ATLA monograph series ; no. 31)
    Includes bibliographical references and indexes.
    ISBN 0-8108-2682-8 (alk. paper)
    1. Salvation outside the church--History of doctrines--Early
church, ca. 30-600. 2. Irenaeus, Saint, Bishop of Lyon. I. Title.
II. Series.
BT759.T54 1993
234--dc20   93-18796

To my wife, Gail, whose encouragement
has contributed significantly to the
completion of this work.

CONTENTS

Editor's Foreword   viii
Preface   ix
List of Abbreviated Journal Titles   xi

1. The Issue   1
A. The Challenge of Religious Pluralism   1
B. Irenaeus and Modern Responses to the
    Challenge of Religious Pluralism   4
C. Karl Rahner and "Anonymous
    Christianity"   11
D. The Scope and Procedure of This Study   28

**2. The Gnostic Heresy: Context of Irenaeus's
Theology of Revelation and Salvation**   35
A. Irenaeus and the Gnostics   35
B. The Quest for Knowledge of the
    Unknown Bythos   47
C. Human Salvation and the Knowledge
    of God   53
D. The *Gospel of Truth*   57
E. The Gnostics and the Salvation of
    the Non-Christian   61

**3. The Missiological Context of
Irenaeus's View of the Unevangelized**   64
A. The Significance of Irenaeus's Perspective
    on the Extent of Evangelization
    for His View of the Unevangelized   64
B. The Geographical Extent of the Church
    at the End of the Second Century   67

C. Early Christian Views of the State of
    Evangelization in the Second Century   74
D. Irenaeus on the Extent of Evangelization   77
E. Conclusion   81

**4. The Father: Incomprehensible, but
    Progressively Making Himself Known   82**
A. The Transcendent Father   82
B. The Father's Life-Giving Self-Revelation   86
C. Concluding Observations Concerning
    the Father and the Unevangelized   123

5. The Son: Exclusive Revealer of the Father 127
A. The Exclusiveness of the Son's
    Mediation of Revelation   127
B. The Universal Revelation of the Father
    by the Word in Creation and Providence   131
C. The Presence of the Word Prior to
    the Incarnation   142
D. Revelation in the Incarnation   149
E. Revelation in the Millennium and
    in Eternity   165
F. Concluding Observations Concerning
    the Son and the Unevangelized   170

6. The Spirit: Revealer of the Son   174
A. The Spirit in Creation and Providence   175
B. The Spirit and Old Testament Revelation   177
C. The Spirit and the Son   179
D. The Spirit and Scripture   181
E. The Spirit in the Church and
    in the Believer   182
F. Concluding Observations Concerning
    the Spirit and the Unevangelized   185

Contents   vii

**7. The Church: Recipient, Preserver, and
   Proclaimer of Divine Revelation**   **188**
A. The Challenge of the Gnostic Claim
   to a "Living Voice"   188
B. The Handing on of the Apostolic Faith
   to the Church   190
C. The Church as the Way of Truth and of Life   206
D. Concluding Observations on the Church
   and the Unevangelized   210

8. The Human Response to Divine Revelation   **213**
A. The Twofold Destiny of Humankind   213
B. Faith: The Saving Response to
   Divine Revelation   226
C. Concluding Observations   244

9. Conclusion   **250**
A. A Summary of Irenaeus's Doctrine of
   Divine Revelation and the Salvation
   of the Unevangelized   251
B. Irenaeus and "Anonymous Christianity"   263
C. A Final Statement   280

Bibliography   **283**
A. Christianity and Non-Christians   283
B. Irenaeus and the Gnostics   292
C. The Missiological Context   296
D. Irenaeus   298

Index of References to Irenaeus's Works   307
Index of Names and Subjects   312
About the Author   318

EDITOR'S FOREWORD

Since 1972 the American Theological Library Association has undertaken responsibility for a modest monograph series in the field of religious studies. Our aim in this series is to publish two dissertations of quality in revised form each year. Titles are selected from studies in a wide range of religious and theological disciplines. We are pleased to publish Terrance Tiessen's study *Irenaeus on the Salvation of the Unevangelized* as number 31 in the ATLA Monograph Series.

Professor Tiessen began his studies at Ontario Bible College and Wilfrid Laurier University, took an M.A. in Biblical Studies at Wheaton Graduate School, and a Th.M. at Westminster Theological Seminary. Following additional graduate study at the University of St. Michael's, Toronto, Tiessen completed the doctorate in systematic and moral theology at Ateneo de Manila University. He is currently Professor of Theology and Ethics at Providence Theological Seminary, Otterburne, Manitoba, Canada.

Kenneth E. Rowe
Series editor

Drew University Library
Madison, NJ 07940
USA

PREFACE

The fate of those who do not hear the gospel has been the focus of much attention in recent years. As theologians have grappled with the question, they have naturally looked to the past for indications of how the Church has responded to the question in previous times. The earliest years of the Church's life, when it was still a small part of the world's population, are a particularly interesting area for study. Among the early theologians of the Church, Irenaeus stands out for his knowledge of Christian Scripture and his efforts to counter the dangerous theological perspectives arising within the Church. The study of his work is certain to enrich the thought of anyone willing to give it some time.

In recognition of the current language conventions, gender-inclusive language has been used in this work. Many of the sources cited, however, were written in a time when masculine pronouns or references to men were used generically. To avoid the distraction of square-bracketed changes or the use of "[sic]," no attempt has been made to update the language in quotations. Readers are asked to bear this in mind.

I am thankful to the Council of SEND International of the Philippines and to the administration of the Asian Theological Seminary for the adjustments made in my teaching assignment which enabled me to devote myself to this study.

Although I must take responsibility for the conclusions which have been reached in this study, I am indebted to Fr. Joseph Smith, S.J., for the help that his

questions and comments provided during early drafts of
this work. His own diligence as a scholar has been a
challenging example. My understanding of Irenaeus's
thought has been greatly enhanced by the opportunity to
discuss my ideas with Fr. Smith.

My own thoughts often become more clear when
I express them to someone else. For this reason, I am
grateful to my wife, who has become a companion and a
participant in the process of trying to understand the
mind of Irenaeus through the writings that he has left
us.

In the course of this study, I have come to admire
and appreciate Irenaeus himself. I am thankful that he
was willing to enter the lists against the Gnostics in
defense of the faith handed down by the apostles. Despite
the many factors that separate me from his own theological context, and in spite of the inevitable differences in
theological methodology, I have been enriched through
the hours spent in his writings.

In my understanding of the work of Irenaeus, I
have been helped by the English translation of Alexander
Roberts and the French translation of Adelin Rousseau
and others who helped in the production of the Sources
chrétiennes series.

I have been very conscious of the providential
assistance of God, both through the instrumentality of
the people already mentioned and in the growth of my
insight into divine truth through the help of Irenaeus
and others whose works I have read in the preparation
of this study. I am thankful for the grace of God that has
blessed me with such rich opportunities to know him in
Christ. I rejoice in the awareness that a day is coming
when God will be worshiped by a great host of people
purchased by the blood of Christ, from every tribe and
language and people and nation (Revelation 5:9).

LIST OF ABBREVIATED JOURNAL TITLES

ATR	*Anglican Theological Review*
BSac	*Bibliotheca Sacra*
CanJT	*Canadian Journal of Theology*
ClerM	*Clergy Monthly*
ClerR	*Clergy Review*
Con	*Continuum*
ConBapt	*Conservative Baptist*
ConTQ	*Concordia Theological Quarterly*
CT	*Christianity Today*
CTJ	*Calvin Theological Journal*
CTTW	*Christ to the World*
DDR	*Duke Divinity Review*
Diak	*Diakonia*
DomSt	*Dominican Studies*
EMQ	*Evangelical Missions Quarterly*
ETL	*Ephemerides theologicae lovanienses*
EvJ	*Evangelical Journal*
EvQ	*Evangelical Quarterly*
EvRT	*Evangelical Review of Theology*
ExpTim	*Expository Times*
FranSt	*Franciscan Studies*
Greg	*Gregorianum*
Hor	*Horizons*
HTR	*Harvard Theological Review*
IBMR	*International Bulletin of Missionary Research*
IJT	*Indian Journal of Theology*
JAAR	*Journal of the American Academy of Religion*
JBR	*Journal of Bible and Religion*
JEcSt	*Journal of Ecumenical Studies*

JETS	*Journal of the Evangelical Theological Society*
JR	*Journal of Religion*
JTS	*Journal of Theological Studies*
LQ	*Lutheran Quarterly*
LV	*Lumière et vie*
Miss	*Missiology*
ModTh	*Modern Theology*
NRT	*La nouvelle revue théologique*
NZM	*Neue Zeitschrift für Missionswissenschaft*
RechSR	*Recherches de science religieuse*
RevExp	*Review and Expositor*
RScRel	*Revue des sciences religieuses*
RSR	*Religious Studies Review*
RUO	*Revue de l'université d'Ottawa*
SEAJT	*South East Asia Journal of Theology*
SecCent	*Second Century*
SJT	*Scottish Journal of Theology*
StudMiss	*Studia missionalia*
StudPat	*Studia patristica*
TD	*Theology Digest*
Th	*Theology*
Thom	*Thomist*
TS	*Theological Studies*
TT	*Theology Today*
TZ	*Theologische Zeitschrift*
USQR	*Union Seminary Quarterly Review*
VigChr	*Vigiliae christianae*
WW	*Word and World*
ZKT	*Zeitschrift für katholische Theologie*
ZMR	*Zeitschrift für Missionswissenschaft ünd Religionswissenschaft*
ZNW	*Zeitschrift für die neutestamentliche Wissenschaft*

1. THE ISSUE

A. The Challenge of Religious Pluralism

Through the centuries, Christianity has been characterized by a strong conviction of the uniqueness of Jesus Christ as the world's Savior. Coupled with this has been an emphasis on the unique role of the Christian Church in the saving work of divine grace, a role frequently described in the words of Cyprian, *extra ecclesiam nulla salus* (outside of the Church, there is no salvation). While Protestant theology has placed less stress on the visible Church as instrument than has Roman Catholic theology, it has been equally emphatic concerning the necessity of the preaching of the Gospel and the necessity of repentance and faith on the part of those who hear it.[1] The work of Christian missions was pursued with zeal and much sacrifice in the conviction that the salvation of millions of individuals depends on their knowledge of Christ through the preaching of the Gospel. Churches were stirred to send and to support missionaries in response to the vision of millions going to hell for lack of an opportunity to hear of Christ.

It would be wrong to suggest that these convictions no longer exist in the minds of many Christian Church members, theologians, and missionaries. At the same time, however, one must take cognizance of the

---

[1]See George Lindbeck, "*Fides ex auditu* and the Salvation of the Non-Christians: Contemporary Catholic and Protestant Positions," in *The Gospel and the Ambiguities of the Church*, ed. Vilmos Vajta (Philadelphia: Fortress Press, 1974), 94.

number of influential theologians and missiologists, Protestant and Catholic, who are troubled by the implications of this stress on the absoluteness of Christianity.[2] Writing in 1966, Hans Küng expressed the uneasiness shared by many of his fellows.[3] He questioned that one could keep on saying that there is no salvation outside of the Church in the face of the statistics concerning the Christian Church. Of the more than three billion inhabitants of the earth, only about five hundred and eighty four million were Catholics. He was troubled by the fact that in India only 2.4 percent were Christians, while in China and Japan the number was even smaller, about 0.5 percent. Furthermore, Küng saw little hope that this situation would change significantly in the future.

While evangelical Protestant theologians have generally continued to take a hard line on the absoluteness and uniqueness of Christ for salvation and on the necessity of explicit faith in Christ, the same may not be as true in the pew.[4] One of the great missionary events for the evangelical church in North America has been the student mission conferences held in Urbana, Illinois, under the auspices of the Inter-Varsity Christian Fellowship. The results of five thousand replies to a questionnaire distributed to eight thousand students at one of these conferences are significant. Only 37 percent

---

[2]Bruce Demarest reviews this denial of the absoluteness of Christianity by Arnold Toynbee and others. *General Revelation: Historical Views and Contemporary Issues* (Grand Rapids: Zondervan, 1982), 17-19.

[3]Hans Küng, *Freedom Today*, trans. Cecily Hastings (New York: Sheed & Ward, 1966), 112-13.

[4]Cf. Lindbeck, 108-9. He suggests that the general failure of Protestant theologians to address the question of the salvation of non-Christians is due to its university orientation. They are unaware of the concern of many people in the churches. In this regard, he considers Catholic theology to be more relevant pastorally.

believed that a "person who does not hear the gospel is eternally lost," and 25 percent believed that "man will be saved or lost on the basis of how well he followed what he did know."[5] A case for the sufficiency of general revelation for the salvation of the unevangelized is also being made by contemporary evangelical writers.[6] Clark Pinnock, for instance, itemizes three "items of useful insight" that lead him to a larger hope than evangelicals have traditionally had. These are "the concept of inculpable unbelief or anonymous faith," the certainty that "God judges the heathen in relation to the light they have," and "the hope of an opportunity to accept Christ's salvation after death."[7]

In spite of great effort on the part of Christian missionaries, aided in the past by the political and economic power of their home countries, the great non-Christian world religions—Hinduism, Buddhism, and Islam—remain. Indeed, they appear in some instances to be gaining fresh vigor. Added to their challenge is that of atheistic Communism, which controls the lives of many more of our contemporaries. To Hans Küng, this persisting religious plurality "makes questionable a claim to be absolute on the part of that faith which, more than, and in a different sense from, any other world religion, claims the support of a uniquely valid revelation of God."[8]

---

[5] J. Ronald Blue, "Untold Billions: Are They Really Lost?" *BSac* 138 (October-December 1981):340-41.

[6] E.g. Norman Anderson, *Christianity and World Religions: The Challenge of Pluralism* (Leicester: Inter-Varsity Press, 1984), 175; Robert Brow, review of *The World Religions*, by Norman Anderson, in *CT* 15 (July 2, 1971):25-26; Evert D. Osburn, "Those Who Have Never Heard: Have They No Hope?" *JETS* 32 (September 1989):367-72.

[7] Clark H. Pinnock, "Toward an Evangelical Theology of Religions," *JETS* 33 (September 1990):367-68.

[8] Ibid., 117.

B. Irenaeus and Modern Responses to the Challenge of Religious Pluralism

As theologians have grappled with the persistent challenge of religious pluralism, responses have varied. M. Blanchard enumerates five theories that have been proposed regarding the relation of Christianity to other religions: 1) selective borrower of good ideas; 2) companion in the evolution of an ultimate universal religion; 3) unique revelation of God to humanity; 4) fulfillment of the good in other religions; and 5) antithesis of other religions, discontinuous from them and often condemnatory of the bad in them.[9] One could doubtless list other modifications of these approaches. However, it is not the purpose of this study to survey, or to develop, a theology of religions as such. Blanchard himself points to the fourth theory as very popular, and suggests that it begins with Justin Martyr and Clement of Alexandria.[10] It is this more optimistic attitude concerning the value of non-Christian religions, and an optimism concerning the salvation of non-Christians, which is the particular interest of this study, especially as appeal is made to the second- and third-century Fathers, and more specifically to Irenaeus, as early examples of this perspective.

In recent years, a number of authors have cited second-century antecedents of an openness to the value of non-Christian religions or, at least, to the salvation of non-Christians. Frequently such references make use of the term "anonymous Christianity" to describe the view

---

[9]M. Blanchard, "Christianity as Fulfilment and Antithesis," *IJT* 17 (1968):5. Another helpful survey of the various perspectives on the respective roles of Christ and the Christian Church in salvation is found in J. Peter Schineller, "Christ and Church: A Spectrum of Views," *TS* 37 (December 1976):545-66.

[10]Blanchard, 7.

that they are presenting and, almost inevitably, credit is given to Karl Rahner for his development of this concept. Rahner's view has had widespread acceptance, but is not without its opponents[11] or its modifiers. Particularly one notes a questioning of the concept of "anonymous Christianity" in favor of a simple acceptance of "anonymous Christians."[12]

A number of the writers who have been favorably impressed by Rahner's concept of "anonymous Christianity," however, have suggested the anticipation of his ideas in the second and third century. James Dupuis, for instance, writes enthusiastically of second-century Logos or Cosmic-Christ theology as establishing "a first regime of salvation, distinct from that given by God to Israel and from the decisive economy of salvation introduced by the incarnation."[13] This cosmic regime of salvation was imperfect and was destined to pass away. Once Christ was announced to the nations they were obligated to turn to him. In the meantime, however, the cosmic regime was "nonetheless willed by God and represented a true economy of salvation established by Him."[14] What is particularly significant for this study is Dupuis's

---

[11]For instance, Paul Hacker, "The Christian Attitude Toward Non-Christian Religions: Some Critical and Positive Reflections," *ZMR* 55 (1971):81-97; Henry van Straelen, *The Catholic Encounter with World Religions* (Westminster, Maryland: Newman Press, 1966), 121-23; and *Ouverture à l'autre laquelle? L'apostolat missionnaire et le monde non chrétien* (Paris: Beauchesne, 1982), 40,65-66,176-218; J. I. Packer, "Are Non-Christian Faiths Ways of Salvation?" *BSac* 130 (April-June 1973):112-14; and Demarest, 194-95.

[12]Henri de Lubac, *The Church: Paradox and Mystery*, trans. James R. Dunne (Staten Island, New York: Alba House, 1969), 87.

[13]James Dupuis, "The Salvific Value of Non-Christian Religions," in *Service and Salvation: Nagpur Theological Conference on Evangelization*, ed. Joseph Pathrapankal (Bangalore: Theological Publications in India, 1973), 218.

[14]Ibid.

statement that "in some passages of Justin, Irenaeus and Clement, it is difficult not to recognize an anticipation of some traits of the present theology of 'anonymous Christianity.' The world religions constitute for the nations authentic ways of salvation, imperfect but real."[15]

In another article, Dupuis studies "The Cosmic Christ in the Early Fathers,"[16] with special attention to the work of Justin and Irenaeus. Summing up Justin's thought, he suggests that the implications are obvious, namely, that "all possession of religious truth as well as all righteous conduct come to all men through a personal manifestation of the eternal Word."[17] He asks then "if this is not, down to the very expression, the theology of 'anonymous Christianity,' even eighteen centuries before K. Rahner."[18] Dupuis does not make so direct a statement concerning the relationship of Irenaeus's work to Rahner's, but he sees Irenaeus as "organizing systematically the theology for which Justin had laid the foundation, in his theology of the Logos-revelation."[19] Irenaeus not only brought out the historical significance of the Mosaic and Christian dispensations, but "he also integrated the pre-Mosaic dispensation in the history of salvation, thus making room for a salvific value of pre-biblical religions."[20]

One finds similar reference to the second-century antecedents in the work of Gerald O'Collins, who is

----

[15]Ibid.

[16]*IJT* 15 (July-September 1966):106-20. The article is also reproduced in *Jesus Christ and His Spirit: Theological Approaches*, ed. James Dupuis (Bangalore: Theological Publications in India, 1977), 3-19.

[17]Ibid., 111.

[18]Ibid.

[19]Ibid.

[20]Ibid.

impressed by the use made of the notion of the *Logos spermatikos.*

> In this vision of things the salvation which was offered to those living before Christ came through the *Word* of God who would be made flesh in the fullness of time. As agent of creation the Word was and is always present at least as a seed (*spermatikos*) in every human being. Thus those who lived before the incarnation were nourished by the divine truth and set on the way of salvation—by the Word of God. This line of thought flowered with Justin, Clement of Alexandria and Irenaeus who saw the Old Testament prophets and the Greek philosophers as "Christians before Christ."[21]

Eugene Hillman, discussing what he calls a "wider ecumenism," is likewise convinced that "anonymous Christianity" is not just some "modern theory" conjured up in order to explain away the widespread disobedience of Christians with regard to the Lord's final command that they should summon his disciples out of every nation.[22] He believes it to be "an ancient belief of Christianity, rooted in Scripture, . . . and clearly formulated as far as back as the days of Justin Martyr."[23] Nor is Justin the only one to whom appeal may be made. Hillman includes Irenaeus, Clement of Alexandria and Origen in "this sympathetic and optimistic application of St. John's Logos theology."[24] This conjunction of Justin, Irenaeus and Clement of Alexandria appears again in the work of Ishanand Vempeny, who considers the Logos theology of these three early theologians to be the guide

---

[21]Gerald O'Collins, *Fundamental Theology* (New York: Paulist Press, 1981), 125.

[22]Eugene Hillman, *The Wider Ecumenism* (New York: Herder & Herder, 1968), 38.

[23]Ibid.

[24]Ibid., 39.

in forming a position with regard to the inspiration of non-biblical scriptures.[25]

Pietro Rossano finds in the christological titles Logos and Wisdom, as used by Justin, Irenaeus, Clement of Alexandria, Origen, St. Augustine, and St. Gregory of Nyssa, "a key for reading and appreciating the entire ethico-religious heritage of antiquity."[26] He asks whether there is revelation in the religions and, if so, what form it takes, and then traces the direction taken by the magisterium back to Irenaeus and other early Fathers.

> The Declaration *Nostra aetate* (no. 2) expresses a general attitude of the Council when it sees in the religions "a ray" of the Word which takes the form of "ways of conduct and life." In fact, the Council itself and later Church documents such as the Apostolic Exhortation *Evangelii nuntiandi* (no. 53) and the Encyclical Letter *Redemptor hominis* (nos. 11-12), while taking no explicit position on the problem, lead the reader to a point from which there seems to be no turning back. A current of theological thought that goes back to Justin, Irenaeus, Clement of Alexandria, and Origen and that has never run dry at any time.[27]

In tracing the historical background of "anonymous Christianity," Maurice Boutin similarly cites patristic anticipation in Justin's concept of the *Logos spermatikos*, as well as Augustine's statement that the true religion existed before Christ's coming, though it was not then called Christian.[28]

---

[25]*Inspiration in Non-Biblical Scriptures* (Bangalore: Theological Publications in India, n.d.), 61.

[26]"Theology and Religions," in *Problems and Perspectives of Fundamental Theology*, eds. René Latourelle and Gerald O'Collins, trans. Matthew J. O'Connell (New York: Paulist Press, 1982), 303.

[27]Ibid., 305.

[28]Maurice Boutin, "Anonymous Christianity: A Paradigm for Interreligious Encounter?" *JEcSt* 20 (Fall 1983):609, citing Augustine's *Retractationes*, I, XIII, 3.

These attempts to provide support for "anonymous Christianity," or other modern theories regarding the state of the non-Christian, by citing antecedence in Justin, Irenaeus and Clement deserve to be examined. It is also apparent, however, as one reads in the theology of religions, that Justin and Clement are considered to be more obviously forerunners than was Irenaeus. Reference is often made to them, without the additional mention of Irenaeus. For this reason, a study of Irenaeus is most needed, in order to establish how rightly he may be cited as anticipating "anonymous Christianity," if only in seed form. For instance, Auguste Luneau has urged us to see the profound value and "the religious richness of every faith"; to value not only individuals, but also the religions they profess. He suggests that, in this regard, "the attitude of a Justin or a Clement is more useful than that of a Jerome or an Augustine."[29] This leaves the reader wondering in which class Irenaeus ought to be placed. Not everyone is convinced that Justin and Clement can be understood in this way,[30] but a study of the justification for doing so

---

[29]"Pour aider au dialogue: les Pères et les religions non-chrétiennes," *NRT* 89 (September-October 1967):927. Cf. André Méhat, "La Philosophie troisième testament? La pensée grecque et la foi selon Clément d'Alexandrie," *LV* 32 (January-March 1983):15-23; George Lindbeck, who suggests that the openness of Rahner and others, including Vatican II's Declaration on Non-Christian Religions, "is a contemporary form of the cosmic logos Christologies of some of the early fathers, beginning already with Justin Martyr in the second-century" (101). One wonders whether Lindbeck would include Irenaeus in his reference to "some of the early fathers."

[30]See for example, Hendrik Kraemer, *La foi chrétienne et les religions non-chrétiennes*, trans. Simone Mathil (Paris: Delachaux et Niestlé, 1956), 55-58; Henri de Lubac, *The Church: Paradox and Mystery*, 68-87; Gustave Martelet, *Les idées maîtresses de Vatican II: Introduction à l'esprit du Concile* (Paris: Desclée de Brouwer, 1966), 47-48; H. van Straelen, *The Catholic Encounter*, 121-23; and Paul

must wait until another time. It will be sufficient for this study to give careful attention to Irenaeus, without passing judgment on the cases of Justin and Clement.

This study will be helpful in the examination of general statements concerning what "the Church Fathers" or "early Christianity" believed, such as one finds in Paul Tillich's work. He says of "the Church Fathers" that "they tried to show convergent lines between the Christian message and the intrinsic quests of the pagan religions," and concerning early Christianity, that it "did not consider itself as a radical-exclusive, but as the all-inclusive religion," its perspective being: "'All that is true anywhere in the world belongs to us, the Christians.'"[31]

More recently, writing within a specifically Asian context, Raimundo Panikkar has made a similar generalization regarding the patristic period:

> Christian theology has always tried, especially in more recent centuries (*in the Patristic period things were different*), to accentuate the differences between Christianity and the "non-Christian" religions and to emphasize the newness of the Christian fact, both as revelation and as an ontological "new creation" [italics supplied].[32]

Such generalizations need to be examined by the study of *specific* Fathers and representatives of "early Christianity."

Hacker, "The Religions of the Gentiles as Viewed by the Fathers of the Church," *ZMR* 54 (1970):253-64. Hacker gives a negative reading on Justin and Clement and does not even include Irenaeus in his study.

[31]Paul Tillich, *Christianity and the Encounter of the World Religions* (New York: Columbia University Press, 1963), 34-35.

[32]*The Unknown Christ of Hinduism: Towards an Ecumenical Christophany*, revised and enlarged edition (Maryknoll, New York: Orbis Books, 1981), 164.

Heinz Schlette has made an important study of the judgment passed on the religions in the history of the Church. Concluding his survey of those various approaches, he suggests that it "brings out all the more urgently the need to take up and work out possible starting points, perhaps in the teaching of Scripture and the Fathers, for a positive evaluation of non-Christian religions."[33] It is hoped that this study will contribute a response to that broad challenge, in the case of one of those early Fathers.

C. Karl Rahner and "Anonymous Christianity"

Since it is specifically the view of Rahner that is identified as foreseen in Irenaeus and his contemporaries, a brief exposition of Rahner's position is in order. This will provide a framework with reference to which the doctrine of revelation in Irenaeus can be studied as to its possible correspondence with Rahner's position.

1. The reason for Rahner's theory

Karl Rahner is not concerned about the name which one gives to the concept he has labeled "anonymous Christianity." He would be willing to accept a better name, if one were suggested, but feels that no better designation has yet been proposed. It is to the concept rather than the name that he is committed.[34] Rahner rejects as ridiculous any suggestion that the

[33]Heinz Robert Schlette, *Towards a Theology of Religions*, trans. W. J. O'Hara (Freiburg: Herder, 1966), 28.

[34]Karl Rahner, "The One Christ and the Universality of Salvation." in *Theological Investigations*, (London: Darton, Longman & Todd, 1979), 16:218. (Hereafter *Theological Investigations* is cited as TI.)

notion is designed to console members of the Christian
Church regarding the diminishing percentage of those
who confess explicit Christian faith. On the contrary, the
theory arose from a need to correlate two facts of Catholic
teaching, as expressed by the Second Vatican Council.
The first fact is that a possibility of supernatural salvation has been granted to non-Christians, even if they do
not become Christian. The second is that "salvation
cannot be gained without reference to God and Christ."
It must be "a theistic and Christian salvation."[35] The
theory of "anonymous Christianity" which is here
reviewed is thus an attempt to provide an explanation of
how these facts may be understood without contradiction.

2. A definition of "anonymous Christianity"

Rahner defines the "anonymous Christian" as
"the pagan after the beginning of the Christian mission,
who lives in the state of Christ's grace through faith,
hope and love, yet who has no explicit knowledge of the
fact that his life is oriented in grace-given salvation to
Jesus Christ."[36] Elsewhere, he suggests that "anonymous
Christianity" is "what we call the condition of a man who
lives on the one hand in a state of grace and justification,
and yet on the other hand has not come into contact with
the explicit preaching of the Gospel and is consequently
not in a position to call himself a 'Christian.'"[37] To the
objection made by de Lubac, that it is acceptable to speak
of an "anonymous Christian" but not of "anonymous
Christianity," Rahner responds that if Christianity is

---

[35]Ibid.

[36]"Observations on the Problem of the 'Anonymous Christian,'" in
TI, Vol. 14 (Baltimore: Helicon Press, 1979), 283.

[37]"Atheism and Implicit Christianity," in *TI*, Vol. 9 (London:
Darton, Longman & Todd, 1972), 145.

understood as "the 'being Christian' of an individual Christian," then we can rightly speak of "anonymous Christianity."[38]

3. The foundation in Rahner's doctrine of grace

As Paul Hacker points out, Rahner's theory is understandable only on the basis of his doctrine of grace and of his philosophy.[39] Particularly important are his understandings of the nature of human existence, of divine revelation, and of the effect of the incarnation of Christ upon human beings. Rahner discerns two principles which must be kept in mind, namely "the necessity of Christian faith and the universal salvific will of God's love and omnipotence." These can be reconciled only by saying that "somehow all men must be capable of being members of the Church."[40] Furthermore, this capacity must be understood as "a real and historically concrete one," and not merely in the sense of an "abstract and purely logical possibility."[41] The revelation of the Word in Christ

> is not something which comes to us from without as entirely strange, but only the explicitation of what we already are by grace and what we experience at least incoherently in the limitlessness of our transcendence. The expressly Christian revelation becomes the explicit statement of the revelation of grace which man always experiences implicitly in the depths of his being.[42]

---

[38]"Observations on the Problem," 281.

[39]Hacker, 85.

[40]"Anonymous Christians," in *TI*, Vol. 6 (London: Darton, Longman & Todd, 1969), 391.

[41]Ibid.

[42]Ibid., 394.

The sincere will of God that all people should be saved is a fundamental point in Rahner's approach to the non-Christian. This will persists "in spite of original sin and also the personal sinfulness of man," and is the reason why God "offers every man, whatever the circumstances of life in which he finds himself, a genuine possibility of attaining to his own salvation."[43] Nor is this merely a "natural" beatitude; it is Christian salvation "that comes to him through supernatural grace and consists in a sharing in the life of God."[44] People never exist in a state of "pure" nature. They are "placed all along in the sphere of history and it is here that they are summoned by God."[45] This being true, it

> necessarily follows that "historical" man *as such* and "historical" revelation are in a positive sense mutually conditioning entities. The offering of salvation by God is already in existence prior to the practical proclamation of it, and it is the intrinsic factor that makes it possible.[46]

Rahner therefore believes that "saving history or its opposite, the history of perdition, is taking place wherever man of his own free decision either voluntarily undertakes his own mode of existence or alternately protests against it."[47] This is because of the fact that "this 'supernatural existential,' considered as God's act of

---

[43]"Church, Churches and Religions," in *TI*, Vol. 10 (New York: Herder & Herder, 1973), 33; cf. "Jesus Christ in the Non-Christian Religions," in *TI*, Vol. 17 (New York: Crossroad Publishing Co., 1981), 40.

[44]"Church, Churches and Religions," 33.

[45]"Anonymous Christianity and the Missionary Task of the Church," in *TI*, Vol. 12 (London: Darton, Longman & Todd, 1974), 167, n. 12.

[46]Ibid.

[47]"Church, Churches and Religions," 36.

self-bestowal which he offers to men, is in all cases grafted into the very roots of human existence."[48]

Rahner thus perceives two sides to the revelational event, a transcendental and an historical aspect. The first is this "supernaturally elevated transcendence" which is a person's "permanent though grace-given destiny."[49] It is operative at all times and in every place and is "present even by the very fact of being rejected."[50] Although everyone may not be able to express it at will and objectively in concepts, it is the "transcendental experience of the absolute and merciful closeness of God."[51] Although it is not possible to know for certain, Rahner hopes that the majority of people accept the free, gracious, divine self-revelation which is always a reality because of the offer of God's grace to all people "in all ages for Christ's sake."[52] It is efficacious by the fact of its being offered and because of what happens "in the inmost core" of spiritual people even when they are not able to reflect on it.[53]

> This grace alters man's consciousness, gives him, in scholastic terminology, a new, higher, gracious but non-reflexive "formal object" (transcendence to God's absolute being as beatitude); because at least the horizon of man's spiritual being, that infinite question with the infinite answer that is himself.[54]

---

[48]Ibid.
[49]Karl Rahner and Joseph Ratzinger, *Revelation and Tradition*, trans. W. J. O'Hara (New York: Herder & Herder, 1966), 13-14.
[50]Ibid.
[51]Ibid.
[52]*Concise Theological Dictionary*, 1965 ed., s.v. "Revelation," by Karl Rahner and Herbert Vorgrimler.
[53]Ibid.
[54]Ibid.

The second side of this revelation event is "the historical mediation, the explicit expression of the supernaturally transcendental experience."[55]

4. The nature of faith

Because God is active in a supernatural self-bestowal, raising and reorienting the transcendental dimension of the human spirit by the power of grace, we may say that "'revelation history' is always and everywhere taking place."[56] Although a person may not have recognized this supernatural self-bestowal, and may not have reflected upon it in conscious thought, "nevertheless it still constitutes an element in his transcendental awareness."[57] It is in this context, then, that the exercise of genuine faith in revelation, necessary for salvation, may be understood as taking place in the non-Christian. Because this human self-transcendence is necessarily directed towards God and is raised up by grace, faith in revelation is made available "although possibly without thematic reflection."[58] If people freely accept their own unlimited transcendence, "which is raised up by grace and directed to the immediate presence of God as its final goal," it is legitimate to say that they have genuine faith.[59]

Rahner is not surrendering the necessity of faith. He is not content, however, to appeal to a natural knowledge of God, since this course was rejected by

---

[55]Rahner and Ratzinger, *Revelation and Tradition*, 14.

[56]Ibid.

[57]Ibid. See also *Concise Theological Dictionary*, 1965 ed., s.v. "Revelation."

[58]"Anonymous and Explicit Faith," in *TI*, Vol. 16 (London: Darton, Longman & Todd, 1979), 55.

[59]Ibid.

Innocent XI, Pius XII and Vatican II. Nor does he appeal to a primitive and ultimate kind of revelation. This he sees as impossible because of the findings of modern paleontology and anthropology.[60] This possibility of exercising genuine faith is a gracious ability. Whether people recognize it or not, whether they reflect upon it or not, they are "oriented towards the immediacy of God as their final end."[61] This is because of the grace which is offered to them and implanted in them as their "freedom in the mode of a formal object and of a spiritual perspective of an *a priori* kind."[62]

> When man of his freedom accepts himself together with his *a priori* awareness which is already revelation, then that is present which can in the true and proper sense be called faith, even though this faith has not yet been objectively explicitated or conceptualized as the absolute openness of man to the immediacy of God in his act of self-imparting. Yet this *a priori* awareness of man (called revelation) is always accepted in faith wherever and whenever an individual in unreserved faithfulness to his own moral conscience accepts himself in freedom as he is, and so too in the as yet unrecognizable implications of the dynamism underlying the movement of his own spirit.[63]

---

[60]"Observations on the Problem," 286. See also Rahner and Ratzinger, *Revelation and Tradition*, 16.

[61]"Observations on the Problem," 288.

[62]Ibid.

[63]Ibid., 290. As J. A. DiNoia has pointed out, Rahner uses the concept "implicit faith" in quite a different sense from the normal use in theology. Traditionally, the term has designated "one who is a member of the community, who accepts what is taught in it as right, true and good and who undertakes to pattern his life in accord with these teachings *even though* he may not be able fully to articulate all the teachings of his community in their totality and complexity." "Implicit Faith, General Revelation and the State of Non-Christians," *Thom* 47 (April 1983):233.

5. Application to the situation of the atheist

The outworking of this concept of human existence in a state of revelation and grace is seen clearly in
Rahner's explanation of the statements of *Lumen
gentium* concerning the possibility of salvation of atheists
whose position is not regarded as the result and the
expression of personal sin and who act in accord with
their consciences.[64] Whether or not people have accepted
the grace, they are "always in a Christ-determined
situation," due to "the grace of Christ (as possibility and
obligation), which is at least a constant offer."[65] "What
we commonly call 'knowledge of God' is not . . . simply
the knowledge of God, but already the objectified concep-
tual and propositional interpretation of what we constantly know of God subjectively and apart from reflection."[66] The offer of supernatural grace and the free
acceptance of it which is thereby made possible are

> *always* and *everywhere* present (on account of God's desire for
> universal salvation, not because of the natural goodness of a
> moral act) where a man freely accepts his own
> transcendentality—which includes an implicit, transcendental
> theism—by means of a moral decision in absolute faithfulness to
> his conscience. . . . [Rahner assumes that] under these conditions
> there is always an occurrence of what Thomas calls *infusio et
> acceptatio gratiae*. . . . The concrete order of salvation together
> with the freely accepted transcendental theism which can even
> be found in an atheist, produces *implicit* Christianity.[67]

Rahner points out that theology has traditionally
thought only of a "natural" morality as possible in a
"heathen's" life. This is because of the valid assumption

---

[64]"Atheism and Implicit Christianity," *TI*, Vol. 9 (1972), 145-64.
[65]Ibid., 146.
[66]Ibid., 154.
[67]Ibid., 161.

that "justification is impossible without revealed faith" and that a *fides virtualis* cannot be a substitute for it; and because "it was thought impossible to imagine such a revealed faith in the case of a 'heathen,' let alone an atheist."[68] However, Rahner finds the possibility of revealed faith in the thesis of Thomism that

> every supernaturally elevated moral act on a man's part has, in connection with its essential elevation, a supernatural formal object which cannot be reached in any merely natural intellectual or moral act on his part, even if in both cases the material object, the objective, *a posteriori* content of the act is the same.[69]

Rahner sees his own view as similar to that of Thomas in that

> the elevation through grace of man's freely accepted transcendentality is in itself revelation, because it involves an *a priori* formal object of man's mind, not necessarily reflected in consciousness, which, *qua* formal object, cannot be reached by any natural intellectual ability but arises from God's self-communication in grace.[70]

Hence, "a theism which is elevated through grace and which is freely accepted (by the grace supplied by the possibility of faith) is a justifying theism and hence an implicit Christianity."[71]

6. The role of the Church in salvation

Even if one accepts Rahner's conceptualization of universal salvific grace and revelation, and the possibility of genuine faith as a person's acceptance of personal

---

[68]Ibid.
[69]Ibid., 162.
[70]Ibid., 163.
[71]Ibid.

transcendence (graciously directed, as it is, towards God), one may still be left wondering how the Church plays a role in salvation, particularly so exclusive and significant a role as has traditionally been ascribed to it. Rahner suggests that the two principles of "no salvation outside the Church" and of the possibility of being saved outside the visible church can be reconciled

> by saying that the real full membership of the Church is neces-
> sary as a means for salvation in the sense that it can also, under
> certain circumstances, be supplied for by an (explicitly or
> implicitly) desired membership of the Church. And in this sense
> actual full membership of the Church is necessary with a
> *conditional* necessity of means.[72]

The framework within which Rahner understands this Church membership is the doctrine of the Incarnation. By the fact that God the Son became man,

> the one human race became thereby fundamentally and radically
> called to share the life of God supernaturally. This calling to
> share supernaturally in the life of the triune God is fundamental-
> ly already given as a real fact in the world (and not merely as
> God's "intention" and "law") by simple fact of the Incarnation of
> the Word.[73]

Furthermore, because of this fact of the Incarnation, and by the natural unity of the human race, "humanity has already in advance become ontologically the real sanctification of individual men by grace and also the people of the children of God."[74] By virtue of this "consecration,"

---

[72]"Membership of the Church According to the Teaching of Pius XII's Encyclical 'Mystici Corporis Christi,'" in *TI*, Vol. 2 (1963), 45.
[73]Ibid., 81.
[74]Ibid., 82-83.

there is already a "'people of God' which extends as far as humanity itself."[75] When a person

> accepts the concrete reality of his nature totally, in the free act of a *supernatural* justification by faith and love, the *membership of the people of God* becomes *the expression of this justifying act.* . . . [In that case,] the act of justification itself . . . finds expression in something really different from itself, viz. in membership of the people of God, which, in its turn, is in reality ordained to the membership of the Church in the proper sense. . . . Precisely because man as a concrete, bodily human being is a blood-relation of Christ, the *votum Ecclesiae* does not at all take place in a purely extra-sacramental and invisible interiority of grace. Rather, it is essentially, as an act of the concrete human being, an acceptance of the quasi-sacramental structure which by reason of the divine incarnation is necessarily proper to humanity and hence to the individual human being, considered as the people of God or member of this people respectively. The *votum Ecclesiae*, therefore, does not replace real membership of the Church by being "good will" towards the Church. It replaces it by being the personal acceptance of that membership of the people of God which is already a fact on the historical and visible plane and in which is already given a real reference to membership of the Church as an established society.[76]

There is an apparent incompatibility between "the fact of the necessity of the Church as a means for salvation" and "the fact of the possibility of salvation for someone outside the Church."[77] However, Rahner sees a solution to this problem in the assumption of a "certain stratification in the reality of the Church."[78] The Church ("as something visible and as a sign of the union with God by grace")[79] is composed of a twofold reality, "viz. Church as an established juridical organization in the

---

[75]Ibid., 83
[76]Ibid., 84-85.
[77]Ibid., 86.
[78]Ibid.
[79]Ibid.

sacred order and 'Church as humanity consecrated by
Incarnation.'"[80] When considered in these terms there
can be no

> belonging to the visible Church (i.e. not yet membership) which
> is *merely* "invisible," because merely constituted by the metahis-
> torical possession of grace and by the necessary justifying human
> acts for this in an unbaptized person, *considered* as merely
> personal acts. For basically every personal act finds also a
> historical expression (a constitutive sign) for the fact of its being
> a *votum Ecclesiae* in the concrete nature of man and in its
> incarnate act. Hence, the justified person who belongs (or is
> "referred" to the Church without being a member of it), belongs
> "invisibly" to the visible church by grace *and* has a "visible"
> relation to this Church, even when this relation is not constituted
> by baptism or by an externally verifiable profession of the true
> faith (as in the case of the catechumen).[81]

Rahner elsewhere speaks in similar terms concerning the dialectical tension between the statements in
numbers 16 and 14 of *Lumen gentium*; he suggests a
reconciliation by the doctrine of the Church as the basic
sacrament for the salvation of the world. "The Church is
the concrete historical *manifestation*, in the dimension of
a history that has acquired an eschatological significance,
and in the social dimension, of precisely *that* salvation
which is achieved through the grace of God throughout
the length and breadth of humanity."[82]

7. The value of non-Christian religions

This understanding of revelation and of grace
provides the context in which non-Christian religions are

---

[80]Ibid.

[81]Ibid., 87.

[82]"The New Image of the Church," in *TI*, Vol. 10 (New York:
Herder & Herder, 1973), 14.

understood by Rahner. He feels that one of the defi-
ciencies of contemporary dogmatic Christology is that it
does not pay enough attention to the general history of
religions.

> The point of such a study would be to examine the history of
> religions from the standpoint of our knowledge of the historical
> Incarnation, and from this standpoint alone, the only one to offer
> a really illuminating interpretation of a history otherwise
> unintelligible in itself; and to examine this history with a view to
> seeing whether and how far man in fact shows himself in history
> for what he unquestionably is in the depth of his concrete nature:
> a being who in the course of his history looks for the presence of
> God himself. When the early fathers kept a lookout for such an
> activity of the Logos, the beginnings of his Incarnation, as it
> were, in saving history before Christ (at least in the Old Testa-
> ment), they were better advised than we are, for whom God rules
> there simply from heaven.[83]

From the perspective of those early fathers, religions
"were an unconscious Yes or No to the Word of God who
was to come in human flesh."[84]
        In Rahner's perception, non-Christian religions,
before Christ, in themselves and "in principle were
positively willed by God as legitimate ways of salvation"
which were overtaken and rendered obsolete by the
coming of Christ and His death and resurrection.[85]
However, Rahner feels that we cannot define the precise
moment at which that obsolescence takes place in the
experience of any particular people and their religion.[86]
It happens only at the point at which "Christianity in its
explicit and ecclesiastical form becomes an effective

---

[83]"Current Problems in Christology," in *TI*, Vol. 1 (1961), 189.
[84]Ibid.
[85]"Church, Churches and Religions," 46.
[86]Ibid., 48.

reality,"[87] that is to say, when the Church asserts "its claims in history in the relevant cultural sphere to which the non-Christian religion concerned belonged."[88] Therefore, the non-Christian religion which an individual has inherited from past history,

> is only abrogated as the authentic way of salvation for him at that point at which the message of Christ so penetrates into his own conscience as an individual that it is only through a grave fault of his own that he can no longer reject it as the way of salvation offered by God and as the fulfilment that goes beyond anything that his former religion had to offer.[89]

In short, Rahner believes that "every way by which a man travels from genuine motives of conscience is a way leading to the infinitude of God."[90]

Rahner has spelled out his understanding of the relationship between Christianity and the non-Christian religions in four theses. First, he postulates that Christianity is the absolute religion and that it has a temporal and spatial starting point in Jesus of Nazareth.[91] As already noted, however, he questions

> whether this moment, when the existentially real demand is made by the absolute religion in its historically tangible form, takes place really at the same chronological moment for all men, or whether the occurrence of this moment has itself a history and thus is not chronologically simultaneous for all men, cultures and spaces of history.[92]

---

[87]Ibid., 47.

[88]Ibid.

[89]Ibid., 48.

[90]Ibid., 49.

[91]"Christianity and the Non-Christian Religions," in *TI*, Vol. 5 (1966), 118-19.

[92]Ibid., 119

Granting, therefore, that "as regards destination, Christianity is the absolute and hence the only religion" for all people, Rahner leaves open the question when exactly this absolute obligation of the Christian religion comes into effect for a particular person or culture, "even in the sense of the *objective* obligation of such a demand."[93]

Rahner's second thesis is that

> until the moment when the gospel really enters into the historical situation of an individual, a non-Christian religion (even outside the Mosaic religion) does not merely contain elements of a natural knowledge of God, elements, moreover, mixed up with human depravity which is the result of original sin and later aberrations. It contains also supernatural elements arising out of the grace which is given to men as a gratuitous gift on account of Christ. For this reason, a non-Christian religion can be recognized as a *lawful* religion (although only in different degrees) without thereby denying the error and depravity contained in it.[94]

From this thesis two conclusions follow. First, that it is "*a priori* quite possible to suppose that there are supernatural, grace-filled elements in non-Christian religions."[95] Second, that "the actual religions of 'pre-Christian' humanity . . . must be seen as quite capable of having a positive significance."[96] They must not be regarded, from the beginning, as simply illegitimate. "The religions existing in the concrete must contain supernatural, gratuitous elements, and in using *these* elements the pre-Christian was able to attain God's grace: presumably, too, the pre-Christian exists to this day, even though the possibility is gradually disappearing *today*."[97]

---

[93]Ibid., 120.
[94]Ibid., 121.
[95]Ibid.
[96]Ibid., 121.
[97]Ibid., 130.

The third thesis states that "it would be wrong to
regard the pagan as someone who has not yet been
touched in any way by God's grace and truth."[98] If a
person has experienced the grace of God, if

> he has already accepted this grace as the ultimate, unfathomable
> entelechy of his existence by accepting the immeasurableness of
> his dying existence opening out into infinity—then he has
> already been given revelation in a true sense even before he has
> been affected by missionary preaching from without.[99]

Rahner concludes that if a person who becomes the object
of the Church's missionary efforts may already be
someone on the way towards salvation, and even "someone who in certain circumstances finds it, without being
reached by the proclamation of the Church's message,"
and if this salvation which reached such a person is truly
Christian salvation, which it would have to be, "since
there is no other salvation," then it follows that "it must
be possible to be not only an anonymous theist but also
an anonymous Christian."[100]

In his fourth thesis, Rahner formulates what the
self-perception of the Church ought to be, given this
saving revelation outside of her own proclamation.

> The Church will not so much regard herself today as the
> exclusive community of those who have a claim to salvation but
> rather as the historically tangible vanguard and the historically
> and socially constituted explicit expression of what the Christian
> hopes is present as a hidden reality even outside the visible
> Church.[101]

---

[98]Ibid., 131.
[99]Ibid.
[100]Ibid., 132.
[101]Ibid.

8. Rahner on patristic anticipation

Reference has been made to Rahner's belief that, in the perspective of the early fathers who were aware of the pre-incarnate activity of the Logos, religions "were an unconscious Yes or No to the Word of God who was to come in human flesh."[102] However, he later comments that "the testimony of the Fathers, with regard to the possibility of salvation for someone outside the Church, is very weak."[103] He cites an anonymous author of a work entitled *De rebaptismate*, from the time of Cyprian, who stated that the Centurion Cornelius had "a baptism in the Holy Ghost, without water."[104] He notes that Ambrose, in a funeral oration for Emperor Valentinian, who died without baptism, said that Valentinian's piety and goodwill had washed him clean.[105] Rahner also suggests that it is possible to establish the doctrine of such a baptism of desire from the time of Augustine, "at least in certain periods."[106] Taking note of the negative attitudes of Gregory of Nyssa and Gregory of Nazianzus toward the "justifying power of love or of the desire for baptism,"[107] and of the fact that Augustine, in his last (anti-Pelagian) period, no longer maintained the possibility of a baptism of desire, Rahner concludes that there is no "*consensus dogmaticus* in the early Church regarding the possibility of salvation for the non-baptized, and especially for someone who was not even a catechumen."[108] He sees as reasons for this the fact

---

[102]"Current Problems in Christology," in *TI*, Vol. 1 (1961), 189.
[103]"Membership of the Church," 40-41.
[104]Ibid., 40.
[105]Ibid.
[106]Ibid.
[107]Ibid., citing *Patrologia Graecae* (Hereafter, *PG*) 36,389; 46,424.
[108]Ibid.

that the early Church did not initially make a very
explicit or clear distinction between material and formal
guilt and the fact that during the period of the preaching
of the gospel they more or less assumed that every pagan
remained a pagan through personal fault.[109]

D. The Scope and Procedure of This Study

The rationale for this study should now be clear.
Theologies of mission and theologies of religion are
attempting to provide for Christians a proper perspective
on non-Christian religions and on the condition of the
individual non-Christian. An interest has been noted in
the teaching of early Church Fathers whose perspective
is believed to be helpful to the modern theologian struggl-
ing with these questions. This work makes a careful
study of Irenaeus's theology of revelation in an attempt
to discern his answer to the questions posed by our
modern situation. It will be necessary to come to a
thorough understanding of his doctrine of divine revelation in and outside of Christ. Particularly significant is
his teaching regarding the salvific value of the revelation
of the divine Word prior to the Incarnation. Also important will be his understanding of salvation, of the means
to salvation, and particularly of the nature and role of
faith. Careful attention will be given, therefore, to
questions such as: Is God the Father knowable? Was He
known by Christ? Was He known before Christ? Was He
made known by Christ and, if so, how, when and to
whom? And what was the role of the Church in regard to
salvific revelation?

---

[109]Ibid.

Paul Knitter has pointed out that while "many Protestant theologians, in varying terminology, admit some form of revelation within the religions," they generally do not see the revelation as salvific. He asks:

> Is the distinction to be between *general* revelation (without salvation) and *salvific* revelation (with salvation)? Can the two be separated? If we can admit the *fact* of revelation outside of the Christ-event, must we not also admit the *possibility* of salvation? Does not the very nature of revelation include the possibility of our receiving salvation?[110]

These are highly significant questions and it is hoped that some perspective on them can be obtained from a study of the theology of Irenaeus.

P. de Letter has rightly emphasized the significance of one's concept of revelation in answering the question whether true supernatural revelation is found also in non-Christian religions. He considers it important whether one conceives of revelation as "a formal speaking of God to men, . . . a communication of God's truth" or as "self-communication," God giving himself.[111] In the first sense, he suggests,

> the one true revelation is the Judeo-Christian revelation, beginning historically with the election of Israel and the old covenant, and completed with Christ in the new. The primitive revelation or the Noah revelation was a preparation of that historical revelation and so also a preparation of God's revelation in Christ. It is generally added that no such historical supernatural revelation is found in other religions. This is correct in the sense that the supernatural revelation is derived from and pointing to Christ. (This need not exclude exceptional cases of "private revelations"

---

[110]Paul Knitter, "European Protestant and Catholic Approaches to the World Religions: Complements and Contrasts," *JEcSt* 12 (Winter 1975):26.

[111]P. de Letter, "Revelation in Non-Christian Religions," *ClerM* 29 (December 1965):466.

to non-Christians, nor, perhaps "traces" of the primitive or Noah revelation.)[112]

But de Letter views the situation differently in the second sense because everyone believes that

> divine graces are given, through Christ and His Church, also to followers of other religions. God's universal salvific will entails such universal dispensation of graces, not independently from Christ and the Church, in hidden ways known to God alone. Accordingly, when such grace is given to non-Christians and when they respond to it and are led to what we are wont to call the (implicit) "baptism of desire," then they receive a self-communication of God and so also a self-revelation of God, truly supernatural and truly Christian. . . . In that sense, since we know that non-Christians are being given graces, it is not incorrect to speak of revelation in non-Christian religions.[113]

Without pronouncing judgment on the validity of de Letter's particular analysis of the consequences of which of the two senses one understands by "revelation," it is clear that the concept of revelation is fundamental to one's judgment on non-Christian religions. The rationale for concentrating on Irenaeus's doctrine of revelation thus becomes obvious.

It would be impossible, in a study like this, to critique all the various modern theories from the perspective of Irenaeus's theology of revelation. Reference has been made, however, to the thesis that anticipations of Rahner's theory of "anonymous Christianity" are to be found in the theology of Irenaeus. It was this suggestion that prompted the study of Irenaeus. Therefore, while the main purpose of this book is to study the theology of Irenaeus in its own right, a second objective is to analyze Irenaeus's view in order to determine to what extent one

---

[112]Ibid., 467.
[113]Ibid., 467-68.

may legitimately cite him as an antecedent of "anonymous Christianity." This detailed study of Irenaeus will also provide a means of critiquing generalizations regarding "second-century theologians," or "the early Fathers," and their position on the state of the unevangelized or the value of non-Christian religions.

Time and space have made it necessary to focus on only one patristic author. Irenaeus has been selected for two main reasons. First, he was chosen because he is less often cited as a helpful antecedent than Justin and Clement. That indicated to this writer that the situation in regard to Irenaeus was less clear than in the work of the other two and made a study of Irenaeus more necessary. Second, he was selected because of his importance. The views of just two modern commentators give some indication of his significance and such comments could be multiplied. Leonard de Moor has suggested that Irenaeus's view of revelation "may be taken as eminently representative of the view of the early Church on Revelation when it definitely came to self-consciousness."[114] L. S. Thornton says:

> As an exponent of Catholic orthodoxy St. Irenaeus stands out as the most representative teacher of his time. . . . He is our most reliable guide to the structure of orthodoxy as it appears just after the last personal contacts with the apostolic age have been finally severed. In this way he is the authoritative exponent of a tradition which is continuous with the New Testament and which overlaps it.[115]

---

[114]"The Idea of Revelation in the Early Church. Part 2," *EvQ* 50 (1978):230.

[115]*Revelation and the Modern World, Being the First Part of a Treatise on the Form of the Servant* (London: Dacre Press, 1950), 28. J. B. Lightfoot remarks on the "exceptional advantages" of Irenaeus and suggests that on certain points "his testimony must be regarded as directly representing three churches at least," the Churches of Asia, Rome and Lyons (*Contemporary Review* [1876], cited by H. B. Swete,

In an historical study of this nature, there is a grave danger of anachronism. Interesting as it is to pose the questions of our day to a theologian of an earlier time, we must always beware of reading him out of context and hence "discovering" our own answers rather than his.[116] The question being posed by contemporary theologians is that of the medium and extent of divine revelation, namely, whether authentic divine revelation is to be found in non-Christian religions. That was not the question which specifically interested or troubled Irenaeus. For this reason, a careful attempt will be made to consider Irenaeus's doctrine of revelation within its own context.[117] Primarily, the situation that elicited his

---

The Holy Spirit in the Ancient Church: A Study of Christian Teaching in the Age of the Fathers [London: Macmillan & Co., 1912], 84). Such scholarly references to Irenaeus's importance could be multiplied.

[116]Nathan O. Hatch has well described the dangers of appeal to history, as well as the value of history to the present. "Yesterday: The Key that Unlocks Today," *CT* 27 (August 5, 1983):18-21.

[117]André Benoit has rightly objected to attempts made to synthesize or systemize Irenaeus's theology, because his work was not a systematic theology. He writes: "It is necessary to avoid posing to him arbitrary questions which, for us, are perhaps of major interest, but which, for him, were not at all." He contends that an attempt to pose to Irenaeus questions which were not of his time, and to which he did not wish to respond, is arbitrary and results in a partial and ambiguous response (*Saint Irénée: Introduction à l'étude de sa théologie* [Paris: Presses Universitaires de France, 1960], 13). Benoit's warning is well taken, but it is our conviction that it does not illegitimate this study. The questions of revelation and salvation were very much of interest to Irenaeus. It is our intention to follow Benoit's advice to take the context of Irenaeus's theology very seriously and not to force him into a contemporary framework.

Benoit has complained that Friedrich Loof's influential work on Irenaeus, from the perspective of source research, has not really increased our knowledge about Irenaeus (viz. *Theophilus von Antiochien Adversus Marcionem und die anderen theologischen Quellen bei Irenaeus* [Leipzig: J. C. Heinrichs, 1930]). He considers it

teaching regarding divine revelation was the error of Gnosticism. It will be necessary, therefore, to have clearly in mind the Gnostic position against which Irenaeus opposed his own theology of the knowledge of God. A second item of context which must be borne in mind is the second-century situation of the Church relative to paganism, and particularly Irenaeus's perception of the state of the missionary task of the Church. An important stimulus to the question of the salvation of people who do not hear the gospel has been the minimal impact of Christian missions upon the adherents of the great world religions. It is the thought of billions condemned to eternal punishment for lack of saving knowledge of God that has raised, in the minds of many, a query concerning the legitimacy of so exclusive a claim to divine salvific revelation and religion. To what extent did the situation of the Church in Irenaeus's day parallel the situation in our own day? To the degree that it was similar, Irenaeus's perspective on divine revelation and salvation relative to non-Christians will be significant in its contribution to our own understanding on the question. On the other hand, should Irenaeus be found to take a position rather different from that of "anonymous Christianity," his differences might be dismissed as insignificant on account of the difference between his missionary context and ours. For this reason also, it is imperative that we develop a clear picture of the missionary situation of the Church in the second century, and particularly of Irenaeus's perception of that situation.

---

an autopsy which did not bring Irenaeus to life (34). Hopefully, this study of Irenaeus's work itself, in the light of its context, will be more successful in "bringing Irenaeus to life." The weaknesses of Loof's source-critical approach have been further examined by F. R. M. Hitchcock, "Loof's Theory of Theophilus of Antioch as a Source of Irenaeus," *JTS* 38 (1937):254-66.

The next two chapters will therefore provide the context in which Irenaeus's theology of revelation and the non-Christian must be viewed. Gnosticism constitutes the context of his doctrine of revelation and salvation, and the missionary situation of the second-century Church is the context of his view of the non-Christian. Following this careful analysis of the contextual location of Irenaeus's theology, his doctrine of revelation will be developed, with an eye especially to the significance of this doctrine to the question of the salvation of the unevangelized. In keeping with Irenaeus's own biblical-theological focus, his doctrine of revelation will be examined in relationship to the economy of the Trinity, focusing on the respective roles of the Father, the Son and the Holy Spirit in divine revelation, and on the bearing of these on the state of the non-Christian. Because of the emphasis that has been traditionally placed on the role of the Church in revelation and salvation, a chapter will be devoted to this matter. Finally, a careful study will be made of Irenaeus's view of the human response to divine revelation, and of the effects of this response for salvation.

It is recognized that we are asking a question which Irenaeus did not himself consciously undertake to answer. It is the writer's conviction that the procedure is valid, provided justice is always done to the context in which Irenaeus developed his doctrines of revelation and salvation and to the questions which Irenaeus explicitly addressed. Again, it is not wrong to ask of Irenaeus questions that he did not ask of himself. In doing so, however, it is essential to be careful to ensure that it is Irenaeus who is answering and not our own echo that is being heard.

2. THE GNOSTIC HERESY: CONTEXT OF IRENAEUS'S THEOLOGY OF REVELATION AND SALVATION

A. Irenaeus and the Gnostics

1. Gnosticism: threat to Christian truth

Considering the length of Irenaeus's *Adversus Haereses* and the care with which he described the teachings of the Gnostics and refuted them, it is clear that Irenaeus perceived them to be a great threat to the Christian Church. He complained that "they falsify the words of the Lord and become evil interpreters of what has been well said,"[1] and destroy the faith of many by turning them away under the pretext of a knowledge which others do not have.

a. The nature of the Gnostic threat

Morton Smith has complained that Irenaeus used the term "Gnostic" indiscriminately, applying the name to all of his enemies or presenting them as descendants and secret followers of the creed.[2] That this is not a fair

---

[1]*Adversus Haereses* I, Pref. 1. All references to *Adversus Haereses* will hereafter be designated AH, and will be included parenthetically in the text. Translations are this writer's unless otherwise noted.

[2]Morton Smith, "The History of the Term *gnostikos*," in *The*

assessment has been demonstrated by M. J. Edwards.[3] What made the task of Irenaeus particularly difficult was the fact that the Gnostics were not a clearly defined and organized sect. Debate continues as to whether Gnosticism was a distinctively Christian sect or whether it had pre-Christian origins.[4] The origin and development of Gnosticism remain something of a mystery.[5] Until at least the early part of the second-century, the lines of division between orthodox and heretic were not yet clearly drawn,[6] and even the Gnostic movements which did exist in the time of Irenaeus were fragmented and disunited.[7] There were no universal principles of ideology upon which they agreed to be integrated.

Rediscovery of Gnosticism, ed. B. Layton (Leiden, 1981), ii, 796-807.

[3]M. J. Edwards, "Gnostics and Valentinians in the Church Fathers," *JTS*, ns 40 (April 1989):27-30.

[4]A case has been made for Gnosticism as a Christian heresy by Edwin Yamauchi, *Pre-Christian Gnosticism: A Survey of the Proposed Evidences* (Grand Rapids: Baker, 1983), and a more recent summation of the case has been provided by Simone Pétrement, *Le Dieu séparé: Les origines du gnosticisme* (Paris: Cerf, 1984). Others argue for a pre-Christian form of Gnosticism. See, e.g., Birger A. Pearson, "Jewish Elements in Gnosticism and the Development of Gnostic Self-Definition," in *Jewish and Christian Self-Definition*, Vol. 1: *The Shaping of Christianity in the Second and Third Centuries*, ed. E. P. Sanders, (Philadelphia: Fortress Press, 1980), 159; and "Early Christianity and Gnosticism: A Review Essay," *RSR* 13 (Jan 1987):3.

[5]R. McL. Wilson, "Slippery Words II: Gnosis, Gnostic, Gnosticism," *ExpTim* 89 (July 1978):300. See also Marvin Meyer, *The Nag Hammadi Library in English; Translated by Members of the Coptic Gnostic Library Project of the Institute for Antiquity and Christianity* (San Fransisco: Harper & Row, 1977), 6; and George W. Macrae, "Why the Church Rejected Gnosticism," in *Jewish and Christian Self-Definition*, ed. E. P. Sanders, 1:127.

[6]Ibid., 299.

[7]Henry Alan Green, "Suggested Sociological Themes in the Study of Gnosticism," *VigChr* 31 (1977):175.

Their stratified system of salvation negated all those who were not ontologically *pneumatic*, and within the particular Gnostic individual movements, internal schisms dictated new directions rather than an authoritative institutional structure. Given all these characteristics the experience of *gnosis* is by definition anti-institutional. It became a vehicle for internal migration rather than institutional external migration.[8]

Irenaeus was thus dealing with something of a guerrilla movement. Though its origins were pre-Christian, the expansion of Christianity had "resulted in the appropriation of Christian theologoumena into Gnosticism . . . and the creation of Gnostic Christian groups."[9] With teachings that were clearly different from those which the apostles handed on to the Church in their writings, the Gnostics were drawing many away from the tradition which Irenaeus, Bishop of Lyons, was called upon to guard. They thereby threatened the very life of the Church. Yet, while van Unnik seems accurate in describing Gnosticism as a "world religion,"[10] it appears clear that the particular Gnostics with whom Irenaeus contended "considered themselves members of

---

[8]Ibid., 176. See also Pheme Perkins, *The Gnostic Dialogue: The Early Church and the Crisis of Gnosticism* (New York: Paulist Press, 1980), 10.

[9]Birger A. Pearson, "Jewish Elements in Gnosticism," 159. Pearson postulates that "the earliest Gnostics were Jewish intellectuals eager to redefine their own religious self-understanding and convinced of the bankruptcy of traditional verities." R. M. Grant also proposes apocalyptic Judaism as the origin of Gnosticism (*Gnosticism and Early Christianity* [New York: Harper & Row, 1966], 39). An extensive survey of opinions regarding the source of Gnosticism can be found in G. van Groningen, *First Century Gnosticism: Its Origin and Motifs* (Leiden: E. J. Brill, 1967).

[10]Willem Cornelis van Unnik, *Newly Discovered Gnostic Writings: A Preliminary Survey of the Nag Hammadi Find*, Studies in Biblical Theology (Napierville, Illinois: Allenson, 1960), 23.

the larger Christian community."[11] To Irenaeus himself
it was at best a Christian heresy and possibly even a
false religion.[12] He believed them to be worse than the
heathen. Although they claimed to have knowledge of all
things, they described the Creator as the fruit of a defect,
as having animal nature and without knowledge of the
Power which is above him. The heathen, at least,
ascribed first place in deity to the God who made the
universe, even if they actually worshiped the creature
rather than the Creator (AH II,9,2). In fact, Irenaeus
accused the Gnostics of syncretism in their use of heathen thought. He charged that they gave names to their
Aeons which were recognizable and credible to the
heathen by association with their own gods. They then
proposed that the heathen gods were actually images of
their twelve Aeons (AH II,14,9).

Gustaf Wingren has made the interesting proposal that "the structure of the [Apostle's] Creed is determined by the struggle against the Gnostics."[13] It con-
fesses what the Gnostics deny, holding together creation
and redemption. Such a proposal certainly emphasizes
the extent to which Gnosticism was viewed as a threat,
but also the influence that it had on the development of
the orthodox position. Irenaeus established the Church's
approach, dealing first with creation and then with the
Incarnation, "in order that the whole may be seen as the
restoration of creation (*recapitulatio*)."[14]

---

[11]Perkins, *The Gnostic Dialogue*, 12.

[12]van Groningen, *First Century Gnosticism*, 15.

[13]Gustaf Wingren, "The Doctrine of Creation: Not an Appendix but
the First Article," trans. E. M. Carlson, WW 4 (Fall 1984):357.

[14]Wingren, "Doctrine of Creation," 357.

b. The historical development of Gnosticism

Irenaeus traced the history of the Gnostics back to Simon Magus (Acts 8:9 ff.), whom he considered to be the "originator of all heresies" (AH I,23,2), and developed a genealogy of Gnostic teachers that posed a heretical alternative to the orthodox successors of the apostles. Simon was succeeded by Menander, who also did magic and claimed that he was sent by invisible beings to save humankind. Through his magic, one would be able to attain knowledge which would give the power to overcome the angels who made the world. By being baptized into him, his disciples would receive resurrection and achieve immortality (AH I,23,5). Saturninus followed Menander in Syria, and Basilides in Alexandria (AH I,24,1), and next came Carpocrates and his disciples (AH I,25,1). Irenaeus also dealt with some who were not technically Gnostics: Cerinthus (AH I,26,1), the Nicolaitans, and the Encratitae. He also described a couple of non-Valentinian sects, the Barbeliotae and the Ophites (AH I,29-30). However, his major attention was devoted to the Valentinians. It was after reading the *Commentaries* of the disciples of Valentinus, and particularly of the disciples of Ptolemy, that Irenaeus set himself to present their teaching in coherent form and to give a definitive refutation of it (AH I, Pref. 2).

Valentinus of Alexandria had taught in Rome, about 135-165, and led a movement which flourished in the Mediterranean world, with particular influence in Alexandria and Rome, as well as the regions of the Rhone valley where Irenaeus was Bishop.[15] About A.D. 140, he made an attempt to get himself elected as Bishop of Rome and, having failed in the attempt, formed a sect

---

[15]O. Reimherr, "Irenaeus and the Valentinians," *LQ* 12 (February 1960):55.

with his followers, some ten years later.[16] Among his
followers were Ptolemaeus, Heracleon and Marcus the
Magician. It was his pupil Marcus who was particularly
active in the Rhone valley where Irenaeus ministered,
and when Irenaeus refers to the Valentinians he generally means Ptolemaeus and Marcus. The other major
object of Irenaeus's polemic was Marcion, who flourished
as a heretic under the bishopric of Anicetus (AH III,4,3).
The Church Fathers frequently coupled Valentinus with
Marcion as one of the archheretics, and his supporters
existed in Asia and Egypt well into the fourth century, in
spite of the work of Irenaeus to combat heresy. In fact, it
is Henry Green's conviction that Gnosticism ultimately
died out, not because of the effectiveness of the attack
upon its teachings but because of its failure to develop an
integrated structure such as the orthodox Church developed.[17] The threat of Gnosticism may, therefore, have
been defeated, not theologically, but sociologically.

c. The fundamental errors of Gnosticism

The focus of this chapter will be on the Gnostic
doctrine of revelation and its relationship to salvation. No
attempt will be made to present a full summary of the
Valentinian system as Irenaeus described it, with its
elaborate and complex scheme of emanations among the
Aeons. It should be noted also that Irenaeus himself,
though aware of the divergences between the various
Gnostic schools, endeavored to treat primarily the ideas
they held in common, and particularly those of
Ptolemaeus and Marcus, with considerable reference also
to Marcion. Gérard Vallée has helpfully pointed out that
Irenaeus was particularly concerned with two essential

---

[16]van Unnik, 61-62.
[17]Green, "Suggested Sociological Themes," 175-80.

aspects of the Gnostic system: "its emanationistic scheme expressed in the doctrine of aeons and, secondly, its dualistic outlook."[18] Vallée observes rightly that Irenaeus focused his attack on the second problem, and he suggests seven types of dualism which troubled Irenaeus.[19] Brief mention of these will provide a larger context for the attention given here to the Gnostic doctrine of revelation. Irenaeus attacked: 1) theological dualism, that is, the split between God and the demiurge (AH III,25,3; II,31,1); 2) Christological dualism, which separated Christ from Jesus (AH IV, Pref. 3; IV,2,4; III,16,2; III,17,4), the Logos from the Savior (AH III,9,3; III,16,8; IV, Pref. 3), and Christ above from Christ below (AH III,11,1; III,17,4); 3) soteriological dualism, which distinguished one way of salvation for the spiritual and another for the psychical; Irenaeus insisted rather that "there is only one economy, which is universal and on the basis of which Christ will recapitulate all things";[20] 4) Scriptural dualism, which separates the New Testament from the Old Testament and the God of the Old Testament from the God announced by the Savior; 5) ecclesiastical dualism, which distinguishes between simple believers and pneumatics, thus dividing the unity of the Church (AH IV,33,7; IV,26,2); 6) social dualism, which perceives some as good and others as evil by nature (AH IV,37,2); and 7) practical dualism, which was manifested either in a rigorism attainable only by a few or in libertinism of the so-called superior people.

---

[18]Gérard Vallée, "Theological and Non-Theological Motives in Irenaeus's Refutation of the Gnostics," in *Jewish and Christian Self-Definition*, 1:180. See also Hans Jonas, *The Gnostic Religion: The Message of the Alien God and the Beginnings of Christianity*, revised edition (Boston: Beacon, 1963), 42.
[19]Ibid., 179-80.
[20]Vallée, "Theological and Non-Theological Motives," 179.

2. The reliability of Irenaeus's description of Gnostic teaching

a. The sources of Irenaeus's exposition of Gnosticism

Until the relatively recent discovery of the Gnostic texts at Nag Hammadi, scholars were largely dependent on the early Christian apologetic writings for their knowledge of Gnosticism. Given the nature and purpose of apologetic writing, this might well have left a question regarding the validity of the account given of the teaching of the "heretics." It is Irenaeus who provides us with the "earliest extant clear and explicit exposition of the Church's case against the Gnostics," and much of the work that followed is clearly dependent on him.[21] It is clear that Irenaeus intended to give a detailed and accurate exposition of the Gnostic teachings, diverse as they were, in order to provide the Church with an adequate critical response. He indicates that he wrote his apology after reading some of the *Commentaries* of the disciples of Valentinus, and particularly of the disciples of Ptolemaeus (AH I, Pref. 2). In regard to the reliability of Irenaeus's representation of Gnosticism, he has not been without his detractors, notably Elaine H. Pagels.[22] For purposes of this study, which focuses particularly on the theological perspective of Irenaeus himself, his reliability as an interpreter of Gnosticism is not critical. On the whole, however, the Nag Hammadi discoveries appear to have confirmed Irenaeus's reliability, and have

---

[21]MacRae, "Why the Church Rejected," 127.

[22]Elaine H. Pagels, "Conflicting Versions of Valentinian Eschatology: Irenaeus's Treatise Versus the Excerpts from Theodotus," *HTR* 67 (1974):35-53.

demonstrated his knowledge of various Gnostic traditions which appear in these manuscripts.[23] Irenaeus knew, for instance, of the Gnostic Petrine tradition, found in the *Apocalypse of Peter,* which portrays Peter as a true Gnostic (AH III,12,1-7; III,13,2).[24] Of particular interest have been two texts, namely, the *Apocryphon of John* and the *Gospel of Truth.* As early as 1907, Carl Schmidt identified the *Apocryphon of John* as a source book for Irenaeus[25] and, more recently, Hans Jonas and H. C. Puech have identified this work as the source of Irenaeus's account of the Barbelo Gnostics.[26] Perkins describes the work as,

---

[23]Simon Tugwell, "Irenaeus and the Gnostic Challenge," *ClerR* 66 (April 1981):127. Pheme Perkins provides a helpful survey of the texts found at Nag Hammadi and indicates numerous points of similarity to the exposition by Irenaeus, in *The Gnostic Dialogue,* as well as her earlier article "Irenaeus and the Gnostics: Rhetoric and Composition in Adversus Haereses Book One," *VigChr* 30 (1976):193-200. Jean Daniélou likewise confirms the authenticity of Irenaeus's account of Gnostic vocabulary, as attested by the manuscripts from Nag Hammadi (*Gospel Message and Hellenistic Culture: A History of Early Christian Doctrine Before the Council of Nicaea,* Vol. 2, trans. and ed. John Austin Baker [Philadelphia: The Westminster Press, 1973], 339). Further support for the reliability of Irenaeus is found in J. F. McCue, rev. of *The Rediscovery of Gnosticism* (Proceedings of the International Conference on Gnosticism at Yale, March 28-31, 1978), vol. 1: *The School of Valentinus,* Studies in the History of Religions, Supplements to *Numen,* 41, ed. Bentley Layton (Leiden: E. J. Brill, 1980) cited by Einar Thomassen in *JAAR* 50 (June 1982):298. M. J. Edwards concludes from comparison of the *Apocryphon of John* and the work of Irenaeus (especially AH I,29) that Irenaeus was "an honest reader and capable critic," "Gnostics and Valentinians in the Church Fathers," *JTS* ns 40 (April 1989):37.

[24]Cf. Perkins, *The Gnostic Dialogue,* 115-18.

[25]Cited by van Unnik, 13,71.

[26]Jonas, *The Gnostic Religion,* 22; H. C. Puech, "The Jung Codex and the Other Gnostic Documents from Nag Hammadi," in *The Jung Codex, a Newly Recovered Gnostic Papyrus; Three Studies,* ed. Frank Leslie Cross (London: Mowbray, 1955), 22.

among the revelation dialogues, the "most complete and most catechetical in its presentations of gnosis,"[27] and points out that "it follows a pattern of topics similar to that in Irenaeus's exposition of Valentinianism."[28] W. C. van Unnik questions the dating of the *Apocryphon* which would allow it to be a source for Irenaeus's exposition. While granting that there are passages common to Irenaeus and the *Apocryphon*, he finds it remarkable that these should be confined to one section of the *Apocryphon*. The latter part of the *Apocryphon* is not used by Irenaeus, and van Unnik concludes that the work is probably a compound of a number of different pieces. He concludes that Irenaeus and the *Apocryphon* were more likely independent of each other, but that both borrowed from the same source.[29] Whatever may have been the exact relationship, it remains true that in the sections where the *Apocryphon* has parallels in Irenaeus, the reliability of the account by Irenaeus has been confirmed.

The *Gospel of Truth* is an even more interesting case, because of the reference Irenaeus makes to a work of that name—*Veritatis Evangelium* (AH III,11,9). Although it is impossible to prove, there is general consensus that this is probably the same work.[30]

---

[27]Perkins, *The Gnostic Dialogue*, 93.

[28]Ibid., citing AH I,1-8.

[29]van Unnik, 71.

[30]W. C. van Unnik, "The 'Gospel of Truth' and the New Testament," in *The Jung Codex, a Newly Recovered Gnostic Papyrus; Three Studies* (London: Mowbray, 1955), 96; Martin Krause, "Introduction to the 'Gospel of Truth,'" in *Gnosis: A Selection of Gnostic Texts*, Vol. 2: *Coptic and Mandean Sources*, ed. Werner Foerster, trans. and ed. R. L. McL. Wilson (Oxford: Clarendon Press, 1974), 54; Jonas, *The Gnostic Religion*, 309; George W. MacRae, "Introduction to the 'Gospel of Truth,'" in *The Nag Hammadi Library in English; Translated by Members of the Coptic Gnostic Library Project of the Institute for Antiquity and Christianity* (San Francisco: Harper & Row, 1977), 37; van Unnik, *Newly Discovered*, 60.

Interestingly, Irenaeus's reference is simply a comparison of the Gnostic *Gospel* with the canonical Gospels, demonstrating their dissimilarity. He does not actually make use of the book in describing the Gnostic teaching. Nevertheless, the great similarity between the teaching of this work and the Valentinian doctrine which Irenaeus presents makes this a very interesting find, and specific attention will be given to the teaching of this work, later in the chapter.

b. Defense of Irenaeus's reliability

It is only fair to note that, while the reliability of Irenaeus is generally affirmed by contemporary students of the Gnostic manuscripts, he is not completely without detractors. Elaine Pagels finds significant differences between Irenaeus's description of Valentinian eschatology and that of the excerpts from Theodotus. She further contends that the recent Gnostic finds tend to support the version of Theodotus rather than Irenaeus. Although the same elements are found in the account by Irenaeus, he tends to ignore them in stating his summary of the Valentinian position. Pagels concludes that those who mistake *Adversus Haereses* for a fairly straightforward presentation of Valentinian theology that is essentially parallel to the *Excerpts from Theodotus* "have underestimated Irenaeus's ability to 'subvert and destroy' the theology of those he considers a serious threat to the unity of the Church."[31] The particular point at issue is whether there are ultimately two categories of mankind, the saved and the lost, or three, with an eternal distinction being made between the destiny of the pneumatics

---

[31]Elaine H. Pagels, "Conflicting Versions of Valentinian Eschatology: Irenaeus's Treatise Versus the Excerpts from Theodotus," *HTR* 67 (1974):53.

and the psychics. Irenaeus depicts them as being
eternally separate, in the Valentinian scheme. Pagels
believes that "Irenaeus ignores the contrast Valentinians
describe between the situation of mankind in the
oikonomia and in the eternity."[32]

In defense of Irenaeus, Perkins contends that
Pagel's treatment of Irenaeus ignores "the demands of
the rhetorical genre in which he writes."[33] She also
points to the possibility that he was dependent upon
"sources like the *Apocryphon of John*, which do teach a
threefold separation at the consummation."[34] J. F.
McCue also argues that "Pagel's hypothesis that Irenaeus
distorted the soteriological status of the psychics cannot
be sustained."[35]

In the final analysis, the reliability of Irenaeus's
account of Valentinian doctrine is not critical for this
study. What matters is the teaching of Irenaeus in the
context of his own presentation of the Gnostic doctrine
which he combats. However, it is the conclusion of this
writer that the reliability of Irenaeus is evident, particularly given the great diversity of Gnostic teaching, to
which Irenaeus himself testified (AH I,11,1-4). Irenaeus
does not appear to have been attacking a straw man or
an enemy of his own devising. Naturally, however, he
wrote as one deeply concerned to unmask the error of his
Gnostic opponents. He endeavored to present the danger
of their position in the clearest manner, without under-
mining his own polemic by obvious misrepresentation.

---

[32]Ibid., 52.

[33]Pheme Perkins, "Irenaeus and the Gnostics: Rhetoric and
Composition in Adversus Haereses Book One," *VigChr* 30 (1976):193,
n. 1.

[34]Ibid.

[35]Cited by Einar Thomassen, rev. of *The Rediscovery of Gnosticism*,
298.

B. The Quest for Knowledge of the Unknown Bythos

1. The unknown Bythos

Pheme Perkins claims that the emphasis placed upon the radical transcendence and unknowability of the highest God, by Gnostic thinkers, was unparalleled by either their pagan or Christian counterparts. "Such radical transcendence is founded on a discontinuity between God and the cosmos in which human beings find themselves."[36] Jean Daniélou aptly describes the difference between the Gnostic view of the unknowability of God and the perspectives of the Jew or the Platonist.

> For a Jew to say that God is transcendent is to say that he cannot be measured by any created thing, and is therefore incomprehensible to the creaturely mind; but at the same time it is to assert that his existence can be known. For the Platonist, to say that God is ineffable is to say that he surpasses any conception of him that the mind can form in terms of the sensible world; but it is also to affirm that, if only the mind can shake itself free from all conceptions of that kind, it will be able to grasp his essence. For the Gnostic, however, the matter goes far deeper. God is unknown absolutely, both in his essence and in his existence; he is one of whom, in the strictest sense, nothing is known, and this situation can be overcome only through the Gnosis. It is, therefore, a question of radical dualism, distinguishing between the God of whom the world enables us to form some idea (who is merely the Demiurge) and the God who has no connection whatever with the world, and who can be known only by means of himself.[37]

The God who was *agnōstos* was not "the hidden God of the Bible, nor . . . the Platonist God who is hard

---

[36]Perkins, *The Gnostic Dialogue*, 167.
[37]Daniélou, *Gospel Message*, 335-36.

for [people] to grasp, but . . . the God of whose very existence [people] are totally ignorant."[38] Most commonly he was described as *akataléptos*, the incomprehensible Father, known only by Nous.[39] By a term that seems to have been peculiar to Gnosticism, he was described as *ho anennoétos*, the inconceivable one (AH I,11,5; I,14,1).[40]

Thus, Irenaeus begins his exposition of the doctrine of Ptolemaeus with a description of the perfect, pre-existent Aeon, called *proarchén kai propatora kai bython*, invisible, eternal and unbegotten (*achóréton kai aoraton, aidion te kai agennéton [AH I,1,1]*). Only Nous (Mind) was capable of comprehending his father's greatness, having been brought forth by Bythos (Depth) through the deposit of a seed in Sige (Silence). He was also called Monogenes (only begotten), Father and Beginning of All Things (AH I,1,1). So began a process of unions and generations which ultimately produced thirty Aeons (AH I,1-3), but to all of these Aeons except Nous, the Propator (Forefather) was invisible and incomprehensible (AH I,2,1).

The Propator was also unknown to people prior to the descent of Soter on the Christ of the economy. He announced a different Father from the Creator of the universe (AH I,19,1). No divine providence in the universe created by the Demiurge revealed the distant Bythos. Isaiah's statement that "Israel has not known me" was taken as a reference to human ignorance of the invisible Bythus (AH I,19,1, citing Isa 1:3; Hos 4:1; Rom 3:11-12; Ps 14:13). The prophets had known only the Creator (AH I,19,1) but the Lord made known the Father who was unknown to everyone, and it is he whom the Gnostics proclaimed, rather than the Creator of the

---

[38]Ibid., 337 (commenting on AH I,2,1-3).
[39]Ibid., 339.
[40]Cf. Daniélou, ibid.

world, whom people had always known. Matthew
11:25-27 was a favorite passage of the Gnostics in
support of their teaching concerning the unknown God
and the novelty of the revelation by Christ (AH I,20,3).
Irenaeus says:

> But these people who wish to be more clever than the apostles
> transcribe in this way: "No one knew the Father except the Son,
> nor the Son except the Father, and the one to whom the Son
> wished to reveal him," and they interpret it as if the true God
> was known to no one before our Lord's coming, and that God who
> was announced by the prophets, they say, is not the Father of
> Christ (AH IV,6,1).

2. The quest among the Aeons

Nous had wanted to reveal to the other Aeons
how great the Father was, but Sige had restrained him,
in keeping with the will of the Father, because she
wanted to lead the other Aeons to knowledge and to the
desire to examine their Father (AH I,2,1). However,
Sophia (Wisdom), the last and youngest Aeon of the
duodecad generated from Anthropos (Man) and Ecclesia
(Community), had a great passion to know the greatness
of the Father. Since this was impossible, she suffered
great agony of mind and there was a danger that, in her
continued quest, she might dissolve into the universal
substance. To prevent this, Horos (Limit), who supports
the Aeons and keeps them outside of the inexpressible
Greatness, restrained Sophia and convinced her that the
Father was incomprehensible (AH I,2,2). Some Gnostics
contended that, in this agonizing but impossible quest,
Sophia produced an amorphous substance which was the
beginning of material substance. It therefore had its
origin in ignorance, sorrow, fear, and confusion (AH
I,2,3). This inborn idea of Sophia's was then separated off
by Horos and expelled from the Pleroma of the Aeons
(AH I,2,4).

Lest any of the other Aeons should be taken by a similar passion, Nous, acting in keeping with the providence of the Father, produced another couple, the Christ above and the Holy Spirit. These were to strengthen and consolidate the Pleroma, and Christ instructed the Aeons that the Father could be known only by Nous (AH I,2,5). The whole Pleroma of Aeons, with one will and thought, and with the concurrence of Christ and the Holy Spirit and the approval of the Father, then brought forth what each had that was most excellent, most beautiful and precious. They put all this together and made, in honor of Bythos, a creature of great beauty, the star and perfect fruit of the Pleroma, Jesus. He was called Savior, Christ, and Logos from the name of his fathers, and also Everything, because he had been produced by all of them. Angels were made as his bodyguard (AH I,2,6).

3. The superior knowledge of the Gnostics

According to Irenaeus, the Gnostics distinguished three classes of people, the pneumatic or spiritual, the psychic, and the material. They themselves were the spiritual, people who possessed perfect knowledge of God and had been initiated into the mysteries by Achamoth (AH I,6,1). What disturbed Irenaeus was the means by which they supposedly received this greater knowledge. He complained that their system was not taught by the prophets, the Lord, or the apostles, but that they used sources other than the Scriptures (AH I,8,1). The Gnostics did try to prove their system out of the Scriptures (AH I,9,1), but they also appealed to traditions coming down to them from Christ and the apostles. They believed, for instance, that after the resurrection, Jesus stayed on earth another eighteen months. At that time knowledge descended into him and he taught the clear truth. He instructed a few of his disciples who had the capacity to understand such great mysteries before he was taken up into heaven (AH I,30,14). Thus, when people like Irenaeus refuted the Gnostic teaching from Scripture, the Gnostics would turn to tradition, to the "living voice" (*zōsēs phōnēs*). In so doing, Irenaeus complained, they rejected the tradition of the apostles and the revelation of the Lord (AH III,2,1). They could do this because of their claim that they had pure, sure knowledge of the hidden mystery (AH III,2,2). They had a key which had been revealed at first by the apostles and had then been transmitted in secret.[41]

The Nag Hammadi manuscripts also indicate this emphasis on a tradition handed down particularly among the Gnostics, and the identification of Jesus and the apostles as Gnostics. Irenaeus was aware of the Gnostic Petrine tradition which depicted Peter as a true Gnostic (AH III,12,1-7), a position set forth in the *Apocalypse of Peter*. The writing invokes Peter's authority against "the combination of Pauline doctrine and Petrine ecclesiology being advanced by the author's opponents."[42] It depicts Peter as the witness to the true meaning of the sufferings of Jesus. Peter's revelation is presented as the source of the Gnostic community, and all attempts made by others to claim such a foundation are dismissed as counterfeit. It is the Gnostic Peter who is the foundation of the true Church and, therefore, only those who are a part of the Gnostic community are united to the Savior.[43]

The *Apocryphon of James* presents James as the only one who had the true tradition concerning the teaching of Jesus. Since the other apostles rejected this teaching, the work presents the Gnostic understanding, which comes from James, as superior to the general

[41]Cf. Daniélou, *Gospel Message*, 143.
[42]Perkins, *The Gnostic Dialogue*, 117.
[43]Ibid., 121.

apostolic tradition.[44] In similar fashion, the *Gospel of
Mary* depicts Mary as the Gnostic leader, and presents
Peter as hostile to her.[45] However, the *Letter of Peter to
Philip* emphasizes the unity of the apostles in teaching
gnosis. Perkins suggests that this was probably a
response to the orthodox polemic against the diversity of
Gnostic preaching.[46] In fact, her study of the Gnostic
dialogues finds at least half of them appealing to a
common apostolic tradition. She concludes that "the
Gnostic position on apostolic tradition is much closer to
the general second-century view than is sometimes
admitted."[47] Only in the Thomas and James traditions
do we find claim to transmission from a single disciple to
the Gnostic, without the involvement of other disciples.

> These Gnostic writings reflect the liturgy, teaching, preaching
> and polemic of their respective communities. But they never
> claim to do more than to embody true tradition. They never claim
> to be the textually authoritative source of reflection, authority or
> even contact with the divine. The revelation about which they
> speak may put an individual in touch with the truth about God,
> about the cosmos, about himself or herself, or about salvation,
> but that truth is not definitively embodied in any inspired text.
> Gnostic interpretation is still the hermeneutic of an oral tradi-
> tion. It does not provide the formalized interpretation of a text
> that would sponsor a systematized and rational account of Chris-
> tian theology such as that proposed by Irenaeus or Origen.[48]

The particular appeal, and threat, of Gnostic
systems thus becomes apparent. In the context of a
theology that strongly emphasized the incomprehensibility of the ultimate God, the Propator, they presented

---

[44]Ibid., 133.
[45]Ibid.
[46]Ibid., 124; cf. AH I,10,2.
[47]Ibid., 196.
[48]Ibid., 201-2.

the possibility of knowledge through the revelation by Jesus. By making a sharp distinction between the God revealed by the prophets and the one revealed by Jesus, they established their superiority to the Jewish religion. By claiming a superior knowledge of the teaching of Jesus, through traditions handed on orally from the apostles in general, or a particular apostle, they set themselves above the teaching of the Church as represented by Irenaeus. What made this special knowledge even more attractive was its alleged role in human salvation.

C. Human Salvation and the Knowledge of God

Hans Jonas identifies as a common feature of the many sects in which the Gnostic movement expressed itself, "the emphasis on *knowledge* as the means for the attainment of salvation, or even as the form of salvation itself, and the claim to the possession of this knowledge in one's own articulate doctrine."[49] He points out that in more radical systems, like the Valentinian, "the 'knowledge' is not only an instrument of salvation but itself the very form in which the goal of salvation, that is, ultimate perfection, is possessed."[50] "Knowledge and the attainment of the known by the soul are claimed to coincide."[51]

In Irenaeus's understanding, the Gnostic doctrine of salvation is closely related to its anthropology. There are three kinds of people—spiritual, psychical, and material—represented respectively by Seth, Abel, and

---

[49]Jonas, *The Gnostic Religion*, 32. See also Grant, *Gnosticism*, 7-10.
[50]Ibid., 35.
[51]Ibid.

Cain (AH I,7,5).[52] The destiny of the material (hylic) is
corruption, because of an intrinsic impossibility that
material substance should partake of salvation (AH I,6,2;
V,6,1; III,22,1; V,12,2),[53] a conclusion from the metaphysical dualism which characterized Gnostic systems.
The same assumption led the disciples of Valentinus to
deny a genuine incarnation of Christ, in order to exclude
the flesh from salvation (AH V,1,2), and also to distinguish between the fleshly, psychical, and spiritual Savior
in explanations of the crucifixion (AH I,7,2; I,24,4; I,26,1;
I,30,13).[54] The psychical have a choice. If they choose
the better, they will rest in the intermediate place of
Ogdoad, the sphere of the Demiurge. If they are evil, they
will go to destruction. The spiritual, however, are a seed
sown by Achamoth in immature form. When they have
been instructed in this world, they will reach perfection
and be married to the angels of the Savior (AH I,7,5).[55]

---

[52]Perkins contends that the "hard and fast distinctions between the
two types of soul according to substance, *kat' ousian*, emerge in those
situations in which the Gnostic community finds itself under pressure
from the larger group," and "function as an explanation for the
rejection faced by the Gnostic. . . . Such intensified dualism does not
represent Gnostic anthropology generally" (*The Gnostic Dialogue*,
183).

[53]As Perkins points out, it was to counter this Gnostic rejection of
material creation that Irenaeus identified the image of God with the
body. "This image, he claimed, is inseparable from the soul breathed
into the body. . . . Likeness to God comes when the Spirit given by
Christ enables humanity to reach the incorruption, which the earlier
formation by God had made it capable of. . . . Incorruption extends to
the body, which is transformed by the Spirit" (*The Gnostic Dialogue*,
181).

[54]Cf. Perkins, *The Gnostic Dialogue*, 121.

[55]Rather than ascribing deliberate distortion to Irenaeus, as Pagels
has done, it might be better to recognize that there was diversity
among the Gnostics regarding the ultimate destiny of the psychical.
Pagels points to passages within AH, and to excerpts of Theodotus, to
indicate that the psychic and pneumatic elements are ultimately

The final consummation of all things will therefore take place when all that is spiritual has been formed and perfected by knowledge (AH I,6,1).

People of the Church, like Irenaeus, were considered psychical. They may be established by their works and a mere faith, but they do not have perfect knowledge. Without good works such people could not be saved, whereas the Gnostics are saved because they are by nature spiritual and not because of their conduct (AH I,6,2). Continence and good works were thus unnecessary to the spiritual. Whereas the psychical had received grace simply to use, the Gnostic, who is spiritual, possesses that grace from above by an indescribable relationship (AH I,6,4).

Irenaeus notes a diversity of views among the Gnostics concerning redemption, but he discerns a general distinction between the ways in which the work of Christ is effective for the two classes. The baptism instituted by the visible Jesus was for remission of sins and was for the psychical, but the redemption accomplished by the Christ who descended on Jesus was for perfection. The obvious interpretation of the Gospels was for the psychical, but for the spiritual the hidden meaning was communicated, largely through parables. Those who have perfect knowledge must necessarily be regenerated in order to enter the Pleroma (AH I,21,2). Some of the Gnostics used no visible sacramental rite in connection with redemption, contending that perfect redemption is simply knowledge of the inexpressible Greatness (*inenarrabilis magnitudinis* [AH I,21,4]). Because defect and passion come from ignorance, knowledge will abolish everything that issued from ignorance. Knowledge is therefore the redemption of the inner person and is of a spiritual nature. Those who have knowledge of all things

---

united ("Conflicting Versions," 52-53).

need nothing else (AH I,21,4). Through the implantation of the *pneuma* in the human soul and body, "the gnosis itself is finally brought down to a sufficiently readied mankind by Jesus unified with Christos."[56] Christos descended upon the human Jesus at his baptism in the Jordan and departed from him before his passion, thereby deceiving death. As Antonio Orbe demonstrates, the Gnostics stressed the cosmic crucifixion, rather than the crucifixion of Jesus in Jerusalem.[57] Hans Jonas concludes that "the real object of salvation is the godhead itself, its theme the divine integrity."[58] He sums up:

> This is the grand "pneumatic equation" of Valentinian thought: the human-individual event in pneumatic *knowledge* is the inverse equivalent of the pre-cosmic universal event in divine *ignorance*, and in its redeeming effect of the same ontological order. The actualization of knowledge in the person is at the same time an act in the general ground of being.[59]

Pheme Perkins makes observations regarding gnosis and salvation in the Gnostic dialogues of Nag Hammadi which supplement the exposition of Irenaeus, as well as underlining its main thrust. Perkins ascribes an almost magical character to Gnostic salvation. There is none of the "direct conflict between agents of salvation and the demonic powers" which was characteristic of the "creation myths in which the monster of Chaos must be defeated before cosmic and social order can be established."[60] "Revelation and the power of the luminous beings from the light world are automatically victorious

---

[56]Jonas, *The Gnostic Religion*, 195.

[57]Antonio Orbe, *Los primeros herejes ante la persecución*, Estudios Valentinianos, Vol. V (Romae: Apud Aedes Universitatis Gregorianae, 1956), 269.

[58]Jonas, *The Gnostic Religion*, 195.

[59]Ibid., 176. Cf. AH I,21,4.

[60]Perkins, *The Gnostic Dialogue*, 170-71.

over darkness."[61] In the Gnostic scheme, humankind occupies an exalted place, higher even than the Demiurge and the intra-cosmic gods.[62] "Gnostics are the immortals in the midst of mortal humanity. Their original origin is in a heavenly aeon."[63] Revelation is described as a call, "an address being made directly to the believer" to which the hearer responds "with his or her own proclamation either in divine praises or in formulaic celebration of his or her new identity with the divine."[64] The Christian's participation in the victory of Christ over the demonic power of death is located by the Gnostics "in the preaching of Gnosis as the Savior had done."[65]

From the exposition of Irenaeus, and from the Gnostic texts themselves, it is clear then that the knowledge was not only the means to salvation, but it was virtually salvation itself, resulting as it did from events taking place within the Pleroma. A clearer picture of this theme may emerge from brief analysis of the one Gnostic text which we now possess and to which Irenaeus may have made reference, the *Gospel of Truth*.

D. The *Gospel of Truth*

1. The authorship of the *Gospel of Truth*

As indicated above, there is general agreement that the *Gospel of Truth* found at Nag Hammadi is in all

---

[61]Ibid., 171.

[62]Ibid., 172.

[63]Ibid., p. 176, citing *Sophia of Jesus Christ*, CG III,93,23 ff; *Apocryphon of Peter*, CG VII,73,9-14; 77,15-19; *Sophia of Jesus Christ*, CG III,108,15-18; *Dialogue of the Saviour*, CG III,139,16-20; *Zostrianos*, VIII,29,16-21.

[64]Ibid.

[65]Ibid., 180, citing *Sophia of Jesus Christ*, CG III,119,1-9; *Letter of Peter to Philip*, VIII,137,20-25.

probability the work to which Irenaeus referred (AH III,11,9).[66] There is also widespread consensus that this is a work of Valentinian Gnosticism and may even have been authored by Valentinus himself.[67] If the latter is true, it was probably written about 140-45, before the development of the typically Gnostic dogmas,[68] and probably in Rome, sometime before his break with the Church.[69] It is significant that Irenaeus made no real attempt to refute the Valentinian doctrine presented in the *Gospel of Truth*, only making the statement that it is not like the four canonical Gospels. Grant finds the probable reason for this in the closeness of its teaching to some other Christian teaching in the second century, such as the *Shepherd of Hermas*.[70] The work does not include "the peculiarly heretical traits of Gnosticism, such as the distinction between the Unknown God and the lower Demiurge or the enumeration of aeons."[71] This

---

[66]See above, footnote 30.

[67]H. C. Puech, "The Jung Codex," 19; G. Quispel, "The Jung Codex and Its Significance," in *The Jung Codex, a Newly Recovered Gnostic Papyrus; Three Studies*, ed. Frank Leslie Cross, 53; van Unnik, "The 'Gospel of Truth,'" 99, and van Unnik, *Newly Discovered*, 63; Krause, "Introduction to the 'Gospel of Truth,'" 37; Grant, *Gnosticism*, 128. Mention should be made, however, of the strong objection of Antonio Orbe to ascription of the *Gospel* to Valentinus because of the great difference in style between it and the homily of Valentinus quoted by Clement ("Los hombres y el creador según una homilia de Valentin" [Clem., Strom. IV,13,89,1-91,3], *Greg* 55 [1974]:368).

[68]van Unnik, "The 'Gospel of Truth,'" 99.

[69]van Unnik, *Newly Discovered*, 63. Robert Grant attempts to date it in line with his theory that Gnosticism originated out of apocalyptic Judaism. From the lack of explicit criticism of the Jews or of Jewish Christianity, he concludes that "Valentinus was trying to interpret Jewish apocalyptic Christianity as Jewish Gnostic Christianity, and that the occasion for his work, as for that of Marcion, was the apocalyptic catastrophe in the reign of Hadrian" (*Gnosticism*, 128-29).

[70]Grant, *Gnosticism*, 134.

[71]Quispel, "The Jung Codex," 134.

leads Quispel to suggest that it was probably written by
Valentinus while he was still a member of the Church of
Rome and a candidate for the bishop's throne.[72] In any
event, it appears to come from an early stage in the
development of Valentinian doctrine. It is significant to
the theme of this study because of its presentation of the
basic Gnostic teaching regarding revelation and salvation, without emphasis on the other aspects which made
Gnostic teaching so objectionable to Irenaeus.[73]

2. Revelation and salvation in the *Gospel of Truth*

The good news which is proclaimed by the *Gospel
of Truth* is the deliverance of those who were ignorant of
the Father from their darkness, through the ministry of
the Logos.

> The gospel of truth is a joy for those who have received from the
> Father of truth the gift of knowing him, through the power of the
> Word that came forth from the pleroma - the one who is in the
> thought and the mind of the Father, that is, the one who is
> addressed as Savior, (that) being the name of the work he is to
> perform for the redemption of those who were ignorant of the
> Father, while the name [of] the gospel is the proclamation of
> hope, being discovery for those who search for him. . . . This [is]
> the gospel of the one who is searched for, which [was] revealed
> to those who are perfect through the mercies of the Father - the
> hidden mystery, Jesus, the Christ. Through it he enlightened
> those who were in darkness. Out of oblivion he enlightened them,

---

[72]Ibid., 54.

[73]Andrew Helmbold raises the question "whether or not the *Gospel
of Truth* (like the later Valentinian work by Ptolemaeus, a disciple of
the master, entitled *Epistle to Flora*) deliberately disguises, 'soft
pedals,' and otherwise hides the true nature of Valentinianism so that
readers will think it is orthodox Christianity and unthinkingly accept
it" (*The Nag Hammadi Gnostic Texts and the Bible* [Grand Rapids:
Baker, 1967], 41). The answer may never be known.

he showed (them) a way. And the way is the truth which he
taught them.[74]

As was characteristic of Gnosticism generally, sin
is defined in terms of ignorance, and salvation as knowledge. Those who receive the truth, however, are those in
whom are the fallen aeons. They come to self-knowledge,
to know themselves for what they are, thereby returning
to the Father from whom they have been separated by
ignorance. The process of salvation is thus described in
terms of predestination and call. It involves a purifying
of self from involvement in the world, separation from
the material body, and ascension to the Father, to the
place of rest and blessing.

But those who are to receive [are] the living who are inscribed in
the book of the living. They receive teaching about themselves.
They receive it (pl.) from the Father, turning again to him. Then,
if one has knowledge, he receives what is his own and draws
them to himself. For he who is ignorant is in need, and what he
lacks is great since he lacks that which will make him perfect.
Since the perfection of the all is in the Father and it is necessary
for the all to ascend to him and for each one to receive what is
his own, he enrolled them in advance, having prepared them to
give to those who came forth from him.

Those whose name he knew in advance were called at the
end, so that the one who has knowledge is the one whose name
the Father has uttered. For he whose name has not been spoken
is ignorant. Indeed how is one to hear if his name has not been
called? For he who is ignorant until the end is a creature of
oblivion, and he will vanish along with it. . . . Therefore, if one
has knowledge, he is from above. If he is called, he hears, he
answers, and he turns to him who is calling him, and ascends to
him and he knows in what manner he is called. Having knowledge, he does the will of the one who called him, he wishes to be
pleasing to him, he receives rest.[75]

---

[74]"The Gospel of Truth," trans. George W. MacRae, in *The Nag
Hammadi Library in English*, ed. Marvin Meyer, 37-38.
[75]"The Gospel of Truth," 40.

E. The Gnostics and the Salvation of the Non-Christian

Perkins states that

> Gnostics have remarkably little to say about paganism. Its deities seem to be subsumed under the lesser demons. Gnostic attention is focused on the God of the Jews and the orthodox Christians, who, Gnostics argue, is not the true God at all.[76]

Jewish and Christian apologists used the transcendence of God to show the necessity of revelation,[77] and to demonstrate that their religion preserves and propagates that revelation. It appears, however, that the Gnostic emphasis on a radical transcendence and unknowability of the highest God was not made for apologetic purposes, with a view to the conversion of pagans, although the Gnostic did believe that pagan religions do not attain the truth about God. "For the Gnostic, this language is primarily a language of worship, a way of magnifying the being of God,"[78] "The primary—if not the only—target of Gnostic preaching was the larger Christian community."[79]

Irenaeus makes some interesting complaints about the syncretism of Gnostic theology which was presumably done for missionary purposes. He objects, for instance, to their use of names for the Aeons which would have a certain plausibility and credibility to the heathen because they were already used of Greek deities. The Gnostics went so far as to suggest that these Greek deities were images of the Aeons (AH II,14,9). It is fascinating to note that the Gnostics, in turn, described

---

[76]Perkins, *The Gnostic Dialogue*, 179.
[77]Ibid., 167.
[78]Ibid., 168.
[79]Ibid., 208.

the apostles as accommodating their teaching to Jewish error. Irenaeus indicates that some of the Gnostics recognized that the teaching of the apostles concerning Jesus and the Father was the same as that of Irenaeus. However, they asserted that this was because the apostles could not declare a different God to the Jews from the one in whom the Jews believed (AH III,12,6). This served the Gnostics well in responding to accusations that their dualistic and emanationist teaching was different from that of the New Testament. They could simply assert that the apostolic witness to the oneness of God was an accommodation to the beliefs of the hearers and not an essential truth. Such an approach to Scripture would be very conducive to a pluralistic approach to truth and revelation, but the Gnostics did not themselves propose a religious pluralism.

The above analysis of Gnostic doctrine, as presented by Irenaeus, indicates a position alien to "anonymous Christianity." The stress on knowledge rules out the possibility of "implicit faith." Salvation would not be possible apart from the teaching of the Gnostics. Those who accepted this teaching would, furthermore, be only those who were pneumatic or psychical by nature. The class of people who were material had nothing within them that could respond to the divine call.

Perkins has suggested that, at its core, Gnostic teaching was really universalistic. They distinguished only between some who would be saved and others who would not be when conflict with non-Gnostics indicated that not all humanity were going to accept their teaching.

Such intensified dualism does not represent Gnostic anthropology generally. The elevation of humanity above the Creator and the cosmos assures its transcosmic destiny. Metaphors of the true human soul as part of the light lost by the Mother would seem to require that all are eventually to reach that destiny.[80]

However true this construction of original Gnostic anthropology and soteriology may be, it is certainly not what appears in the representation by Irenaeus. He encountered a Gnosticism which clearly set itself apart as the saved and offered some hope to those like Irenaeus who were psychical, but none to the material by nature.

All of this is very significant as the context of Irenaeus's teaching on revelation and salvation. Given the strong Gnostic emphasis on the necessity of knowledge for salvation, the stage is set for Irenaeus to downplay that necessity, if he actually believed it to be unnecessary. A doctrine of implicit faith, or of salvation through means of revelation less developed and complete than in the incarnate Logos, would make an ideal foil to the Gnostic position.

---

[80]Perkins, *The Gnostic Dialogue*, 183.

3. THE MISSIOLOGICAL CONTEXT OF IRENAEUS'S VIEW OF THE UNEVANGELIZED

A. The Significance of Irenaeus's Perspective on the Extent of Evangelization for His View of the Unevangelized

The context of contemporary optimism regarding the saving work of God outside of the Church and its proclamation of the Gospel is an immense number of people who have not heard the Gospel or had contact with the Church. It is not surprising that questions should have been raised, in the minds of modern Christians, concerning the state of those who have no opportunity of explicit faith in Christ. In examining the attitude of second-century writers relative to the salvation of these non-Christians, it is important to determine the similarity, or difference, of their context in this regard. Did they live with the same concern for the salvation or lostness of large numbers of people beyond the reach of the Church's mission? If so, a simple comparison of their views can be made with those of modern theologians of mission. However, if their context, or at least their perception of it, was quite different from our own, that difference must be taken into account in examining their teaching as it bears on the subject of the salvation of the non-Christian. If Irenaeus did not have a consciousness of large groups of people without knowledge of Jesus Christ, his teaching must not be analyzed as though he specifically addressed the same situation that confronts the contemporary theologian who proposes the existence of "anonymous Christians."

Yves Congar points out that the Fathers and the theologians of the Middle Ages knew a religious world in which atheists were exceptional individuals. On the other hand, we know a situation of collective unbelief and a milieu of atheism or at least of negative theism.[1] While Congar is stressing the difference between our situation and that of the early Church, others have stressed the similarity. Although atheism was not a significant factor then, religious pluralism was. As W. C. van Unnik indicates,

> research has made it clear that when Christianity spread through the (known) world it did not do so in a religious vacuum or in the midst of religions that were dying away, but it found itself surrounded and opposed by a rich variety of religious patterns, theological and philosophical schools, which held out to the questing souls of men the promise of security in this world and the hereafter.[2]

Interestingly, Irenaeus used the term atheism to describe belief in a wrong kind of God. He indicated that Anaxagoras was also surnamed "Atheus" and called him irreligious. He says of Thales and Anaximander that they were not original but merely repeated the things which others have said who were "ignorant of God" (*Deum ignorant*) (AH II,14,2).[3]

---

[1] Yves M. J. Congar, "Au sujet du salut des non-catholiques," *RScRel* 32 (January 1958):62.

[2] Willem Cornelis van Unnik, *Newly Discovered Gnostic Writings: A Preliminary Survey of the Nag Hammadi Find*, Studies in Biblical Theology (Napierville, Illinois: Allenson, 1960), p. 30.

[3] See also Harry Austryn Wolfson, *The Philosophy of the Church Fathers*. Vol. 1, *Faith, Trinity, Incarnation*. Third edition revised (Cambridge, Massachusetts: Harvard University Press, 1970), 82. He notes that Justin Martyr and Clement of Alexandria used the term in

Paul Hacker criticizes Rahner for not giving
sufficient notice to this one striking similarity between
the situation of the Fathers and our own. "In the first
four centuries the Church lived in a 'religious pluralism'
scarcely less multiform than the pluralism in which we
find ourselves today."[4] To Hacker, it is very significant
that the vexation which Rahner and the others feel in
face of this fact of pluralism was not expressed by the
Fathers.[5] He concludes that

> our situation resembles that of the Fathers in that we are, as
> they were, constantly faced with the reality of other religions.
> The Fathers knew, and we have to learn anew, that this is even
> the normal situation of Christianity in the world. There is,
> therefore, no reason for a feeling of frustration.[6]

Yves Congar observes that while the Fathers knew that
there were other peoples outside of the areas in which
the Church had taken root, "on the whole they had little
curiosity or disquiet about them," and they "seem to us to
have been little disturbed about the ultimate fate of 'the
others.'"[7]

There is a factor, however, in the "vexation for
Christianity" which Rahner finds in the pluralism of
religions,[8] to which Hacker has not given proper importance, namely, the length of time between those early
Fathers and ourselves. While the early Church was
confronted with a multitude of conflicting religions, it

the same sense.

[4]Paul Hacker, "The Christian Attitude Toward Non-Christian
Religions; Some Critical and Positive Reflections," *ZMR* 55 (191):81.

[5]Ibid., 82-83.

[6]Ibid., 96.

[7]Yves Congar, *The Wide World My Parish; Salvation and Its
Problems* (Baltimore: Helicon Press, 1961), 95.

[8]"Christianity and the Non-Christian Religions," in *TI*, Vol. 5
(1966), 116.

could see progress being made. In the latter half of the second century and during the third century, remarkable expansion of the Church was experienced. What Rahner reflects on is the fact that some eighteen hundred years separate us from those second- and third-century Fathers and yet the major religions persist and grow.

What is even more significant to our study is the claim of Congar that in the eyes of the Fathers and of theologians in the Middle Ages "the Gospel had indeed been proclaimed over all the earth."[9] In other words, although many other religious views existed, the message of the Christian Church had been universally proclaimed. This contention needs to be examined, because such a perspective would constitute an important context for Irenaeus's theology of the non-Christian. Accordingly, a brief survey will be made of the extent of the Christian Church in the second century. More important, the perspectives of early Church writers will be examined, with particular attention to the position of Irenaeus.

B. The Geographical Extent of the Church at the End of the Second Century

1. North and west of Palestine

Of course, the Church existed in Jerusalem, Judea and Samaria, the location of Jesus' earthly ministry, but what of the "ends of the earth," to which Jesus ordered His disciples to carry their witness (Ac 1:8)? The *Acts of the Apostles* describes missionary work that resulted from the dispersion of the Christians after the martyrdom of Stephen, and from the missionary journeys of the Apostle Paul and his companions. The Church at

---

[9]Yves Congar, *The Wide World*, 118; cf. also "Au sujet du salut," 62.

Antioch and churches in Asia Minor were particularly significant. Mention is also made of churches in Greece, specifically in Philippi, Corinth, and Thessalonica. In Italy, Rome plays the major role, while little is known about the Church elsewhere in northern Italy, or in central and southern Italy. Karl Baus claims that the most we can say is that "in the second half of the second century some bishoprics had been established South of Rome."[10] There were certainly Christians in Sicily by the third century, and possibly in the second.[11]

Nothing is known of the introduction of Christianity into Spain. "Legend or tradition pictures the Apostle James as laboring there, declares that Paul made the projected voyage of which he speaks in his letter to the Romans, and reports that Peter sent seven bishops to the country."[12] There is no clear trace of churches and bishops in Spain until the mid-third century.[13]

France appears to have been the mission field for the vibrant Church of Asia Minor. Perhaps, as Lawson suggests, this was because of a natural kinship in race and speech, between the Gauls and the Galatians.[14] Irenaeus himself was a missionary to southern Gaul, having spent his youth in Smyrna, where he was a student of Polycarp. It may have been Polycarp who

---

[10]Karl Baus, *From the Apostolic Community to Constantine.* Vol. 1, *Handbook of Church History,* ed. Hubert Jedin and John Dolan (New York: Herder & Herder, 1965), 210.

[11]Kenneth Scott Latourette, *A History of the Expansion of Christianity,* Vol. 1: *The First Five Centuries* (Grand Rapids: Zondervan, 1970), 96.

[12]Ibid.

[13]Philip Schaff, *A History of the Christian Church.* Vol. 2, *Ante-Nicene Christianity, A.D. 100-325* (New York: Charles Scribner's Sons, 1888), 29.

[14]John Lawson, *The Biblical Theology of St. Irenaeus* (London: Epworth Press, 1948), 3.

persuaded him to go to France to assist Pothinus, then an aging bishop, who had been sent there by Polycarp.[15] He served for some years as a presbyter, during which time he was sent to Eleutherius, Bishop of Rome, with letters from the persecuted Christians in Lyons and Vienne, during the reign of Marcus Aurelius Antoninus, about 177. When Pothinus died in prison, under the persecution, Irenaeus succeeded him as Bishop of Lyons (ca. 179-202).

Irenaeus preached to both Celtic- and Latin-speaking people, and it appears that there was some success in the spread of the Gospel during his time. Maisie Ward reports that "new Christian groups sprang up at Tours, Châlons and Autun," while Dijon, Langres and Besançon "were also probably reached at this time."[16] André Benoit likewise speaks of the large impact of the Church at Lyons on all of Gaul.[17] However, in terms of the total picture of evangelization of the area, the response was relatively discouraging, as viewed from the situation a short time later. "As late as 250, scattered churches in half a dozen communities embraced only a small number of converts. A century later, when Martin of Tours became bishop of the diocese, the surrounding countryside was still largely pagan."[18] That the Church at Lyons was itself small in the time of Irenaeus is

---

[15]William Cave, *Lives of the Most Eminent Fathers of the Church That Flourished in the First Four Centuries with an Historical Account of the State of Paganism Under the First Christian Emperors* (Oxford: Thomas Tegg, 1840), 1:26.

[16]Maisie Ward, *Early Church Portrait Gallery* (London: Sheed & Ward, 1959), 51.

[17]André Benoit, *Saint Irénée: Introduction à l'étude de sa théologie* (Paris: Presses Universitaires de France, 1960), 54.

[18]J. Herbert Kane, *A Concise History of the Christian World Mission: A Panoramic View of Missions from Pentecost to the Present* (Grand Rapids: Baker, 1978), 11.

evident from the fact that, though the persecution of 177 was violent, it took only forty-eight victims, and it is significant that the list of martyrs includes no Celtic names.[19]

Irenaeus spoke of Christian congregations in Germany (AH I,10,2), which Karl Baus takes to be probably "in the Rhenish provinces with their chief towns of Cologne and Mainz."[20] Schaff contends that Irenaeus could only have been referring to parts of Germany belonging to the Roman Empire.[21] Christians among the soldiers in the Danubian provinces may have been responsible for occasional converts.[22] Eusebius reports a miracle experienced in response to the prayer of Christian soldiers in the legion quartered at Melitene under Marcus Aurelius.[23] Tertullian and Origen spoke of the Gospel's extension to Britain "but probably the Church had little serious foothold until the middle of the third century."[24]

2. South of Palestine

A very important movement grew in North Africa, which became the home of Latin Christian literature through the work of Tertullian, and later of Cyprian and Augustine.[25] There was a flourishing church in Carthage, and strong progress was made in lower Egypt,

---

[19]Benoit, 53.

[20]Baus, 211.

[21]Schaff, 30.

[22]Baus, 209.

[23]Eusebius, *The History of the Church from Christ to Constantine*, V,5, trans. with an introduction by G. A. Williamson (New York: New York University Press, 1966), 63.

[24]Henry Chadwick, *The Early Church* (Baltimore: Penguin, 1967), 63.

[25]Latourette, 92.

Alexandria.[26] By the end of the second century a foothold had even been established in upper Egypt.

> Papyrus fragments show that in the second-century the mission had moved far up the Nile Valley. . . . A papyrus find proves that Irenaeus's refutation of Gnosticism was being read at Oxyrhynchus within a very few years of its publication, which suggests much concern in Egypt for the maintenance of orthodoxy.[27]

3. East of Palestine

The Church made further progress eastward. "Whereas southern Arabia appears to have had no Christians for a longer time, northern Arabia or Transjordan shows evidence that Christianity was known there in the first and second centuries."[28] The Gospel was carried at an early date to Edessa, the capital of the small state of Osrhene, in Mesopotamia. A legend recorded by Eusebius traced the origin of the Christian gospel to a request from Abgar, King of Edessa, to Jesus to come and heal him. After the resurrection, Thaddaeus was reportedly sent by Thomas and healed the King, resulting in the faith of the whole city.[29] It is more likely that the Christian message reached Edessa by the trade route from Antioch.[30] Whatever its origin, there was clearly a thriving Syriac-speaking Christian community there in the second century with its own translation of the Gospel and a body of indigenous literature. Its "native kings were Christian before their territory was

---

[26]George Park Fisher, *History of the Christian Church* (New York: Charles Scribner's Sons, 1897), 45.

[27]Chadwick, 64.

[28]Baus, 208.

[29]Eusebius I,13 (65-66); II,1 (72-73).

[30]Latourette, 101.

"native kings were Christian before their territory was
absorbed in the Empire in A.D. 216."[31] From Edessa,
the missionary Adai carried the Gospel further east into
Mesopotamia.[32]

Eusebius reports the tradition of the scattering of
the apostles and disciples "over the whole world. Thomas,
tradition tells us, was chosen for Parthia, Andrew for
Scythia, John for Asia."[33] Mark had reportedly been the
first to take the Gospel to Egypt.[34] A rather well-
founded tradition claims that Thomas first preached the
Gospel in India, in A.D. 52, and was martyred there in
A.D. 72. He was "reputed to have made thousands of
converts during his missionary career."[35] Eusebius tells
us that Pantaenus of Alexandria, "one of the most
eminent teachers of his day," traveled as far as India
about 180.[36] There, "he appears to have found that
Matthew's Gospel had arrived before him and was in the
hands of some there who had come to know Christ.
Bartholomew, one of the apostles, had preached to them
and had left behind Matthew's account in the actual
Aramaic characters.[37] G. A. Williamson notes that

[31]Cyril Bailey et al. *The History of Christianity in the Light of
Modern Knowledge, a Collective Work* (London: Blackie & Son, 1929),
427.

[32]Baus, 208.

[33]Eusebius III,1 (107).

[34]Eusebius II,16 (89).

[35]J. Herbert Kane, *A Global View of Christian Missions from
Pentecost to the Present* (Grand Rapids: Baker, 1971), 108.

[36]Eusebius V,10 (213). Schaff finds this tradition concerning
Pantaenus "more credible" than that of Thomas and Bartholomew
(23).

[37]Eusebius V,10 (213).

"India may mean any country east of Ethiopia."[38] However, the state of contact with India does not make it at all unlikely that the Gospel reached there in the second century. Philip Carrington describes the situation:

> There were three roads to India; by sea from Egypt, by sea from the Gulf of Akaba, which was linked by road with the Roman province of Arabia, and down the Euphrates and Tigris to the Persian Gulf. Communication was slow and difficult and dangerous, but it was established; Buddhist monks had turned up in Egypt in the time of the Ptolemies; Brahmins had visited the court of Augustus; trade missions had come to the court of Antoninus. Towards the end of the second century, the Romans had built permanent trading posts on the Indian coast, and a certain amount of information was disseminated. Romantic pictures of the Brahmins were current; it was understood that they lived naked, abstained from all bodily appetites, and had incredible mental powers.[39]

4. Summary

It is clear then that, by the end of the second century, at the time when Irenaeus was writing, the Church was spread at least from Gaul (possibly Britain) to India, north into Germany, and south into Egypt and North Africa. It spread throughout the Roman Empire and beyond.[40] More significant than this actual geographical spread, however, was the optimism expressed by the early Christian writers concerning the growth of the Church and the extent of evangelization.

---

[38]Ibid., n. 1 (214).
[39]Philip Carrington, *The Early Christian Church*. Vol. 2. *The Second Christian Century* (Cambridge: University Press, 1957), 284.
[40]Ibid., 21.

C. Early Christian Views of the State of Evangelization in the Second Century

1. Justin Martyr

Writing in about A.D. 148, Justin addressed his *First Apology* to the Emperor and others "in behalf of those men of every race who are unjustly hated and mistreated."[41] He described Christians as those "who from every nation, once worshipped Bacchus" and other gods but who "now, through Jesus Christ, even under the threat of death, hold these in contempt."[42] He saw prophecy fulfilled in the universal spread of the Church:

> But the prophecy, "He shall be the desire of nations," meant that people from all nations would look for his second coming, as you yourselves can see with your own eyes and be convinced by factual evidence: for men of every nation look for him who was crucified in Judea.[43]

Even more enthusiastically he wrote:

> There are no people, Greek or barbarian, or of any other race, by whatsoever appellation or manners they may be distinguished, however ignorant of arts or agriculture, whether they dwell in tents or wander about in covered wagons—among whom prayers and thanksgivings are not offered in the name of the crucified Jesus to the Father and Creator of all things.[44]

Of the last statement, Edward Gibbon said that it was "splendid exaggeration . . . of a devout but careless

---

[41]*First Apology* c. 1, in *Writings of St. Justin Martyr*, trans. and ed. Thomas B. Falls. The Fathers of the Church, A New Translation, no. 6 (New York: Christian Heritage, 1948), 33.

[42]*First Apology* c. 25 (60).

[43]*First Apology* c. 32 (68).

[44]Cited by Schaff, 22.

writer."[45] Even given the spread of Christianity indicated above, Gibbon is correct in accusing Justin of exaggeration. The question is: did Justin deliberately use hyperbole or did he actually believe that there were *no* "hidden people" in his day, no group without the gospel, or without Christian presence? Given his apologetic purpose, some hyperbole is quite possible. Yet, his apology would be too simply dismissed if he blatantly stretched the truth concerning the spread of Christianity. It would appear that, however overenthusiastic Justin may appear to have been from our knowledge of the actual missionary situation, he did have a very optimistic view of the spread of the Christian Church and of the gospel, in his day. This is significant because of the obvious recourse that Irenaeus had to Justin's writings.

2. Tertullian

Writing shortly after Irenaeus, but describing the same situation at the end of the second century, Tertullian was as enthusiastic about the triumph of Christianity as was Justin. In his *Apology*, written toward the close of A.D. 197, he describes the potential threat of Christians should they be provoked to rebellion, because of their large numbers and their pervasiveness.

> If we wanted to act as open enemies and not merely as secret avengers, would we lack the strength of numbers and troops? Take the Moors and Marcomani and the Parthians themselves or any tribes at all who, even if they are numerous, still live in one place and inhabit their own territories—are they really more numerous than the Christians who are scattered over the whole world? We are but of yesterday, yet we have filled every place

---

[45]*The Triumph of Christendom in the Roman Empire* (New York: Harper Bros.. 1958), 68, cited by Kane, *A Concise History*, 16.

among you—cities, islands, fortresses, towns, marketplaces, camp, tribes, town councils, the palace, the senate, the forum; we have left nothing to you but the temples of your gods.[46]

In the same vein he wrote: "For now the enemies whom you have are fewer because of the numbers of Christians, inasmuch as nearly all the citizens you have in nearly all the cities are Christians."[47]

Daly notes that "Tertullian here testifies to the rapid spread of Christianity, but he is doubtless indulging to some degree in hyperbole."[48] Granted that probability, however, it is clear that Tertullian too had a very triumphalistic view of the spread of the Gospel.

3. Eusebius

Although writing after the time of Constantine, Eusebius speaks of the second century in the same glowing terms as have been noted in second-century writers. Speaking of those who were the immediate successors of the apostles, he said: "These earnest disciples of great men built on the foundations of the churches everywhere laid by the apostles, spreading the message still further and sowing the saving seed of the Kingdom of Heaven far and wide through the entire world."[49] Describing the situation in Hadrian's time (117-38), he spoke of the circumstances that precipitated Irenaeus's apologetic work: "Like dazzling lights the churches were now shining all over the world, and to the limits of the human race faith in our Savior and Lord

---

[46]*Apology* 37,4 in *Apologetical Works*, trans. Emily Joseph Daly. The Fathers of the Church, A New Translation, no. 10 (New York: Fathers of the Church, 1950), 95.

[47]*Apology* 37,8 (96).

[48]Ibid., p. 95, n. 1.

[49]Eusebius II,37 (148).

Jesus Christ was at its peak"[50] when Menander, Saturninus, Basilides and others rose up within the Church as a trap to the ignorant.

These perspectives now provide a context in which to examine the state of evangelization as Irenaeus viewed it.

D. Irenaeus on the Extent of Evangelization

One of the attractive features of "anonymous Christianity" is its starting point in the good will of God toward people, with regard to their salvation—His "universal salvific will." On the other hand, theologies of the Calvinistic flavor have often met resistance because of a double predestinarian position, or the doctrine of reprobation. It runs counter to a common human sense of fairness to believe that certain people are condemned for eternity because of the lack of gracious disposition of God toward them in His eternal counsel. Even among theologians of a more Arminian bent, where the responsibility for human unbelief is traced clearly to the person who rejects God, there is a resistance to extending God's condemnation to those whose unbelief may be largely the result of a lack of knowledge of the gospel or contact with the Church.

As was seen above, the Valentinians were, in a manner, predestinarian in their view of salvation. The salvation of the pneumatics was determined from birth by their relationship to the Aeons. Likewise, the condemnation of the hylics. For the psychics, however, there was a degree to which their destiny depended on their personal obedience. The position of Irenaeus will be

---

[50]Ibid., IV,7 (158).

developed at a greater length in later chapters, but it is
significant to note, at this point, that he placed the blame
for human condemnation squarely on personal human
choice and not as the consequence of any lack of necessary divine grace. Human beings are free agents who
have power to obey God's command voluntarily (AH
IV,37,1).

> For there is no violence in God, but good will is always present
> in him. And because of this He gives good counsel to all. And he
> has placed in people the power of choice, as also in angels—for
> angels are rational beings—in order that those who have been
> obedient might justly possess the good, given certainly by God,
> but kept by themselves. But those who have not been obedient
> shall justly be not found with the good and shall receive the
> deserved punishment, because God kindly gave the good; but
> they themselves did not diligently keep it precious, but despised
> his supereminent goodness (IV,37,1).

   In placing the blame for people's condemnation
upon their own choice with regard to God, Irenaeus
appears to assume that all have had the opportunity to
respond appropriately. God "gives good counsel *to all*"
(IV,37,1) [emphasis supplied]. If people do not believe in
God, the fault does not lie in God who calls them, but in
those who do not obey (AH IV,39,3). Referring to the
parable of the marriage supper in Matthew 22, Irenaeus
stresses that the Lord has called us *everywhere* by the
apostles, just as He formerly called people by the
prophets (AH IV,36,5; cf. IV,39,3). He appears to have
believed that in the time of the apostles the world had
been evangelized, and that this was in fulfillment of Old
Testament prophecy and in obedience to the commission
of Christ.
   Irenaeus details the manner in which Christ
fulfilled Old Testament prophecy, and concludes that

our belief in him was well-grounded, and true the tradition of the preaching, that is, the witness of the apostles, who, sent by the Lord, preached *to the whole world* that the Son of God was come unto sufferings, undergone for the destruction of death and the giving of life to the flesh.[51] [emphasis supplied]

This universal proclamation had been foretold by David who "says that it was to be preached to all the earth: 'Their sound is gone forth into all the earth, and their words unto the ends of the earth'" (Proof, 86, citing Ps 19:5 as quoted in Rom 10:18). It was after the descent of the Holy Spirit that the apostles were sent "into the whole world and carried out the calling of the Gentiles, showing mankind the way of life, turning them back from idols and from fornication and from selfish pride, purifying their souls and their bodies through the baptism of water and of the Holy Spirit" (Proof, 41). Or, as Irenaeus says elsewhere, "they went to the ends of the earth [*in fines terrae*]" evangelizing or declaring the good news concerning the good things which have come to us from God (AH III,1,1). It would be interesting to know whether Irenaeus had in mind the tradition that the apostles had spread themselves out over the world, but there is no reference to this in his extant writings. He would surely have known of the tradition.

Moving from the days of the apostles to his own, Irenaeus speaks of the Church as spread throughout the whole world. He defended the appropriateness of four Gospels as four pillars of the Church, "since there are four regions of the world in which we are, and four

---

[51]*Proof of the Apostolic Preaching*, 86 (100). Unless otherwise noted, all quotations from the *Proof* are from the translation by Joseph P. Smith, in the series Ancient Christian Writers: The Works of the Fathers in Translation, vol. 16 (Westminster, Maryland: Newman Press, 1952). Henceforth, references will be cited parenthetically in the text as "Proof."

principal [*principales* or *katholika*] winds and the Church
is distributed over all the earth [*katespartai . . . epi pasēs
tēs gēs*]" (AH III,11,8), and has for her columns and
foundation the Gospel of the spirit of life.

Against the diversity of teaching amongst the
Gnostics, Irenaeus pleaded the unity of faith, which was
preserved in the Church which was "dispersed in the
whole world" (AH I,10,2).[52] Although preserved in many
different languages around the world, the content of the
tradition was the same, whether in the churches established in Germany, in Spain, among the Celts in Gaul, in
the East, in Egypt, in Libya, or in those which are
established in the "center of the world," presumably
Rome (AH I,10,2). "As the sun, the creature of God, is one
and the same in the whole world, so also the light, the
preaching [*kērygma*] of the truth shines everywhere and
enlightens all people who are willing to come to a knowledge of truth" (AH I,10,2). Jean Daniélou seems justified
in his comment on this passage that "Irenaeus's ecclesiastical frontiers are identical with those of the known world
of his day."[53]

---

[52]"in universum mundum disseminata."

[53]Jean Daniélou, *Gospel Message and Hellenistic Culture; A
History of Early Christian Doctrine Before the Council of Nicea*. Vol.
2, trans. and ed. John Austin Baker (Philadelphia: Westminster,
1973), 150. Cf. Hans Kung: "At one time—the Fathers of the Church
and the flowering of Patristics—the *ecclesia catholica* extended more
or less throughout the known world. The Church had a secure place
. . . in the whole of the inhabited world; it even seemed for a period
that the whole world was Christian. Given these limited geographical
perspectives, it was easier to formulate an axiom like 'no salvation
outside the Church'. It was taken for granted that more or less every
human being would be brought face to face existentially with the
Christian message" (*The Church*, trans. Ray Ockendem and Rosaleen
Ockendem [London: Burns & Oates, 1967], 313).

E. Conclusion

This brief survey of the missionary situation in the second century has indicated that the Gospel had not in fact reached the whole world, nor had the Church been established throughout the world, at the end of the second century when Irenaeus wrote. However, second-century writers spoke very optimistically about the spread of the gospel, and Irenaeus himself appears to have shared this optimism. In unqualified terms he described the evangelization of the world by the apostles, in their day, and the universal dispersion of the Church in his own. It is clear that Irenaeus did not develop a doctrine of revelation, or of salvation, in a context in which he was conscious of large numbers of people who were out of reach of the gospel or out of contact with the Church. Irenaeus can not be expected to speak explicitly of "anonymous Christianity" because anonymity presupposes lack of knowledge of the gospel or of contact with the Church.[54] It cannot be concluded, therefore, from his lack of such teaching, that he would have rejected such a concept if he had written with an awareness of large numbers of people who were without the Gospel. The remainder of this study will have to determine, from a careful examination of Irenaeus's teaching concerning divine revelation, whether there is in his belief a position which is compatible with "anonymous Christianity" and which could have developed into such a view, if his context (or rather, his understanding of it) had been different.

---

[54]Our conclusions thus accord well with Rahner's own analysis of the patristic context. Cf. "Membership of the Church According to the Teaching of Pius XII's Encyclical 'Mystici Corporis Christi,'" in *TI*, Vol. 2 (1963), 40. See above, ch. 1, C,8.

4. THE FATHER: INCOMPREHEN-SIBLE, BUT PROGRESSIVELY MAKING HIMSELF KNOWN

A. The Transcendent Father

The Gnostics stressed the great distance between humanity and the Father, a gap bridged by the many Aeons. The Father, as distinguished from the Demiurge, or Creator, was completely unknowable by human beings (AH IV,19,3). In countering this distortion of divine transcendence, Irenaeus did not go to the extreme of denying the Father's distance from humanity, his "otherness." Indeed, Irenaeus uses "at least eleven different attributes, and their respective nouns and verbs, to express God's sovereign transcendence regarding human knowledge."[1]

Irenaeus describes God as *immensurabilis* or *impossibile . . . mensurari* (AH III,24,2; IV,19,2; IV,20,1) the God who cannot be measured. He is *incapabilis* or *achōrētos* (AH IV,20,5),[2] beyond the grasp of people;

---

[1]Juan Ochagavía, *Visibile Patris Filius: A Study of Irenaeus's Teaching on Revelation and Tradition*, Orientalia Christiana Analecta, no. 171 (Rome: Pont. Institutum Orientalium Studiorum, 1964), 22.

[2]It should be noted here, and throughout the remainder of this study, that, although Irenaeus wrote in Greek, we have only fragments of the Greek text today. The Latin translation (probably from the third century) appears to be a very literal rendering of the Greek, with the consequence that it is not good Latin. However, that has made reconstruction of the Greek somewhat easier. Rousseau indicates that there are Greek fragments of about 74% of Book I, 3%,

incomprehensibilis or *akatalēptos* (AH II,18,2; III,11,5; IV,20,5), beyond human ability to comprehend him; *indeterminabilis* (AH IV,16,3; II,25,4), that is, infinite, without limit, beyond comprehension. God is also *inenarrabilis*, *arrētos* or *anexēgētos* (AH II,13,4; IV,20,5; Proof 8,70), that is, indescribable[3] or beyond the power of expression, while also having "the nuance of something secret and mysterious, that cannot be revealed."[4] He is *inexcogitabilis*, or *anennoētos* (AH I,14,1), also translated *incognoscibilis*, the one beyond conception (AH I,15,5).[5] He is the inscrutable or unsearchable one, the God who is *investigabilis* or *anexichniaston* (AH IV,20,5; V,36,3).[6] He is invisible (*invisibilis*, *aoratos* [AH I,10,1; III,11,6; V,16,2; Proof 47]), *non transibilis* (AH II,25,4), a God who cannot be surpassed, as the Gnostics supposed in postulating a God beyond the Creator. He is *agennētos*, or *agenētos*,[7] variously translated as *ingenitus* (AH II,34,2),

---

11%, 7% and 17% of the remaining four books, respectively. (SC # 263, p. 61; SC # 293, p. 83). For Books I, III, IV, and V, the editors of the Sources Chrétiennes' critical editions have attempted to reconstruct the original Greek text. This is very helpful to the reader, but it will always have to be kept in mind that, outside of Book I, the Greek cited is largely the product of retranslation.

[3]G. W. H. Lampe, ed., *A Patristic Greek Lexicon* (Oxford: Clarendon Press, 1961), 134.

[4]Ochagavía, 22, n. 7.

[5]Lampe, 134.

[6]"Non praevalentes investigare."

[7]G. L. Prestige has an interesting discussion of the difference in meaning between *agennētos* (ingenerate) and *agenētos* (uncreated), as used by pre-Nicene fathers (*God in Patristic Thought* [London: SPCK, 1964], 37-54). He concludes that "it would seem that there is nothing much to choose between agennetos and agenetos, except a vague sense of the greater propriety of the personal term in connection with the personal being. We are dealing with alternative spellings of a single word, in fact, rather than with two separate terms bearing distinct connotations" (43). His study of these terms in Irenaeus indicates that the Gnostics "habitually employed the double nn," whereas Irenaeus,

infectus (AH IV,38,3), *innatus* (AH IV,38,1), or even trans-
literated as *agennetos* (AH I,11,3). Hence, he is separated
from those who are only created beings and therefore
imperfect. "The *ageneton* exists *per se*: its cause lies
within its own being."[8]

This description of God might appear to separate
him irremediably from human knowledge, but Irenaeus
tempers this in two ways. First, he teaches that, though
God is beyond humans' grasp, he wills to make himself
known. Second, Irenaeus distinguishes between two
orders of knowledge. In relation to the first point, it did
not surprise Irenaeus that the Gnostics had no knowledge of God, because they had cut themselves off from
him by blasphemously imagining that they had "discovered another God beyond God" (AH III,24,2),[9] or
another Pleroma, or a different economy. It is God
himself who provides humankind with the power to
"discover" (*invenire*) him and who illumines people with
a light from himself (AH III,24,2).[10] Precisely because
the Gnostics refuse to admit that the true God, Father
and Creator, has communicated with the human race,
and that he exercises his providence over the details of
human life, thus dishonoring and despising God, they are
bound not to know him (AH II,24,2).

Through God's love and great goodness
(*immensam benignitatem*) toward us, he has come into
the realm of human knowledge. This knowledge, however, is not of his greatness or grandeur (*magnitudinem*)

"when writing in his own person, prefers the form agenetos," to which
infectus corresponds in the Latin (44). Prestige concludes that, for
Irenaeus, "the meaning is the same, but the spelling is governed by an
unconcious sense of the greater propriety of the associations connected
with one or the other distinct derivation" (46).

[8]Prestige, 46.

[9]"Super Deum alterum invenisse Deum."

[10]"Lumen quod est a Deo non lucet eis."

nor of his essence (*substantiam/ousian*) which are beyond human measure or grasp. It is, rather, a knowledge that the only true God is the God who made humankind, and who nourishes us by creation; who established all things by his Word and who coordinates them by his Wisdom (AH III,24,2).[11] Again, in Book IV, Irenaeus draws a distinction between the knowledge of God with regard to his greatness and knowledge with regard to his love.

> Therefore, according to his greatness, it is not possible to know God, for it is impossible to measure the Father; but according to his love (for it is that which leads us to God by his Word) those who obey him always learn that there exists a God so great, and that it is he who by himself has created and made and adorned and contains all things (AH IV,20,1).[12]

This knowledge according to his love is mediated through the Son (AH IV,20,4).[13] It was, furthermore, predicted by the prophets, conforming to the promise of the Lord that people should see God (AH IV,20,5; cf. IV,20,6) not

---

[11]"Agnitionem autem non secundum magnitudinem nec secundum substantiam, nemo enim mensus est eum nec palpavit, sed secundum illud ut sciremus quoniam qui fecit et plasmavit et insufflationem vitae insufflavit in eis et per conditionem nutrit nos, Verbo suo confirmans et Sapientia compingens omnia, hic est solus verus Deus."

[12]"Igitur secundum magnitudinem non est cognoscere Deum: impossibile est enim mensurari Patrem; secundum autem dilectionem ejus—haec est enim quae nos per Verbum ejus perducit ad Deum—obediantes si semper discunt quoniam est tantus Deus, et ipse est qui per semetipsum constituit et fecit et adornavit et continet omnia."

[13]"Unus igitur Deus, qui Verbo et Sapentia fecit et aptavit omnia. Hic est autem Demiurgus, qui et mundum hunc attribuit humano generi, qui secundum magnitudinem quidem ignotus est omnibus his qui ab eo facti sunt—nemo enim investigavit altitudinem ejus, neque veterum neque eorum qui nunc sunt—, secundum autem dilectionem cognoscitur semper per eum per quem constituit omnia. Est autem hic Verbum ejus, Dominus noster Jesus Christus."

according to his greatness and his indescribable glory
(*inenarrabilem gloriam*) but according to his love and
goodness to people (AH IV,20,5)[14] and by his infinite
power. Exodus 33:20 states that "nemo videbit Deum et
vivet," ("no one sees God and lives") but the Lord promised: "Beati mundo corde, quoniam ipsi Deum videbunt"
("Blessed are the pure in heart, for they shall see God"
(AH IV,20,5, citing Mt 5:8). This is possible because "that
which is impossible with mortals is possible with God"
(AH IV,20,5, citing Lk 18:27).

There is, therefore, a tension between the transcendence of God in his incomprehensibility and the
knowledge people have of him through his works as
mediated by the Son according to his love. As Irenaeus
described that tension, in his *Proof of the Apostolic
Preaching*, God was "called in the Law, 'the God of
Abraham and the God of Isaac and the God of Jacob, the
God of the living.' Yet is the sublimity and greatness of
this same God beyond the power of expression" (Proof 8).

B. The Father's Life-Giving Self-Revelation

1. To see God is to live

The significance of human ability to know God
according to his love is found in the life-giving quality
that Irenaeus attributes to the vision or knowledge of
God. There is a progression in people's coming to knowledge of the Father that leads them in successive stages,
through the economic operations of the persons of the

---

[14]Literally "his human kindness" (*humanitatem*), which Rousseau
translates "sa bonté envers les hommes" and reconstructs in the Greek
as *philanthrōpia*.

Trinity, to the point at which they see God and have immortality.

> For God is powerful in all things, having been seen at that time
> through the Spirit in a prophetic mode, and having been seen
> through the Son adoptively, and he shall be seen also in the
> kingdom of heaven in a fatherly manner, the Spirit preparing
> people in the Son of God, the Son leading them to the Father,
> and the Father giving them incorruptibility in eternal life, which
> comes to everyone from the fact of seeing God. For just as those
> who see the light are within the light and participate in its
> brightness, so also those who see God are in God and share in his
> brightness. The brightness of God makes them alive, therefore
> those who see God have a part in life. And this is why he, though
> beyond human grasp and incomprehensible and invisible, made
> himself visible and comprehensible and within human capacity,
> in order to make alive those who receive and see him (*tous
> chōrountas kai blepontas auton*). For just as his greatness is
> inscrutable, so also his goodness is inexpressible; through which,
> having been seen, he gives life, and the means of life come
> through sharing in God, but sharing in God is to see God and to
> enjoy his goodness (AH IV,20,5,6; cf. IV,38,3; III,20,2).[15]

---

[15]AH IV,20,5: "Potens est enim in omnibus Deus, visus quidem
tunc per Spiritum prophetice, visus autem et per Filium adoptive,
videbitur autem in regno caelorum paternaliter, Spiritu quidem
praeparante hominem in Filium Dei Filio autem adducente ad
Patrem, Patre autem incorruptelam donante in aeternam vitam, quae
unicuique evenit ex eo quod videat Deum. Quemadmodum enim
videntes lumen intra lumen sunt et claritatem ejus percipiunt, sic et
qui vident Deum intra Deum sunt, percipientes ejus claritatem.
Vivificat autem Dei claritas: percipiunt ergo vitam qui vident Deum.
Et propter hoc incapabilis et incomprehensibilis et invisibilis visibilem
se et comprehensibilem et capacem hominibus praestat, ut vivificat
percipientes et videntes se. Quemadmodum enim magnitudo ejus
investigabilis, sic et benignitas ejus inenarrabilis, per quam visus
vitam praestat his qui vident eum: quoniam vivere sine vita
impossibile est, subsistentia autem vitae de Dei participatione evenit,
participatio autem Dei est videre Deum et frui benignitate ejus."
  Cf. IV,20,6: "Homines igitur videbunt Deum ut vivant, per
visionem immortales facti et pertingentes usque in Deum" ("Therefore,

This is certainly an important concept to keep in mind as consideration is given to the condition of the non-Christian. If "life" requires vision of God, clearly some means of that vision must be possible to those outside of the gospel if they are to have life.

2. The Father's will to be known

Given the essential incomprehensibility of the Father, it is clear to Irenaeus that no knowledge of God is possible for people by their own power (AH IV,20,5). God can be known only as he wills to be known, and it is humankind's blessing that God chooses to reveal himself to them. When he chooses to be seen by people, he is seen by those whom he wills to see him, when and as he pleases (AH IV,20,5, IV,5,1).[16] Clearly, knowledge of God is the result of a divine initiative toward us, and this initiative is assured by God's continual good will toward humanity (AH IV,37,1).[17] There is something of a

---

people will see God in order to live, being made immortal by the sight and attaining even unto God"); IV,38,3: "Deus enim est qui habet videri, visio autem Dei efficax est incorruptelae, 'incorruptela vero proximum facit esse Deo.'" ("For it is God who has to be seen, and the vision of God procures incorruptibility, and incorruptibility makes us near to God" [Wisdom 6:19]).

Cf. the excellent discussion of salvation as the vision of God by José González-Faus, *Carne de Dios: significado salvador de la Encarnación en la teología de san Ireneo* (Barcelona: Herder, 1969), 43-59. It is helpful to note, as González-Faus does, the close relationship in this passage between the theme of salvation as vision of God and another important theme for Irenaeus—salvation as communion with God.

[16]AH IV,20,5: "Homo etenim a se non videbit Deum; ille autem volens videbitur hominibus, quibus vult et quando vult et quemadmodum vult." AH IV,5,1: "quoniam impossibile erat sine Deo discere Deum."

[17]"Vis enim a Deo non fit, sed bona sententia adest illi semper." Cf.

"universal salvific will" implied here. To know God is life, and it is God's desire to be known by all people. However, he will not force people to obey him. He created humans as free agents, having a certain autonomy from the beginning, with power over their own souls, to follow God's counsel of their own volition and not by force on God's part (AH IV,37,1).[18]

3. The universality of the Father's self-revelation

One of the peculiarities of the Gnostic doctrine of the Aeons was the belief that the Demiurge or Creator of the world was ignorant of the Almighty Father. To Irenaeus this made no sense, since the Demiurge was purportedly a creature of the Father and hence contained by him, and must, therefore, have knowledge of the Father. The same argument would be true also of the angels (AH II,6). Irenaeus was ready to grant that God would be invisible and unknown to his creatures because of his great eminence (*eminentiam*), yet they could not be totally ignorant of him because of his providence (*providentiam*) (AH II,6).

Irenaeus appeals to a universal consensus that God is Creator of the world. This was a truth which the ancients carefully preserved from the tradition of the first created man. The prophets later reaffirmed it, and even the pagans assent to it, having learned it from creation. For the created world itself reveals the God who made it

---

IV,14,2; and Leonard deMoor, "The Idea of Revelation in the Early Church, Part 2," *EvQ* 50 (1978):233.

[18]"Liberum eum Deus fecit, ab initio habentem suam potestatem sicut et suam animam, ad utendum sententia Dei voluntarie, et non coactum ab eo."

(AH II,19,1).[19] Furthermore, the universal Church has accepted this as an apostolic tradition (AH II,19,1).[20] God's providence over the affairs of the world which he created is a further self-revelation accessible to all. It was the denial of this providence of God by the Gnostics which cut them off from knowledge of the true God. What they discovered instead was "the God of Epicurus who does nothing either for himself or for others, that is One who has no providence" (AH III,24,2).

The providence of God is a basic and obvious fact in the thought of Irenaeus, as is the necessary consequence that he is known by those creatures for whom he cares and whom he governs. These creatures are not irrational but have a perception or understanding which is itself received through the providence of God. This explains why some of the pagans (*ethnicorum*) were moved by providence, although feebly, to declare that the Maker of this universe is a Father who takes care of all things and administers our world. Granted, these were the people who had been less enslaved by seductive pleasures and less carried away by idolatrous superstition (AH III,25,1).[21] Nevertheless, they serve as

---

[19]"Et mundus manifestat eum qui se disposuit."

[20]"Ecclesia autem omnis per universum orbem hanc accepit ab apostolis traditionem."

[21]"Providentiam autem habet Deus omnium, propter hoc et consilium dat; consilium autem dans adest his qui morum providentiam habent. Necesse est igitur ea quae providentur et gubernantur cognoscere suum rectorem, quae quidem non sunt irrationabilia neque vana, sed habent sensibilitatem perceptam de providentia Dei. Et propter hoc ethnicorum quidam, qui minus illecebris ac voluptatibus servierunt et non in tantum superstitione idolorum abducti sunt, providentia eius moti licet tenuiter, tamen conversi sunt ut dicerent Fabricatorem huius universitatis Patrem

witnesses to the revelatory value of God's providence. Even Plato confessed God to be just and good, with power over all, and exercising judgment. It could thus be said that he, too, bore witness to the providence of God and thereby showed himself more religious than the Gnostics (AH III,25,5).[22] Scripture attests that God created all things, and creation witnesses to the one God who made and rules it. Therefore, those who blind their eyes to this demonstration are to be considered very obtuse or stupid (AH II,27,2).

Though more will be said about the indispensable role of the Word, in the next chapter, it should be noted here that this knowledge of God through his creation and providence is mediated by the Word who played so critical a role in both of these activities of the Godhead (AH IV,6,1 & 6; IV,20,4).

Particularly revealed in the creative and providential work of God are his power, wisdom and goodness. His power and goodness are seen in that he has voluntarily created and made things which did not previously exist. His wisdom is apparent in that he has made his creature in proportion and harmony. His liberal giving of what is good to his creatures reflects glory upon the Uncreated One who is so overwhelmingly good (AH IV,38,3).[23]

---

omnium providentem et disponentem secundum nos mundum."

[22]In enumerating the natural phenomena which point to God's existence, Irenaeus follows common Stoic arguments (II,30,2-3).

[23]"Circa Deum autem virtus simul et sapientia et bonitas ostenditur, virtus quidem et bonitas in eo quod ea quae nondum erant voluntarie constituerit et fecerit, quae quidem propter immensam ejus benignitatem augmentum accipientia et in multum temporis perseverantia infecti gloriam referunt, Deo sine invidia donante quod est bonum."

4. The nature of human knowledge of God through creation and providence

How is this knowledge of God through his creation and providence obtained by human beings? What is
their capability in this regard? Can they know God
through creation and providence, independent of further
divine revelation, in a way that might be described as
natural knowledge? If there is further revelation, should
it be considered "supernatural"?[24] Is this revelation in
creation and providence salvific, or is other revelatory
activity of the Word necessary for salvation? Such are the
questions which arise in considering the revelatory
character of creation and providence. The most significant, and somewhat controversial, text related to this
issue is in *Adversus Haereses* II,6,1.

> Invisibile enim eius, cum sit potens, magnam mentis intuitionem
> et sensibilitatem omnibus praestat potentissimae et omnipotentis
> eminentiae. Unde etiamsi "nemo cognoscit Patrem, nisi Filius,
> neque Filium, nisi Pater, et quibus Filius revelaverit," tamen hoc
> ipsum omnia cognoscunt, quando Ratio[25] mentibus infixus[26]

---

[24]Charles K. Robinson has posed the question in terms of a choice
between "natural theology" and "general revelation," but these are
terms with varied meaning in contemporary theological discussion
that are likely to confuse the study of Irenaeus, at this point ("St
Irenaeus on General Revelation as Preparation for Special Revelation," *DDR* 43 [Fall 1978]:171). A helpful analysis of the complexity
of the terms, in the context of the theology of religions, has been made
by Antonio R. Gualtieri ("Descriptive and Evaluative Formulae for
Comparative Religion," *TS* 29 [1968]:52-60).

[25]It is significant that Migne does not capitalize *ratio* in his text
(PG 724). This reading is reflected in Roberts' translation. Rousseau
proposes as the Greek retroversion: *ho Logos tois nois emphutos.* SC
293, 220.

[26]In keeping with the decision not to capitalize *ratio*, Migne follows
the Latin manuscripts that read *infixa* at this point (Arundelianus

moveat ea et revelet eis quoniam est unus Deus, omnium Dominus.

Alexander Roberts translates the passage thus:

> For since the invisible essence is mighty, it confers on all a profound mental intuition and perception of His most powerful, yea, omnipotent greatness. Wherefore, although "no one knows the Father, except the Son, nor the Son except the Father, and those to whom the Son will reveal Him," yet all [beings] do know this fact at least, because reason, implanted in their minds, moves them, and reveals to them [the truth] that there is one God, the Lord of all.[27]

As Roberts has translated the phrase "quando ratio mentibus infixa," it appears to indicate a natural knowledge of God, and this understanding has been followed by M. A. Dufourcqu, M. Vernet[28] and Jules Lebreton,[29] among others. Lebreton saw a distinction between the natural knowledge which is derived from creation (Cf. AH III,24,2; IV,19,3), which is certain but imperfect, and other knowledge, compared to which the first seems like ignorance in comparison, namely, the knowledge by love (*secundum dilectionem*), which is granted by means of the revelation of the Word (Cf. AH IV,20,4). Like Robertson, he translated *ratio* as *raison*.[30]

---

and the editions of Erasmus). Rousseau has preferred the reading of Claromontanus and Vossianus.

[27]*Ante-Nicene Fathers*, 1:365.

[28]Cited by Louis Escoula, "Saint Irénée et la connaissance naturelle de Dieu," *RScRel* 20 (May-October 1940):252.

[29]Jules Lebreton, *Histoire du dogme de la Trinité des origines au Concile de Nicée*, Vol. 2 (Paris: Gabriel Beauchesne, 1928), 528ff.

[30]Lebreton, 528.

a. Arguments for the activity of the pre-incarnate Word (*Ratio* or *Logos*)

A number of scholars have argued, more recently, for a different understanding of the passage, as a reference to the revelatory activity of the Logos.

1) Louis Escoula. Escoula has taken issue with Lebreton and presented a number of arguments in favor of his own interpretation.[31] He feels that the translation of *ratio* as reason or *raison* does not properly represent what it is that Irenaeus is designating. Escoula contends that Irenaeus is not dealing with the faculty in the pure state, left to its own force. He is not trying to prove that this reason has by itself the physical power to know God. The affirmation pertains rather to the universality of the faculty of the knowledge of God in beings endowed with reason. It is this faculty which makes us like God, and hence the complete sense might better be rendered "raison éclairée d'en Haut," that is, reason enlightened from Above. In other words, contrary to the Gnostics, who emphasized the incognizability of God, all reasonable beings know that there is only one God, although the knowledge need not be purely natural. Escoula sees a parallel between the proposition here that God is invisible in his essence but known on account of his providence, and the numerous passages in which Irenaeus shows that God is unknowable in the order of his grandeur, but known by means of the Word in the order of his love.[32]

To Escoula, the textual variant in Claromontanus, one of the two oldest and best of the Latin versions, is significant. There, one finds *ratio mentibus infixus*, rather than *infixa*, which Harvey and Migne

---

[31]Escoula, 255-70.
[32]Ibid., 258. See discussions above, and particularly AH IV,20.

preferred. If it is admitted that this is not a copyist's error, then there must be a logical, rather than a grammatical, accord with the word *ratio*, the latter therefore being the translation of the Greek *logos*. In that case, the expression would be equivalent to *Verbum assistens suo plasmati*, which is found frequently in *Adversus Haereses*. The logical accord between *Verbum* and its epithet is also frequent elsewhere, as, for example, in IV,24,2: "Verbum naturaliter invisibilem, palpabilem et visibilem in hominibus factum." Rendered in this way, Escoula is convinced that the text confirms what he set out to demonstrate, that Irenaeus does not have in view a purely natural knowledge of God, but rather a religious knowledge, which is provided by the Word enlightening the mind.[33] It is Escoula's conviction that the dogma of natural knowledge of God is outside of the perspective of Irenaeus's work. Irenaeus deals rather with a knowledge which carries people forward to salvation.[34]

2) Juan Ochagavía. Ochagavía concurs with Escoula in regard to the translation of *ratio mentibus infixus*, accepting the masculine ending of the participle, as in Codex Claromontanus. He suggests that it be rendered: "the Word inherent in the mind," *ratio* being recognized as the Latin for *logos* and *Logos infixus* being a part of Irenaeus's theological vocabulary and referring to the activity of the Word on the level of providence. Precisely because of the personal revealing activity of the Word in creation, a distinction cannot be made between a natural knowledge through creation, and revelation through the mediation of the Word.[35] The idea of divine providence is intimately associated with the Word, in the thought of Irenaeus: "He is the one who rules the world

---

[33]Ibid., 257-58, n. 1.
[34]Ibid., 269.
[35]Ochagavía, 77-79.

and, through His active presence maintains harmony and order."[36] Ochagavía further argues that if *ratio* is reason, it is hard to understand the quotation from Luke 10:22 or Matthew 11:27, since a knowledge achieved by human reason does not seem to demand special revelation such as Matthew and Luke describe. It also seems to contradict IV,6,7, where the universality of the Word's revealing function is so clearly affirmed. He concludes that it is "almost certain" that the expression here refers to the divine Word.

The knowledge of God which people achieve from contemplation of the universe is under the direct personal influence of the Word. It is "revelation" because it "presupposes an impulse of the revealing Word on the human mind through the concrete order of providence."[37] Ochagavía doubts that it is justifiable to speak of this as "supernatural revelation," but neither should it be labeled as "natural knowledge" in the modern sense, since he contends that such questions fall outside the scope and interest of Irenaeus and his predecessors.[38] In other words, the question of "natural knowledge" is anachronous.[39]

3) Albert Houssiau. Houssiau is another who stresses the mediation of the Word in Irenaeus's doctrine of the knowledge of God communicated in nature. Again, he points out that knowledge of God by providence is, in effect, revelation by the Son, or Word, who exercises this providence, and that the revelation of providence is identical to the revelation by the Son, of Matthew 11:27b,

---

[36]Ibid., 78, n. 157.

[37]Ibid., 79-80. Also citing AH III,25,1.

[38]Ibid., 80.

[39]Ochagavía cites, in agreement with his reading of the period, Th.-A. Audet ("Orientations théologiques chez Saint Irénée," *Traditio* 1 [1943]:36): "Une distinction si nette entre naturel et surnaturel nous apparaît prématurée chez Saint Irénée."

although it does not make the Father visible to the creature, because the Word himself is not yet visible.[40] He suggests that it is not only reasonable beings, but *all* beings, including the animals, that recognize the sovereignty of God in submitting themselves to his name, even before the coming of Jesus.[41] He sees the tie between the natural knowledge of God (which all creatures possess) and the mediation of the Son as an appeal to the universal impulse of the Logos, which is identical to the Logos communicated to our intelligences. The Logos who directs the world is participated in by our intelligences.[42]

A question naturally arises here concerning the extent to which Irenaeus ought to be read as carrying on the Stoic Logos concept that seems to have been taken up by Justin Martyr. Stoicism saw a participation of the universal Logos in the individual Logos. In a similar situation to that which Irenaeus faced, Justin appears to have built on this Stoic concept. He addressed the question concerning the salvation of those who lived before the incarnation of the Word. How could people be guilty, if the Word had not manifested himself? As Houssiau interprets Justin, he replied that Christ is the first born of God, since he is the Logos in which all the human race participates, and those who have lived according to the Logos are Christians.[43] The inherent

---

[40]Albert Houssiau, "L'exégèse de Matthieu 11, 27b selon Saint Irénée," *ETL* 29 (1953):334-36.

[41]Ibid., 334. Escoula also made this point, stressing the significance of the neuter *omnia* ("La connaissance naturelle," 256).

[42]Houssiau, "L'exégèse," 335-36.

[43]I Apol. 46, 2-3. However, Houssiau's interpretation of the *logos* as the pre-incarnate Word, in this passage of Justin, is open to question. It may be better understood as human reason, that is, human participation in the divine Logos. Cf. Nestor Pycke: "Le logos qui régit la vie de l'homme est la raison humaine. . . . Il ne faut

seed of the Logos apparently lived, feebly but really, in
Plato and the Stoics.[44] There seems to be general
agreement that the use of the *logos emphutos* in dealing
with the question of pre-Christian religious thought is
characteristic of Justin.[45] The Word of God and the Stoic

cependant pas concevoir la participation au Logos divin comme une
émanation du Logos divin, car ce qui participe à quelque chose en est
par cela même distinct" ("Connaissance rationelle et connaissance de
grâce chez Saint Justin," *ETL* 37 [1961]: 56). Also, 83: "L'expression
'vivre suivant le logos' signifie que l'on vit selon la connaissance de la
raison humaine et qu'on s'efforce de régler sa vie selon ses
injonctions."

[44]II Apol. 13,5. Pycke's understanding of Justin, however, is not
that the seed of the Logos lived feebly in people, but that human
reason sees feebly; that is, it arrives at a knowledge of the truth only
in a confused manner (Pycke, 55-56). Pycke's understanding of Justin
brings Justin closer to Irenaeus as understood by Orbe (see discussion
below) than does that of Houssiau.

[45]Houssiau, "L'exégèse," 337.

In regard to this question of the ability of people to know God by
natural reason, unaided by revelation, S. Harent has emphasized that
when Justin spoke of ancient philosophers like Socrates and
Heraclitus as "Christian" (I Apol. 46) it was his belief that these men
had the Bible (I Apol. 44,59). Clement likewise was convinced that the
philosophers had the Bible, and not just reason (Strom. II,21). Both
men, Harent suggests, were emphasizing the participation of all men
in the Word (II Apol. 13) ("Infidèles," in *Dictionnaire de Théologie
Catholique*, vol. 7, part 2 [Paris: Librarie Letougey et Ané, 1923], cols.
1808-13). However, as H. Chadwick points out, although Justin
explained his positive appreciation of Greek philosophy partly by the
conventional thesis that the Greek philosophers had studied the OT,
his chief appeal was to the doctrine of the divine Logos. "All who have
thought and acted rationally and rightly have participated in Christ
the universal Logos" (citing II Apol. 10,13, in "The Beginning of
Christian Philosophy: Justin: The Gnostics," in *The Cambridge
History of Later Greek and Early Medieval Philosophy*, ed. A. H.
Armstrong [Cambridge: University Press, 1967], 162). Chadwick notes
the same twofold source of philosophy in Clement's work. On the one
hand, there is the suggestion that the Greeks plagiarized Moses and
the prophets. On the other hand, "Clement affirms that the positive

Logos, the universal and the particular Logos, are brought together, in the apologetic presentation of the pre-existence of Christ. The problem of the religious and moral value of paganism led to consideration of the

---

value of philosophy for theology is a simple corollary of the capacity for reason and insight implanted in man by the Creator" (170). "Christ is the uniting principle of all the separate fragments of knowledge (Strom. I,58-59). . . . The Old Testament and Greek philosophy are two tributaries of one great river (Strom. I,28-29; IV,67,117)" (170).

It is Ochagavía's contention that "we should not be too rash in affirming that Justin admitted a 'natural knowledge of God,' as we understand the expression." He suggests that Justin "neither admitted nor denied it: he just did not consider the question." However, he too cites Justin on the historical borrowing from books of the OT (I Apol. 59), the dimness of the philosophers' knowledge of truth (II Apol. 13) and the fact that the knowledge of God presupposed a virtuous disposition and an interior illumination of the Holy Spirit (Dial. 4). Knowledge of God required a grace of understanding from God (Dial. 7) (Ochagavía, 36). As will be seen later, Ochagavía's dismissal of "natural knowledge" in Justin as anachronous is not necessary. His reading of Justin probably needs to be reconsidered in the light of Orbe's work on Irenaeus which is discussed below.

Jean Daniélou also has a fine discussion of Justin's concept of the *logos* as a *sperma emphuton* (*A History of Early Christian Doctrine Before the Council of Nicaea*, vol. 2: *Gospel Message and Hellenistic Culture*, trans. and ed. John Austin Baker [Philadelphia: Westminster, 1973], 41-47). Daniélou suggests that "even though Justin's vocabulary is Stoic, the thought underlying it is Platonist" (43). "The Logos has endowed man with reason, by which is meant essentially the capacity to distinguish between true and false, good and bad," and in addition "every man knows certain fundamental truths," probably innate in the human spirit, in a Platonist manner (44). Still another concept was that the philosophers' borrowings from revelation (e.g. Plato, I Apol. 59,1; 60,1,5,8) were spermata of truth (I Apol. 44,9-10) in the sense of being imperfect rather than because of origination in the action of the Word (45).

On the difference between Justin and Irenaeus, see also Arthur Hilary Armstrong and R. A. Markus, *Christian Faith and Greek Philosophy* (London: Darton, Longman & Todd, 1960), 142-45.

participation of humanity in the universal Logos as a partial participation in Christ, the universal Logos.

Houssiau ventures the opinion that the anti-Ptolemaic response of Irenaeus may be based on these apologetic antecedents, though he does not seem sure that this is so.[46] Jules Lebreton, however, points to a significant difference between Irenaeus and Justin or Clement at this point. Irenaeus makes no mention of the Hellenistic philosophy that Clement compared to a third testament and Justin, a little earlier, had presented as a diffusion of the light in humanity.[47] Lebreton therefore expresses his disagreement with A. Dufourcq, who, like Houssiau, discerned the influence of Justin and the apologists on Irenaeus, as well as a relationship to Clement. Says Lebreton: "I think that he is mistaken: if the pagans are reached by the divine light, it is not by means of philosophy, it is by the sight of creation; St. Irenaeus follows St. Paul here, not St. Justin."[48] As noted earlier, however, Lebreton distinguishes between this knowledge which creation presents to all reasonable beings and that which the Son communicates to the elect of God. So great is the difference between these two that one could almost call the first ignorance, when compared with the second.[49]

4) Adelin Rousseau. Rousseau has chosen also to understand Irenaeus in the sense of the pre-incarnate Logos. He translates "quando Ratio mentibus infixus" (where the capitalization of *Ratio* and the masculine ending of the participle are highly significant) as "le Verbe, inhérent aux intelligences," and renders the Greek

---

[46]Houssiau, "L'exégèse," 337.

[47]Jules Lebreton, "La connaissance de Dieu chez Saint Irénée," *RScRel* 16 (1926):339.

[48]Ibid., 399, n. 8.

[49]Ibid., 387, citing III,24,2; IV,19,3; IV,20,4.

as *ho logos tois nois emphutos.*[50] Rousseau admits the attractiveness of a translation such as "la raison (*logos*) dont sont douées les âmes."[51] However, he believes that would do violence to the context, in which this expression is a commentary on the preceding citation. He understands " . . . *Ratio* . . . revelet" as an echo of "*Filius* revelaverit," and concludes that it is therefore incontestable that it is the Word that Irenaeus speaks of in this phrase. "Irenaeus considers the beings endowed with reason (*logikos*) as possessing in themselves, by virtue of a certain participation, the Word (*Logos*) of God himself. And this Word, thus present in them, reveals to them the Father."[52] Rousseau's interpretation is obviously strongly influenced by Irenaeus's later discussion (AH IV,6,5-7) of the universality of the revelation of the Father by the Word, which provides the ground for the just judgment of all people by God.[53]

b. The argument for natural knowledge (*ratio* or *logos*)

The most thorough work on this aspect of Irenaeus's teaching has been done by Antonio Orbe, and his conclusions are more satisfying than any which have been reviewed thus far.[54] Houssiau attempted to locate

[50]"Notes Justificatives" (SC # 293), 220.

[51]Ibid.

[52]Ibid: "Irénée considère les êtres doués de raison (*logikoi*) comme possédant en eux, en vertu d'une certaine participation, le Verbe (*Logos*) même de Dieu. Et ce Verbe, ainsi présent en eux, leur révèle le Père."

[53]SC # 293, 220.

[54]Antonio Orbe, "San Ireneo y el conocimiento natural de Dios," *Greg* 47 (1966):441-77, 710-47. Given the importance of the critical edition of the text in the Sources Chrétiennes series, it is disappointing that Rousseau, though publishing his work comparatively recently

the work of Irenaeus in the context of Stoic philosophy and the precedents of the Apologists. However, Orbe was convinced that no one had yet (1966) approached the question in the light of the problems and solutions of the adversaries of Irenaeus. No one had asked if the natural knowledge of God was a matter of interest to the heterodox or not, nor if Irenaeus was conscious of their position. It is therefore on that foundation that Orbe establishes his interpretation of Irenaeus in this matter.[55]

1) "Natural knowledge" is not an anachronism. Contrary to Ochagavía and Audet, Orbe contends that to attribute to Irenaeus the concept or language of "natural knowledge" (by reason alone) as opposed to "supernatural knowledge" (by the Son) is not an anachronism in the second century.[56] The Valentinians took up an idea which was widespread among the Stoics, namely, the visibility of God in his providence.[57] Ptolemy did not negate a superior providence, but he assigned it to the Demiurge. The Gentiles or hylics were equally able with the psychics to contemplate the sensible creation.[58] Thus the Gnostics attributed to the Gentiles true worship of God, of a material kind which was appropriate to hylic men, but nonetheless religious. Although erroneous, all worship was based on the idea of an existent God. The majority of people were hylics, mainly heathen Gentiles, but Cain himself, a type of the hylic, was introduced in Genesis as speaking with the Demiurge and offering worship. In short, the Gnostics were ready to grant that the lowest category of people,

---

(1982), makes no mention of Orbe's work, and does not justify his rendering against Orbe's exhaustive analysis of this passage.

[55]Ibid., 441-42.

[56]Ibid., 733.

[57]See n. 43 above.

[58]Orbe, 448.

the Gentiles (hylics), were capable of reasoning from creation to the Creator, of rising from the sensible world to the Demiurge.[59]

Although the Valentinians held the heathen in low esteem, pagan philosophy had its value in regard to the knowledge of the Creator. Their irrationality lay, not in their arguments founded on reason, but in the moral impurities with which they were defective.[60] It was material passions which impeded Cain's worship of the Creator. Likewise, the pagan arguments were acceptable in themselves, but the pagans were contaminated by their position in the human hierarchy and were unable to rise to the heights of pure reason, mediating the perfect and univocal knowledge of the Creator. The majority of the pagan philosophers were content with the way "from effects" and believed it impossible to know directly or immediately, in essence, the author of the sensible world. Consequently, all the popular arguments of Hellenism concerning the essential unknowability of the unknown God passed easily to the mass of the hylics or irrational people.[61]

In Gnostic teaching, although the providence of the Creator is sensibly manifested to the hylics, the providence of the Father is not knowable by the psychics without positive revelation.[62] There is no *natural* way of conveying to hylic and psychic people the knowledge of the Father. Not even the Creator was capable of reaching knowledge of either the essence or the existence of the Father. For psychics and hylics the Word was the unique way to knowledge of the good God,[63] and even for the

---

[59]Ibid., 449-50.

[60]Irenaeus takes a similar view, AH III,25,1 (478).

[61]Ibid., 450.

[62]Ibid., 455.

[63]Ibid., 457.

spiritual, the rational ways, as rational, had no value.
The Old Testament was characterized as psychic, whereas the New Testament was typically spiritual. This
spiritual revelation was manifested in two ways—that of
the Gospels or literary traditions of the Gnostics and that
of individual illumination.[64] But the way from creation
to the Creator, which leads to knowledge of the
providence or existence of the Demiurge, was inadequate
to understand the simple providence and existence of the
true God. Only revelation accomplishes that.[65]

In II,6,1-2, Irenaeus is showing the absurdity of
the Valentinian claim that even the Demiurge and his
angels, creatures of the Father, who live in his house, do
not know the existence of the Father, let alone his
essence. In evidence of the folly of this teaching, Irenaeus
points out that God has granted to all rational beings an
intuition and mental sensibility. This fact is seen by
observation of the experience of all people, of evil spirits,
and even of brute animals, all of whom submit to the
name of the Almighty. The existence of the supreme God
is wrapped up in the power of his name.[66] Even evil
spirits perceived God's power in his dominion and
providence over the world before the coming of the Lord,
and thus bore witness to his existence.

As Orbe points out, Irenaeus was precise in his
terminology, distinguishing sight from knowledge,
invisibility from unknowability. To see (*videre*) is equivalent to contemplating directly or immediately: to have as
an object the thing in itself, the very person or essence of
God. To know (*cognoscere*), by contrast, indicates a simple
knowledge: to have as an object something emanating
from the essence or person of God, such as the power, the

[64]Ibid., 461.
[65]Ibid., 462. Cf. "Letter from Ptolemaeus to Flora."
[66]Ibid., 467.

dominion, the divine providence over the world. Whoever sees or contemplates God in his eminence, apprehends him just as he is. Whoever knows God in his providence understands his manifestations of power and dominion over the world. The first knowledge (visual) belongs uniquely to the Son, whereas the second is extended to all.[67]

To know God in his providence is not necessarily to see him, but rather to understand the footprints of power and wisdom that he has left in the universe, and to rise up from them to the existence of the one unique God. That was a method in use among the theologians of the second century, such as the Alexandrian Jews, who believed that God was knowable in his existence, though not in his essence.[68] Orbe contends, therefore, that according to II,6,1, the supreme God, by the sublimity of his invisible essence, has an exceptional virtue and, according to it, he gives power to all rational beings (*a fortiori* the Demiurge and his angels), namely, a sensibility and penetration of mind capable of discovering his presence.[69] Neither the evil spirits nor the brutes will ever *see* God. They are incapacitated to contemplate the essence of the Almighty, by evil in the first case, and irrationality in the second. But, nonetheless, they

---

[67]Ibid., 465-66.

[68]Ibid., 446.

[69]Cf. Ibid. For this reason Charles Robinson says: "if by 'natural' one means an intimate and organic relation which is integral to and constitutive of the essential nature of humanity, then this knowledge of God is in the highest sense natural, because it is the actualization of the personal grace of the Creator in dynamic relatedness with the rational creature" (171). Later, commenting on II,9,1 and II,10,1, he remarks: "Even those very persons who 'speak against' the one Creator nevertheless, in the God-given *a-priori* structure of rational human thought, must 'accept' him; those who 'take no account' nevertheless 'consent'" (177).

perceive the powerful eminence of the Almighty in the efficacy of his name.

Against the Gnostics, Irenaeus argues that if the providence of the Demiurge is already perceived in the material world, even by irrational beings, *a fortiori* the providence of the first God—though not his essence—must impress itself upon the Demiurge himself. The Gnostic, on the other hand, granted that God has *power* to confer upon the Demiurge and his angels intuition and sharpness of mind to discover his providence in the universe, but denied the *fact*.[70] They argued that God did not want to give himself by a physical way, but declared himself only by revelation, by means of the announcement of the Savior. He was thus completely unknown throughout the Old Testament (AH I,7,4). The providence of the Father escaped the knowledge of the Demiurge, who served as a blind instrument (AH I,5,6).

It is clear that there were antecedents to Irenaeus, both in the Stoic philosophers and in the teachings of his Gnostic adversaries, concerning a knowledge of the existence of God by rational argument from his providence or the demonstration of his power.

2) "Ratio mentibus infixa" examined in context. Coming specifically to the phrase *ratio mentibus infixa*, Orbe is willing to grant that an accurate retroversion of *ratio* would be *logos*. However, he contends that it should not be understood with the excessive significance of the *Verbum* of God, but rather as *verbum mentis*.[71] He further suggests that it is arbitrary to claim the support of the word *revelar*, as it figures in the text of Luke (*revelaverit*) and in the clause of Irenaeus (*et revelet eis*), in order to confuse its significance and import

---

[70]Ibid., 469.
[71]Orbe, 714.

in the context.[72] There is a true contrast between the citation of Matthew 11:27 and the *ratio* clause. The first refers to a kind of knowledge leading to the Father or the Son, whereas the second is a rational knowledge—common to rational beings, human beings and evil spirits—which leads to knowledge of the existence of only one God, Lord of the Universe.[73]

Orbe is correct in appealing to Irenaeus himself for the authentic interpretation of his lines.[74] In II,6,2 Irenaeus gives confirmation of the knowledge by all beings of the existence of the one God, by citing the submission of all beings to the invocation of the Almighty. The knowledge which he assigned to the evil spirits and demons was a particular case of the generic proposition which he repeated twice in II,6,1 and formulated in the final lines:

1) hoc ipsum *omnia* cognoscunt . . . quoniam est unus Deus, omnium Deus.

2) cum scirent (terreni spiritus aut daemones) quoniam est qui est super omnia Deus.

Although the evil spirits were unwillingly subject to the invocation of the Most High, they understood that there is only one God, Lord of the universe. *Ratio mentibus infixa* moved them to the recognition of this truth. As Orbe rightly observes, it would be absurd to attribute to the evil spirits and demons a reason enlightened from above to know the Most High, that is, a supernatural revelation.[75]

---

[72]As Rousseau has explicitly done. See above, B,4,a,4).
[73]Orbe, 714.
[74]Ibid.
[75]Orbe, 715.

Orbe thus situates the clause of Irenaeus within
the context of the Stoic doctrine of the *prolepsis*. *Ratio
mentibus infixa* is thus the discursive reason or *logos*
impressed in every intellectual being (*nous*), and distinct
from the Intellect as the immanent reason.[76] Neither
the Intellect as such, nor its discursive faculty, have the
capacity to lead anybody to knowledge of God apart from
information from the outside that sets them in motion. It
is the providence of God, contemplated in the universe,
which produces this effect. Without any superior illumination, reason moves intellectual beings, to whom God
grants "magnam mentis intuitionem et sensibilitatem," so
that they understand "quoniam est unus Deus omnium
Dominus."[77] They are all led to the knowledge of God,
Lord of the universe, because reason impressed in them
moves them, manifesting that thing to which they are
moved, not in a blind manner, but as becomes rational
beings.[78]

Although Irenaeus elsewhere dwells on the
universal immanence of the Logos (AH V,8,3), Orbe suggests that we ought not let that fact prejudge the nature
of its activity and efficacy in this context.[79] The Word
that gives cohesion to the material world accommodates
himself to the nature of the beings in his governing of
them. He moves believers to saving knowledge of God
(AH IV,13,1), and the Jews or those rebellious in unbelief
he conducts (as He does the evil spirits) to a purely
rational, not a saving, knowledge.[80] Reason will be
moved, among intellectual beings, according to its own
condition of physical and moral life. It will always be

---

[76]Ibid., cf. AH II,13,2.
[77]Ibid.
[78]Ibid., 716.
[79]Orbe, 716.
[80]Orbe, 716.

under the higher dominion, and even the motion, of the Word of God, but not, therefore, by superior enlightenment.[81]

3) The rational knowledge of God by means of providence. Irenaeus maintains vigorously the pagan argument for knowledge of God from providence. He grants, according to the Gospel text, that no one knows the Father (*secundum eminentiam vel magnitudinem*) except the Son, nor the Son except the Father and those to whom the Son reveals him (by strictly supernatural revelation).[82] Nevertheless, beside this special knowledge, there is the simple rational knowledge accessible even to the terrestrial spirits, of the existence of God, Lord of the universe. According to the Valentinians, the Wisdom of the Word moves upon the Demiurge, imprinting in him, blindly, his ideas relative to the world, without revealing the existence of superior Being (AH I,5,3). Irenaeus contends that the *verbum mentis* moves the mind in view of the providence or dominion of God perceptible in the world, and reveals to it the existence of only one God, the provident One, Lord of all creation.[83]

A constant theme in Irenaeus's work against the Gnostics is the identity or unity of God the Father and the Creator (or Demiurge). To know the Creator is to know the Father. To this basic truth Irenaeus adduces five testimonies (AH II,9,1): 1) universal consent; 2) the Patriarchs, by a tradition going back to Adam himself; 3) the Israelites, who were so taught by the prophets; 4) the pagans, by argument *ab ipsa conditione*; and 5) the

---

[81]Ibid.

[82]Ibid.

[83]Orbe, 716-17. Orbe points out that Irenaeus uses "et *revelet* eis" by attraction to the "revelaverit" of the later Gospel citation, but in the context he might just as well have said "et *ostendat* eis," i.e. displays or manifests (716).

universal Church which received the tradition from the apostles. In his study of this important passage, Orbe notes that, in contrast to the triple "positive" tradition (numbers 2, 3, and 5 above), Irenaeus emphasizes the knowledge of God beginning from creation possessed specifically by the Gentiles or heathen.[84] This was a knowledge accessible to the nations apart from all "positive" tradition and, as such, was natural, proceeding by way of reason. The believer has other ways of arriving at knowledge of God, but this was a way accessible to all people, even pagans, who were not too depraved to confess the providence and good disposition of the sensible world (Cf. AH III,25,1), people such as Plato (AH III,25,5).[85] Contrary to the Gnostic dualism, such unity in the cosmos, and such simple harmony, would be inexplicable if the world were subject to two providences, one of the Father and another of the Demiurge.[86]

---

[84]Orbe, 718. Orbe interestingly draws out a Trinitarian significance from the manner in which Irenaeus describes three aspects of the knowledge of God, according to three modes of considering the created world: 1) ascending from the first creation (*conditione*) to the Creator (God the Father); 2) from the second creation or *demiurgia* (*factura*) to the immediate Demiurge (the Word of God); and 3) from order and perfection (*mundus*) to the One who arranges and gives the ultimate touch (the Holy Spirit).

Orbe also points out that Irenaeus did not appeal to an argument from the contingency of created being, nor from analogy (as Tertullian did, for instance [Adv. Prax. V, especially V,5]). The Valentinians explained the procession of the only begotten and of his perfections according to Stoic psychology, but Irenaeus denied all analogy between humanity and God as incompatible with the simplicity (II,13,8-9; II,28,5-6; III,19,2) and transcendence of God (II,13,4). Following the method of the Stoics, he placed more emphasis on such aspects of the world as spontaneously lead to the idea of the provident Creator (cf. Sap. 13, 1ff.) (720-21).

[85]Orbe suggests that Irenaeus probably included in this class the Stoics, and maybe even the middle-Platonists (719, n. 91).

[86]Cf. Orbe, 720.

4) The relationship between knowledge of the Creator by creation and knowledge of the Father by the Son. Granted that Irenaeus delineates two ways to know God: from tradition and from creation, it is significant that he never identifies the first with the way *per Filium* and the second with the way *per rationem.* Orbe rightly concludes that in both ways, therefore, Irenaeus finds a way of introducing the Son (or Word) between humankind and God.[87] The difficulty that confronts us, therefore, is to discern the harmony between knowledge of the Creator *ab ipsa conditione* and that of the Father *per Filium,* keeping in mind the unique role of the Son in mediating *all* knowledge of God. Orbe aptly sets aside a few unsatisfactory attempts at resolution of the difficulty,[88] and then proposes what he considers the most adequate solution.

The Gnostics often cited Matthew 11:27b, or Luke 10:22, to demonstrate that before the coming of the Son no one knew the true God and that consequently the one who was announced by the ancient prophets or the patriarchs was another god (AH IV,6,1). Irenaeus, in his exegesis of the text, in IV,6,3ff., was not content with the theme (*aoratos-oratos*) of Hellenism, in its common application: God, in himself invisible, is made visible in the world. He raised it to a much higher level, assigning it to the personal relations between Father and Son.[89] God the Father, unknowable in himself by human beings, made himself visible by means of the Son. The Son, in his time personally knowable, possessed many ways of manifestation to the world, and, in consequence, many

---

[87]Ibid., 723.

[88]Orbe does not indicate who has proposed these solutions. Perhaps they are attempts of his own which he came to reject, in the search for a more satisfying answer.

[89]Orbe, 226.

ways of revealing the Father (AH IV,6,5).[90] The Father
is revealed to all by his Word, made accessible even to
the Gentiles. The Word, by his personal visibility,
manifests the Father and the Son to all, pagan and non-
pagan. Citing the text as *cognoscit* (*epignōskei*), rather
than *cognovit* (*egnō*, as per the Gnostics), Irenaeus insists
that the Son has been revealing the Father ever since the
beginning, so that even Adam knew that God was, by
means of the Son (AH IV,6,7).[91] This was too basic a
point in orthodox doctrine for Irenaeus to have changed
his position out of any polemic necessity, between Books
II and IV. The doctrine of IV,6,1ff. and that of II,6,1 are
in harmony. The indispensable mediation of the Son for
knowledge of the Father is clear from Luke 10:22 and
Matthew 11:27, quoted in both passages. What needs to
be defined more precisely is the exact nature of such
mediation in its various forms.

The knowledge of the Creator by his works does
not escape the universal efficacy of the Son. There is
clearly a sense in which the Word *illumines* the Gentiles
for the manifestation of God the Creator. Irenaeus sees
in this a particular case of the universal Gospel proposition that no one knows the Father except the Son and
anyone to whom the Son reveals the Father. But he uses
the term *revelare* without exalting the knowledge *per
conditionem* to the privileged position of the patriarchal
theophanies, nor equating it with the triple "positive
tradition" of Adam, the prophets and the apostles. Yet
everything that is ordered to the knowledge of God the
Father is governed by the Word, and is under his
influence.[92] The revealer is always the Word. The media
by which God is manifested, and the aspects of his being

---

[90]Cf. Orbe, 726.

[91]Cf. Orbe, 726.

[92]Orbe, 728.

which are revealed, vary. Thus: 1) by means of creation, God the Creator is revealed; 2) by means of the world, the Lord or Demiurge of it is revealed; 3) by means of the human body, the Artificer or Maker is revealed; and 4) by means of the Son, the Father who engendered him is revealed. Four aspects—God the Creator, the Maker of the world, the Maker of humankind, the Father of the only-begotten Son—are manifested indirectly, by means of universal creation, the sensible world, the human form and the Son. The four media are objective and are offered to human consideration.[93] The genius of Irenaeus's teaching is his distinction between seeing the objective medium and seeing *by revelation of the Word*.[94] He carefully distinguishes objective revelation, that is, the quadruple way for ascending to God; and the saving revelation by means of which people get to God. From this arises the repeated formula: 1) all have seen, but not all have believed (AH IV,6,5); 2) all are addressed by the Word, but not all believed (AH IV,6,6); 3) all the people heard alike, but not all believed alike; 4) all saw and spoke of the Son and the Father, but not all believed.

Even the demons saw and heard the Son, and in him the Father, as the Pharisees and unbelieving scribes

---

[93]José González-Faus notes a gradation in the verbs which Irenaeus uses in IV,6,6 (448). Thus we read: "per ipsam conditionem *revelat*"; "per Legem et Prophetas . . . *praedicabat*"; and "per ipsum Verbum *ostendebatur*." González-Faus suggests that the first alludes to the simple, objective manifestation that needs yet to be perceived and interpreted. The second enters by the senses, in this case by the ears. And the third is by sight itself. What González-Faus sees as important here is that the Incarnation is not an isolated episode, interesting only in so far as it gives a view of the horizon of the possibility for the salvation of human beings. It is rather a link in a horizon of possibilities still opening up, in the chain which goes from creation toward the "vision," a chain which is an economy of the Word (155-56).

[94]Orbe, 728-29.

saw and heard, and as the disciples of Jesus saw and heard, but not all equally believed in him. The objective medium and the aspect which is understood by it do not change. The difference (and also the solution which Orbe presents to the difficulty) is in the subjective element, namely, the Word that gives eyes and ears to one to see and hear savingly, and does not do so to another.[95] Even the evil spirits were capable of reasoning from the visible to the invisible, from creation to the Creator (AH II,6,2; IV,6,6), from the image to the one who molded it, from the Son to the Father, *but not savingly*. The revelation to which faith responds reaches only to believers, to those whom the Word illuminates.

The synoptic phrase is thus seen to refer to a *saving revelation*. The Son reveals the Father, thus, uniquely to those who receive his teaching in *faith*.[96] In fact, Irenaeus practically identifies *gnosis* with *pistis* in his exegesis of Matthew 11:27.[97] One may also know the Son, and by him the Father, with a revelation, or generic manifestation, to which a purely rational acceptance is the response. Such was the case of the unbelieving Jews and the demons. However, to know the creation, the world, the human form and the Son himself, by revelation of the Word, is to know savingly God the Creator, Maker, Framer, and Father. The revelation of the Word does not supplement (or take the place of) the causal order, in the physical world, as if the objective medium were not sufficient physically to manifest God. But the mere physical knowledge is not salutary, as it is when

---

[95]Orbe, 730.

[96]Orbe, 731.

[97]Antonio Orbe, "La revelación del Hijo por el Padre según san Ireneo (Adv. Haer. IV,6). Para la exegésis prenicena de Mt. 11,27," *Greg* 51 (1970):84.

accompanied by supernatural revelation by the Word.[98]
It is within this framework that one can understand
Irenaeus's comments regarding the necessity of a moral
disposition if one is to rise to confession of one God the
Father and Creator, from observation of providence (AH
III,25,1). The Word could not reveal the saving knowledge of God while people were guilty of an idolatrous
spirit and dominated by concupiscence. Thus the testimony of an Epicurus regarding the existence of God does
not enter the category of Irenaeus, not precisely because
he denies providence, but because—given his dissolute
way of life—he was incapable of a saving knowledge, just
as the demons were.[99]

Reason imprinted or implanted in the mind is
thus sufficient to discover the causal nexus between
creation and the Creator, between the world and its
Maker, but it was not this to which the Lord referred in
the Gospel. In Matthew 11:27, Jesus alludes to the way
of saving knowledge which affects equally the knowledge
of the Creator *per conditionem* and the knowledge of the
Father *ex generatione Filii*. The causal nexus between the
world and its Author is self-evident, whether or not there
is "revelation" by the Word, but by virtue of the illumination of the Son it becomes salutary.[100]

5) Conclusion. Orbe therefore disagrees with
Audet's and Ochagavía's proposition that to find a
distinction between natural and supernatural knowledge
is premature or anachronistic. In contrast to the
Valentinians who established a difference between the
psychic and the pneumatic order, Irenaeus distinguished,
as pagan theologians did, between a knowledge of the
existence of God and of his essence. It is Orbe's conviction

---

[98]Orbe, "Conocimiento natural," 731.
[99]Orbe, "Conocimiento natural," 732.
[100]Ibid.

that the contrast between: 1) the non-saving knowledge
(by logical deduction) of the pagans, unbelieving Jews
and evil spirits, and 2) the saving knowledge (by faith)
positively granted by the Word, is exactly equivalent to
the modern distinction between natural and supernatural.[101]

Orbe insists on distinguishing *propter
providentiam* from *secundum dilectionem*. In the physical
order, the divine manifestation *propter dilectionem* comes
first, and then the knowledge of providence by human
beings. In the cognitive order it is reversed. First the
individual knows God by means of his providence, and
then by the love which explains the generous manifestation of God to humankind. Providence is a means of
knowledge. The love of God moves the economy of which
providence is a part. Orbe thus disagrees with Escoula,
who argues from this situation that the knowledge itself
(by providence) is of the order of grace. This is to confuse
the impulse of the gracious dispensation of salvation
(*propter dilectionem*) with the medium of the knowledge
of God by human beings.[102] The cognitive way (*propter
providentiam* [II,6,1]; *providentia eius moti* [III,25,1])
should not be confused with the generic *propter
dilectionem*. This is ultimately not a human way of
knowledge, but a generic principle of all the divine
economy in which many cognitive ways participated.
Here are included both the "positive," directly divine
ways (tradition, Scripture or written revelation, faith, the
spirit of prophecy, the spirit of adoption and the paternal
or strict spirit of vision), and the "natural" ways,
including the knowledge *ex providentia*, which is
accessible to all rational beings (good angels and evil,

---

[101]Ibid., 733-34.
[102]Ibid., 744-45.

people before and after Christ, Jews as much as pagans).[103]

Orbe's conclusion is clear and credible. According to Irenaeus, the Word, in his universal efficacy, manifests the Father in many ways according to his action upon all beings. By a rational way, he makes known the Creator by means of creation, just as, by way of faith, he reveals the Father by means of the Son. There is "revelation" and there is "revelation." The first is generic, a simple manifestation of God, assigned to the Word in His universal efficacy over creation. The other is specific, a saving revelation to which faith corresponds in men. One can know the Son, and by him the Father, through a generic revelation, to which corresponds an acceptance without faith, purely rational. This was the knowledge of the scribes and Pharisees and the evil spirits. Likewise, in regard to the knowledge of God by creation, the Word does not have to add anything to the causal order of the physical world, as if the objective medium were not sufficient, naturally known, to manifest God. "Reason implanted in the mind" is enough to discover the causal nexus between the world, wisely governed, and its Creator. Thus Irenaeus distinguishes the indispensable universal efficacy of the Word in the cognitive order, the objective medium of knowledge (*propter providentiam*), and the initial motive of the economy (*secundum dilectionem*). While acknowledging that the unknown God made everything by means of the Word, and that the actual economy is governed by the Benignity and Love of the Father, he does not eliminate, among the objective media of the knowledge of God, the natural ways.[104]

---

[103]Ibid., 745.

[104]Ibid., 746-47. Cf. also José González-Faus: "La afirmación de que todo conocimiento de Dios es *per Verbum* no pretiende negar que se da una diferencia fundamental entre el conocimiento sobrenatural de

We conclude that Irenaeus did speak of a "natural knowledge" of God, a knowledge which is attained by natural human powers on the basis of the self-manifestation of God in creation and providence. This is not in conflict with the revelatory work of the Word, which will be examined in the next chapter, nor does it ignore the necessity of the Word's special illumination for any revelation to be salutary.[105]

5. The progressive nature of divine self-revelation

a. The "economy" of God

One last item of significant interest in regard to the universality of the divine self-revelation is Irenaeus's emphasis on the *oikonomia* or *dispositio* of God. It provides the framework which unites all of God's working with humanity, allowing for diversity and progression, while underlining the oneness of God's universal plan which is realized in history. It enables Irenaeus to rejoin creation and redemption and to unite the Old Testament and the New Testament in one integrated perspective. It considers history as one, from beginning to end, and provides a total vision in which everything is subsumed

---

Dios—por revelación—y un cierto conocimiento natural—o por razón. Y probablemente Ireneo no desconoce ni niega esa diferencia. Pero como en otros muchos puntos . . . Ireneo está mas atento a señalar la continuidad—que también existe—que la diferencia" (154).

[105]Nor does this conflict with Dai Sil Kim's conclusion that Irenaeus's epistemology proceeds from revelation to reason "based on his conviction that the very nature of God and of human beings makes it impossible for humans to attain the perfect knowledge of God, since they are inferior to and later in existence than God" (citing AH II,28,2, "Irenaeus of Lyons and Teilhard de Chardin: A Comparative Study of 'Recapitulation' and 'Omega,'" *JEcSt* 13 [Winter 1976]:71).

under the one plan of God.[106] The Gnostics did not
understand the economy of God (AH III,12,12) but had
instead a multiplicity of economies—one of the Pleroma,
one of the Savior, one of the Demiurge, one of the Christ,
one of creation and one of redemption (AH I,6,1; I,7,2;
I,14,6; I,15,3; II,30,7; III,11,3).[107] Where they spoke of
"the dispensation of the Pleroma," Irenaeus turned the
phrase inside out and described the "fulfilling of the
dispensation."[108] Closely related to the all-encompass-
ing unity of the economy was the doctrine of recapitulation, which will be discussed later.

André Benoit rightly indicates that the concept of
the economy is not unique to Irenaeus.[109] The term was
used twice in the Epistle to the Ephesians with reference
to the plan of God concerning the coming of Christ.[110]
Justin used the term with reference to the Incarnation
and Passion[111] and to the prefigurative acts of the Old
Testament.[112] The concept was always oriented to the
event of salvation.[113] It appears to have been Irenaeus's
contribution to maintain the Christological orientation,
but then to enlarge it to a universal vision.[114] It is
within the context of this universal and integrated vision

---

[106]André Benoit, *Saint Irénée; introduction à l'étude de sa théologie*,
Etudes d'histoire et de philosophie religieuses, no. 52 (Paris: Presses
Universitaires de France, 1960), 220.

[107]Cf. Benoit, 220.

[108]Benoit, 221.

[109]Benoit, 223.

[110]Ibid.

[111]Dial. 45,4; 30,3; 31,1; 103,3; 67,6; 87,5.

[112]Dial. 104,2; 141,1.

[113]Benoit, 223.

[114]Ibid: "l'économie, ce n'est pas seulement la venue du Christ, ce
ne sont pas seulement les prédictions de l'Ancien Testament
concernant cette venue, mais c'est tout le plan de Dieu réalisé par le
Christ depuis la création jusqu'à la fin, plan qui englobe
naturellement l'événement du salut."

of God's working with his creation that the unfolding of
his self-revelation is to be considered in studying the
thought of Irenaeus. This was the answer to Marcion's
radical distinction between Judaism and Christianity.
Within the one plan of God, by a sort of pedagogy, "God
led mankind on till it was able to bear full divine
revelation, till it was in some degree ripe for Christ."[115]
This concept of the progressive education of humanity is
another important aspect of the ongoing self-revelation of
God. It views the Testaments, Law and Gospel, as two
moments of the education of humanity, and underlines
the unity of God and his plan, in opposition to
Marcion.[116] As Jules Lebreton rightly observes, the
characteristic mark of Irenaeus concerning the knowledge
of God is that it is certain but very imperfect and slowly
growing.[117]

---

[115]Jean Daniélou, *Advent*, trans. Rosemary Sheed (London: Sheed
& Ward, 1950), 7. Daniélou sees a similar continuity between pagan
civilizations and Christianity. "They all fit into the same design, . . .
they are the work of the same God. . . . It was the same Word who
was secretly at work in the non-Christian world, and in the Jewish
world." Having taught people to know his way, he then adapted
himself to the human way. Thus, "it was necessary—according to St.
Irenaeus's most beautiful line of thought—for man to take on divine
habits, and God to take on human because the Incarnation itself was
not something put up in a hurry, and every part of God's work upon
us takes place in time." There is a certain attractiveness and
symmetry in this analogy between Judaism and the pagan civilizations, in their relationship to Christianity, but there is insufficient
evidence to attribute it to Irenaeus. Perhaps Clement is better cited
in this regard (Strom. 1,5) but, as Harent points out, although
Clement parallels philosophy and the Old Testament, even he does not
establish an equality between the two pedagogues (col. 1812).

[116]Jean Daniélou, "Saint Irénée et les origines de la théologie de
l'histoire," *RScRel* 34 (1947):229-30. See also Albert Houssiau,
Christologie, 93.

[117]Jules Lebreton, *Histoire de dogme de Trinité des origines au
Concile de Nicée*, (Paris: Gabriel Beauchesne, 1928), 2:531.

Irenaeus is not consistent in his delineation of the various steps in the divine pedagogy. On one occasion, he speaks of it in trinitarian terms: the prophet saw God by a prophetic vision given by the Spirit; the adoptive children see the Son who was announced in figure by the Spirit; and the children will see the Father immediately in the final kingdom. The Spirit prepares people in the Son and the Son leads them to the Father who gives them eternal life as a consequence of the vision of God (AH IV,20,5).[118] In a different place, Irenaeus describes four testaments or covenants (*testamenta* or *diathēkai*) that God made with humankind: 1) with Adam, prior to the flood; 2) with Noah, after the flood; 3) with Moses on Sinai, in the giving of the Law; and 4) "that which renews humanity and recapitulates all things in itself, which, by the Gospel, elevates and bears people in flight to the heavenly kingdom" (AH III,11,8).[119]

Auguste Luneau discerns a four-step pedagogy. The first is a period from Adam to the double gift of circumcision and the Law, which Luneau designates as "natural law." Although Irenaeus distinguishes two testaments, of Adam and Noah, because the context demands it, the second adds little to the first. The second period is intimated with Abraham, whose call was a turning point in history, but it is definitely opened with Moses and specifically prepared for Christ, lifting a people originally pagan to a new height. The prophets added their action to that of the Law. Thirdly, the Word

---

[118]See Latin text above, n. 15.

[119]Cf. Gustave Thils (*Propos et problèmes de la théologie des religions non-chrétiennes* [Paris: Casterman, 1966], 67), who sees this theme as progressing to an absolutely universal perspective. He contends that it is wrong to identify the Old Testament with the Mosaic covenant because it is prejudicial to other covenants relative to the non-Jews, but it is doubtful that Irenaeus shared his concern.

himself came in human form, and, finally, all things are renewed or summed up in him at his return.[120]

b. The sufficiency of the Old Testament

An interesting exegetical position arises from Irenaeus's attempt to refute the Gnostic (and particularly the Marcionite) division between the two Testaments, which stressed the newness of revelation in the New Testament. They taught a new God (the Father), a new Son (the Word), a new Spirit (that of adopted sonship), a new human race, and a new salvation by means of the new intuitive gnosis.[121] Irenaeus contended instead that the Father makes *no* new revelation concerning himself or the Son, but that it was already contained in the Old Testament. Therefore, the believer does not look for new knowledge of the Son, but for harmony between the Testaments and the fulfillment of prophecy in history.[122]

To maintain this position, Irenaeus has to explain the instances in the New Testament where the Father is spoken of as "revealing" things to people regarding Christ. The Gospel of John records Nathaniel's recognition of Jesus as the Son of God (Jn 1:49). Peter, likewise, recognized Jesus as "the Christ, the Son of the living God," and Jesus declared that this had been revealed to him by his Father in heaven (Mt 16:16-17). However, Irenaeus denies that this was an immediate revelation, because the Father always acts through the Son

---

[120]Auguste Luneau, *L'histoire de Salut chez les Pères de l'Eglise: La doctrine des âges du monde*, Théologie historique, no. 2 (Paris: Beauchesne et ses fils, 1964), 96-100.

[121]Orbe, "La revelación del Hijo," 86.

[122]Ibid., 86.

(AH III,6,2).[123] Nor was it a new revelation given by a
new impulse. Rather, the apostles recalled the Old
Testament prophecies (Peter remembering Isaiah 42:1-4
[AH III,11,6]), and understood that these things were
fulfilled in Jesus. Without any new revelation, they
responded in faith.[124] The same was true of Joseph (AH
III,16,2; cf. III,9,2). The angel did not reveal the mystery
of the virgin birth to him, but "made him see that the
revelation contained in Isaiah 7:14 was fulfilled in his
wife."[125] The angel's message would have been useless
if Joseph had not understood the prophecy beforehand.

As Houssiau points out, the "Seed of Christ" in
the Scriptures, for Irenaeus, is the announcement of
Christ in the Old Testament, not the insertion of the
Word in the creature as in the Stoic idea of *logos
spermatikos*.[126] Thus, in an exposition of John 4:36-38,
Irenaeus identifies the sower with the prophets and the
patriarchs. The seed sown is the prediction of the coming
of the Son of God and the reaping is done by the Church,
which experiences the presence of Christ and his Kingdom (AH IV,25,3).[127]

C. Concluding Observations Concerning the Father and the Unevangelized

There are factors in Irenaeus's portrayal of the
Father's self-revelation which could be considered
positive indicators for a doctrine of "anonymous
Christianity." The Father's will to be known is the most
obvious. Since knowledge of God is the way of life, God's

[123]Cf. Orbe, "La revelación del Hijo," 52-74, summary, 85.
[124]Orbe, "La revelación del Hijo," 81-82, summary, 85.
[125]Orbe, "La revelación del Hijo," 85.
[126]Albert Houssiau, *Christologie*, 83; cf. AH IV,10,1 (492).
[127]See also Houssiau, *Christologie*, 85.

initiative in self-revelation, and his desire that *all* should
know him, reminds one of the oft-mentioned "universal
salvific will" of "anonymous Christianity." The emphasis
on the universality of revelation is certainly a significant
factor, particularly the teaching of II,6,1 and III,25,1
regarding the accessibility to all people, by reason alone,
of a knowledge of the existence, the uniqueness, the
power of God the Creator, through His providence.
Irenaeus's stress on the importance of the moral disposition of the pagan is also echoed in "anonymous Christianity."

There are aspects of Irenaeus's teaching seen in
this chapter which pose problems to the identification of
Irenaeus as a forerunner of "anonymous Christianity."
Some of these may be simply the result of the specific
context which Irenaeus addressed, and the difference
between his situation and that of the contemporary
theologian. However, there are features of Irenaeus's
thought which do seem to tend in a direction quite
different from a theology of "anonymous Christianity."
Mention was made earlier of the Father's will to be
known, but there is an important difference that has
been evident in this chapter. The theology of "anonymous
Christianity" speaks of the "universal salvific will of God"
as efficacious, meaning, thereby, that God makes a
supernatural revelation available to all people, thus
giving all people the necessary means to attain salvation.
However, it is clear in the above discussion that
Irenaeus, while speaking positively of the universal self-
revelation of the Father, and of a natural knowledge of
God through creation and providence, describes a special
activity of the Word which leads to faith, and which is
not universally experienced. There is not a strong
indication of the possibility of that illuminating activity
for the pagan. It must be remembered, however, that
Irenaeus conceived of a world in which, at least in his

own day, everyone had supernatural revelation through the proclamation of the Church.

An important theme in Irenaeus's works is the progression of humankind towards maturity and perfection and the vision of God. This is closely related to the economic operations of the Trinity and the unfolding of the divine self-revelation in successive stages or economies of God's working with humanity. Irenaeus describes the situation as it existed for the second-century person in the Judeo-Christian context. For such a person, there was a clear line in history leading from the creation of Adam in immaturity, and his subsequent fall, through the illuminative work of the Spirit and the adoptive work of the Son, to final vision of the Father. This was paralleled by a continuity in the positive tradition of God's self-revelation, from Adam, through the Patriarchs, the Law and the prophets, and the apostles. But what of the pagan who stood outside of the Trinitarian operations that brought about this revelation? How would the pagan who did not have the advantage of the threefold positive tradition progress toward vision of God? Can one move from knowledge of God through his providence to the vision of the Father, without going through the stage of knowledge of the incarnate Word?

The only aspect of revelation that the "pagan" has is that of providence. Irenaeus is positive regarding the value of that revelation. It is an objective medium, sufficient in its own right to lead a morally upright person to recognition of the existence of one God, Creator and Lord of all, through reason alone. However, Irenaeus clearly distinguishes between this objective revelation in providence and an internal operation of the Word, an illumination or special revelation that gives saving knowledge of the Father. Is Irenaeus suggesting, however, that if the inner working of the Word (revealing the Father) were present, the self-revelation of God in

providence would be salutary? In other words, is there
only a formal insufficiency of the knowledge of God
through providence, by reason, or is there also a material
insufficiency? Is the revelation of the Father in providence, if received by faith (and hence through the revealing operation of the Son), and not only rationally, sufficient to lead a person to *vision* of the Father? Was such
a "subjective" work a possibility for the pagan who, like
Plato or some of the Stoics, was of a moral disposition? It
is premature to answer these questions, but we shall
keep them in mind as the study proceeds.

5. THE SON: EXCLUSIVE REVEALER OF THE FATHER

A. The Exclusiveness of the Son's Mediation of Revelation

Against the heretics, Irenaeus insisted that God could be known. With equal strength, he emphasized that God could be known only as he made himself known through the Son. In witness of this fact, he cited John 1:18:

> "No one has ever seen God except the unique Son of God who is in the bosom of the Father, he has declared him." For he, the Son who is in the bosom, declares (*enarrat*) to all the Father who is invisible. Therefore, they know him to whom the Son reveals (*revelaverit*) him (AH III,11,6).

Further evidence is seen in Matthew 11:27 and Luke 10:22: "neither does anyone know the Father except the Son, and the one to whom the Son wishes to reveal him" (AH IV,6,1 and elsewhere). "For no one can know the Father without the Word of God, that is to say unless the Son reveals him, nor [know] the Son without the good pleasure (*beneplacito* or *eudokia*) of the Father" (AH IV,6,3; cf. Proof 47).[1] The Word knows the invisible and

---

[1]Juan Ochagavía points out that *eudokia*, which appears 12 times in AH, "refers always to the historico-salvific dispositions of the Father with regard to man, and more particularly to the Incarnation." *Visibile Patris Filius: A Study of Irenaeus's Teaching on Revelation and Tradition*, Orientalia Christiana Analecta, no. 171 (Rome: Pont.

infinite Father and does the good pleasure of the Father by making him known to us. In fact, the Son reveals the Father by revealing himself, since manifestation of the Son gives knowledge of the Father (AH IV,6,3).[2]

One sees here the great importance to Irenaeus of the identity of the Father and the Son in revelation. There is a reciprocal revealing by Father and Son, but both the Father and the Son are made known by means of the Son. The Father, who alone knows the Son, reveals the Son to human beings by the visible manifestation of the Son, who at the same time reveals the Father.[3]

Institutum Orientalium Studiorum, 1964), 66.

[2]"Et patrem quidem invisibilem et indeterminabilem, quantum ad nos est, cognoscit suum ipsius Verbum, et cum sit inerrabilis, ipse enarrat eum nobis. . . . Et propter hoc Filius revelat agnitionem Patris per suam manifestationem. Agnitio enim Patris est Filii manifestatio: omnia enim per Verbum manifestantur."

[3]Frederick Loofs has distinguished two concepts of the term *logos* in the second-century. One is represented by the Apologists Ignatius, Irenaeus, and Theophilus of Antioch; the other by Clement and Origen. He attributed the difference to the Asiatic origin of the first group, and spoke of "the identity of Revelation between the Father and Son as the hall-mark of this tradition." The emphasis of the second group was on the Discarnate Logos. Loofs suggests that whereas for Irenaeus the Word is God himself revealing himself in Christ (II,16,4), for Justin he is another, or a second God (cited by H. E. W. Turner, *The Patristic Doctrine of Redemption. A Study of the Development of Doctrine During the First Five Centuries* [London: A. R. Mowbray & Co., 1952, 36-38]). The last comment of Loofs regarding Justin should be accepted cautiously, however. Cf. the discussion by E. F. Osborn which stresses Justin's insistence on the unity of God. Though different in number, the Logos was the same in substance with the Father (*Justin Martyr* [Tubingen: J. C. B. Mohr, 1973], 30-32; cf. especially Dial. 11,1).

As H. A. Wolfson indicates, Irenaeus rejected the two-stage theory of the Logos which Justin held, in which the Logos was first in the mind of God and then generated. Irenaeus denied a beginning of generation to the Logos and interpreted the words "In the beginning was the Logos" to mean that the generation of the Logos was from

Both the Jews (AH IV,6,1) and the Gnostics mistakenly believed that they could come to know God without the mediation of the Son. It was against this error that Irenaeus stressed the necessity of the Son's mediatorial work of revelation. The Ptolemaeans further erred in their teaching that what the Savior declared was not knowledge of the Father but the impossibility of knowing and seeing God. They, and the Marcionites, drew a distinction between the God known and seen in the Old Testament and the unknowable Father announced by the Savior. Thus, they cited Matthew 11:27 and Luke 10:22 to demonstrate that Jesus announced a God who was unknown until that time.

Irenaeus cites this Gospel text nine times in seven passages (AH I,20,3; II,6,1; II,14,7; IV,6,1,3,7; and IV,7,4), including three instances in which it is cited in the Gnostic form (AH I,20,3; II,14,7; IV,6,1). Robert Luckhart's careful study of these passages finds three significant differences: 1) a change in the tense of *cognosco* from *cognoscit* to *cognovit*; 2) a difference in the order in which the Father and the Son are named; 3) two different forms of the verb in the final clause: "voluerit revelare" and "revelaverit."[4] However, he discovers only one constant difference. The Gnostics used *cognovit* where Irenaeus uses *cognoscit*, or *egnō* (aorist of *ginōskō*)

---

eternity (*The Philosophy of the Church Fathers*, vol. 1: *Faith, Trinity, Incarnation*, 3rd. ed. rev. [Cambridge, Massachusetts: Harvard University Press, 1970], 200). For Irenaeus, the Logos "from eternity coexisted with God as a generated being" (ibid., 201). In fact, "Irenaeus thinks that the analogy between the generation of the Logos and the uttered Logos of the Stoics is the source of the Gnostics' erroneous conception of the generation of the logos as a physical process" (ibid., 299, citing AH II,28,5-6; II,13,8).

[4]Robert Luckhart, "Matt. 11:27 in the *Contra Haereses* of St. Irenaeus," *RUO* 23 (April-June 1953):67.

rather than the present, *epiginōskei.*[5] For Irenaeus, this was the statement of an eternal truth. It is not that the Son now makes known a Father who was previously unknown, but that no one has ever known the Father (although he *was* previously known) except by the means of the Son's manifestation. Rather than announcing the unknowability of the Father, Matthew 11:27 declares the exclusive role of the Son as revealer of the Father. The coming of the Son would have been without purpose if it were only to announce an unknowable Father.[6] Thus, from the beginning, the Son, who co-existed with the Father eternally, revealed the Father to the Angels, Archangels, Powers, Virtues, and to all whom he willed (AH II,30,9; cf. IV,6,7).

Irenaeus illustrated this truth by reference to the preaching of the apostles to those who had not previously been instructed about God. If Peter had agreed with the Gnostics, he would have declared to Cornelius and his household that the God of the Jews and the God of the Christians were different, and they would have believed him because of the impact made upon them by the vision of the angel. However, Peter did not do so. He declared that Jesus called the Christ was the Son of God, without rejecting the God they knew (AH III,12,7). It was likewise when Philip preached Jesus to the eunuch of the queen of Ethiopia and the eunuch confessed Jesus Christ to be the Son of God, the one God whom the prophets proclaimed (AH III,12,8).

---

[5] Luckhart, 72. Cf. AH I,20,3.

[6] See discussion by André Benoit, *Saint Irénée; introduction à l'étude de sa théologie.* Etudes d'histoire et de philosophie religieuses, no. 52 (Paris: Presses Universitaires de France, 1960), 185; Albert Houssiau, *La christologie de saint Irénée* (Louvain: Publications Universitaires de Louvain, 1955), 72-75; and Antonio Orbe, "San Ireneo y el conocimiento natural de Dios, Part II," *Greg* 47 (1966):712, 725-27.

As was clear in the previous chapter, Irenaeus was no Christomonist (in the manner of Karl Barth). He is not saying that only Christ is a revelation of the Father, to the exclusion of revelation in nature, but he is insisting that all the forms of divine self-revelation are by the agency of the Son. He is thus a clear witness to the absoluteness of Christ in the knowledge of the Father. Although he never specifically addressed the question, it is clear that Irenaeus would not conceive of revelations found in non-Christian religions as *alternative* means of knowing God *apart from* revelation through the Son. Whatever knowledge of God might be had by means of Hinduism or Buddhism would have to be mediated by Christ and be the result of the Father's will to make himself known to them for salvation.

B. The Universal Revelation of the Father by the Word in Creation and Providence

1. The continuous presence of the Word

Irenaeus had a very clearly enunciated doctrine of revelation by means of God's handiwork in creation and providence. The God who created all things, who was separated from his creatures by his transcendent greatness, had nonetheless made himself known to his creatures by means of his provision for them.[7] The creatures who experience God's government and benevolent care in the world have perception of him on account of that providence, so long as they are not blinded to this manifestation of God by a sinful manner of life or by idolatry (AH III,25,1). However, what is important to our

---

[7]AH II,6,1; cf. above discussion.

study, at this point, is the clear teaching that the work of
God in creation and providence is very much a revelation
of the Father *by the Son*.

> For *by creation itself the Word reveals God the Creator*; and by
> the world the Lord the Maker of the world, and by the thing
> formed the craftsman who formed it, and by the Son the Father
> who generated the Son.
>   . . . The Son, serving the Father, brings all things to
> completion, from the beginning to the end, and without him no
> one is able to know God. For the Son is the knowledge of the
> Father, on the other hand, the knowledge of the Son is in the
> Father and is revealed through the Son. And this is why the Lord
> said: "No one knows the Son except the Father, neither the
> Father except the Son and those to whom the Son shall reveal
> him." For "shall reveal" does not exclusively have a future sense,
> as if the Word had only begun to manifest the Father when he
> was born of Mary, but it is stated generally, referring to all time.
> For, *from the beginning, the Son, who has been present to that
> which he formed, reveals the Father* to all to whom the Father
> wishes and when and how he wishes. And this is why, in all
> things, and through all things, there is one God the Father, and
> one Word [the Son], and one Spirit, and one salvation to all those
> who believe in him (AH IV,6,6-7).[8] [italics supplied]

---

[8]"Etenim per ipsam conditionem revelat Verbum Conditorum
Deum, et per mundum Fabricatorem mundi Dominum, et per plasma
eum qui plasmaverit artificem, et per Filium eum Patrem qui
generaverit Filium.
    . . . Omnia autem Filius administrans Patri perficit ab initio
usque ad finem, et sine illo nemo potest cognoscere Deum. Agnitio
enim Patris Filius, agnitio autem Filii in Patre et per Filium revelata.
Et propter hoc Dominus dicebat: 'Nemo cognoscit Filium nisi Pater,
neque Patrem Filius, et quibuscumque Filius revelaverit.' 'Revelaverit'
enim non solum in futurum dictum est, quasi tunc inceperit Verbum
manifestare Patrem cum de Maria natus, sed communiter per totum
tempus positum est. Ab initio enim assistens Filius suo plasmati,
revelat omnibus Patrem, quibus vult et quemadmodum vult Pater. Et
propter hoc in omnibus et per omnia unus Deus credentibus in eum."

Irenaeus thus stresses the role of the Son in all self-manifestation of God, by emphasizing his mediatory role in the work of the Father. The same Word who was incarnated, crucified and resurrected is the one who was active in creation[9] and continues active in providence. It is the Word who reveals God the Creator by creation. It is he who has been present with that which he formed, revealing the Father from the very beginning.[10] The Son's role as revealer of the Father is not restricted to his human life, but extends to his continuous presence with his creatures, an idea that is synonymous with the providential presence of God.[11] His presence with God is correlative to his presence with humankind (AH III,18,1).[12]

2. A life-giving revelation

In AH IV,20,7, Irenaeus again underlines the revelatory role of the Son *from the beginning*, since he was *present* with the Father from the beginning. The

[9]See also AH I,22,1, citing Ps 33:6 and Jn 1:3; III,18,1.

[10]Irenaeus elsewhere refers again to the idea of God's presence with humankind, e.g. III,12,13: "Deum ab initio usque ad finem variis dispositionibus adsistentem humano generi (i.e. *symparonta tē anthrōpotēti*)." In V,16,1, he speaks of God's *voice* as being present with his image or handiwork from beginning to end. Rousseau appropriately capitalizes *Voix*, in his French translation, as well as in his Greek retroversion (215). In AH V,5,2, Irenaeus writes of the *hand* of God as present with the three men thrown into the furnace by Nebuchadnezzar, making use of the concept expressed elsewhere that the Word was the hand of God doing the Father's work in creation and the idea of providence by the notion of presence (*pareinai*), Irenaeus is following Hellenic usage from Homer to Plotinus ("L'exégèse de Matthieu 11,27b selon saint Irénée," *ETL* 29 [1953]: 350).

[11]Cf. Houssiau, *La christologie*, 109-10.

[12]Cf. Houssiau, *La christologie*, 110.

Word dispensed the Father's grace for the benefit of
human beings, revealing God to people and presenting
people to God through a variety of economies. This
revelation is necessary to human life, which consists in
the vision of God, as seen earlier. Particularly significant
is the fact that Irenaeus considers the manifestation of
God which is made by means of creation to be life-giving,
although it is not as valuable as the revelation of the
Father which comes "through the Word and gives life to
those who see God" (AH IV,20,7).[13] The above-cited
passage in AH IV,6,6-7 also clearly treats of the manifestation of the Father by the Word through creation and
providence (presence) as something that must be believed
unto salvation, or else as bringing condemnation upon
those who do not believe. José González-Faus describes
the last phrase of AH IV,20,7 as a "surprising parallelism," because it indicates that revelation in creation is
already salvific, at least germinally.[14] This seems to be
true. Irenaeus did not appear to have an awareness of
people who were restricted to that revelation in creation,
but assumed that everyone had further modes of revelation, even in Old Testament times. His emphasis in
IV,6,5-6 is that there are some who reject revelation even
at this basic level. Nevertheless, he clearly speaks of the
life-giving character of the revelation in creation. It might
be suggested that the life that is given in the revelation
of creation (understood appositionally: revelation, namely,
creation) is physical life, but that does not seem to do
justice to the parallel that Irenaeus makes in the context
of life as the vision of God.

----

[13]"Si enim quae est per conditionem ostensio Dei vitam praestat
omnibus in terra viventibus, multo magis ea quae est per Verbum
manifestatio Patris vitam praestat his qui vident Deum."

[14]*Carne de Dios: significado salvador de la Encarnación en la
teología de san Ireneo* (Barcelona: Herder, 1969), 52.

Later, Irenaeus stresses the importance of providence (along with the coming of Christ) to the salvation
of those who lived before the incarnation (AH IV,22,2).
Christ did not come only for those who lived at the time
of Tiberius Caesar, as though only they could benefit
from the revelatory work of the Word. More significantly,
the Father did not only exercise his providence for those
who were alive at the time of the incarnation and later.
These two important aspects of divine self-revelation
were

> for all people without exception who, from the beginning, accord-
> ing to their capacity, in their generation, both feared and loved
> God, and practised justice and piety toward their neighbor, and
> desired to see Christ and to hear his voice (AH IV,22,2).[15]

Such people will be raised first, at Christ's return, and
given a place in his kingdom. Because of the conjunction
of the coming of Christ with the exercise of God's providence, and because of the context before and after this
passage, which treats particularly of the patriarchs, it is
difficult to know how much weight one ought to give to
the role of providence. Irenaeus does speak of *all people*
and of varying capacities (*virtutem*). Does he mean,
thereby, to distinguish between the capacity of those who
experienced theophanic appearances of the pre-incarnate
Word and the capacity of those who perceived God only
by the Word's manifestation in creation? Natural revelation, including the human conscience, would provide
sufficient "capacity" for a certain fear and love of God and
a certain practice of justice toward one's neighbor.[16] But

---

[15]"Sed propter omnes omnino homines qui ab initio secundum
virtutem suam in sua generatione et timuerunt et dilexerunt Deum,
et juste et pie conversati sunt erga proximos, et concupierunt videre
Christum et audire vocem ejus."

[16]Cf. the "pagans" of AH III,25,1.

what capacity would such people have to "desire to see Christ and to hear his voice?" No definitive answers are possible at this point, but the significance of the questions must not be dismissed.

3. The cosmic cross

An important aspect of Irenaeus's thought regarding the presence of the Word in his creation is the manner in which he describes this as a cosmic crucifixion of the invisible Word. His teaching in this regard is found primarily in two passages:

> For the Maker of the world is truly the Word of God. However, this is our Lord, who in the last times was made man, existing in this world, and in an invisible manner he contains (or gives cohesion to) all created things, and is imprinted in the form of a cross[17] upon the entire creation, since the Word of God

---

[17]The Latin simply reads "in universa conditione infixus," which Roberts translates: "inherent in the entire creation" (ANF, 546). A more literal translation might be "impressed" or "imprinted" upon the entire creation. However, Rousseau translates the phrase "imprimé en forme de croix dans la création entière" (245) and argues convincingly for his rendering (SC 152; 296-302). He considers the Greek original to have been *kechiasmenos* (p. 296) and not *estaurōmenos* as Houssiau proposes (*La christologie,* 108, n. 5), since there is not ground for such a retroversion in either the Armenian or the Latin translation. Rousseau's retroversion is founded on a perceived relationship to Proof 34 and to Justin's I Apol. 60, a relationship which he claims is "admitted by all authors." (He cites W. Bousset, "Platons Weltseele und das Kreuz Christi," *ZNW* 14 [1913]:273-85.) Rousseau finds it easy to understand the Latin translator's rendering of the Greek participle as *infixus,* translating "d'une manière large," a Greek expression which seemed to him to be too abrupt. Rousseau therefore suggests as the essence of Irenaeus's passage: "Parce que . . . Le Verbe se trouvait déjà invisiblement *disposé* (tracé, imprimé . . .) *en forme de croix* dans l'univers créé en tant que le soutenant par sa puissance et le gouvernant par sa providence, il a fallu que ce même Verbe fût suspendu visiblement au bois de la croix" (297).

governs and arranges all things; and this is why "He came to his own" in a visible fashion and "was made flesh," and hung upon the tree, in order to recapitulate all things in himself (AH V,18,3).[18]

And the sin that was wrought through the tree was undone by the obedience of the tree, obedience to God whereby the Son of man was nailed to the tree, destroying the knowledge of evil, and bringing in and conferring the knowledge of good; . . . So by the obedience, whereby he obeyed unto death, hanging on the tree, he undid the old disobedience wrought in the tree. And because he is himself the Word of God Almighty, who in his invisible form pervades us universally in the whole world, and encompasses both its length and breadth and height and depth—for by God's Word everything is disposed and administered—the Son of God was also crucified in these, imprinted in the form of a cross on the universe;[19] for he had necessarily, in becoming visible, to bring to light the universality of his cross, in order to show openly through his visible form that activity of his: that it is he who makes bright the height, that is, what is in heaven, and holds the deep, which is in the bowels of the earth, and stretches forth and extends the length from east to west, navigating also the northern parts and the breadth of the south, and calling in all the dispersed from all sides to the knowledge of the Father (Proof 34).

a. The source of Irenaeus's symbolism

There would appear to be a number of different influences upon Irenaeus in his conception of the visible

---

[18]". . . et secundum invisibilitatem continet quae facta sunt omnia, et in universa conditione infixus, quoniam Verbum Dei gubernans et disponens omnia, et propter hoc 'in sua' invisibiliter [Rousseau necessarily keeps the "invisibiliter" but points out that it is impossible in the context; the Armenian text has the same mistaken reading, which points to a common mistake in the Greek, where *oratōs* became *aoratōs*; it is a confusion found often in AH (SC 152, 302)] 'venit, et caro factum est,' et perpendit super lignum, uti universa in semetipsum recapituletur."

[19]Rousseau suggests as the Greek retroversion: "*kai eis tauta estaurōthē ho Huios tou theo kechiasmenos en tō panti*" (SC 152, 301).

crucifixion of Christ on a cross of wood as representing a
relationship which Christ bore to the universe from the
very beginning. Rousseau sees an allusion to, or even an
implicit citation of, Justin,[20] who in turn was citing
Plato.[21] Without denying the importance of Justin's
influence, however, there would seem to be an even more
immediate source in the writings of the Gnostics whose
teaching Irenaeus was refuting. The Valentinians
explained the passion as a visible indication or demonstration of the passion of the last of the Aeons (AH I,8,2).
The passion of Christ was an indistinct reflection of the
"crucifixion" of the Christ above, who took pity on
Achamoth (the fruit of the passion of Sophia) and
deposited in her a spiritual form (AH I,4,1).[22] González-
Faus concludes that "the cosmic crucifixion which
Irenaeus affirms is no more than the orthodox version of
the Gnostic crucifixion."[23] It is important to note, therefore, that Irenaeus's "economic" exegesis of the cross in
no way negates its historical facticity.[24]

---

[20]I Apol. 60: "kai to en tō para Platōni timaiō physiologoumenōn
peri tou Huiou tou Theou, hote legei: 'Echiasen auton en tō panti,'
para Mōuseōs labōn homoiōs eipen." (And that which is treated
physiologically, in Plato's *Timaeus*, concerning the Son of God, where
he says: "He impressed him in the form of the letter in all things," he
likewise took from Moses.) Justin goes on to say that Plato had read
how Moses made a cross of brass in order to save the Israelites from
the poisonous serpents. However, Plato had not accurately understood
that it was a cross, and therefore spoke of it as a letter *chi*.

[21]SC 152, 299.

[22]Cf. González-Faus, 277-78.

[23]González-Faus, 229. He finds this in keeping with an attitude of
Irenaeus found throughout his work, namely, a desire to formulate
correctly rather than simply to contradict the Gnostic version of
Christian truth.

[24]Ibid. In this regard, Irenaeus was very different from the
Gnostics who stressed the cosmic crucifixion but not the Logos union,
crucified in Jerusalem. Cf. Antonio Orbe, *Los primeros herejes ante la*

b. The meaning of the symbolism

The purpose of Irenaeus's reference to the imprinting of the Word upon the universe is to indicate the cohesion which the invisible Word gives to all things. Orbe suggests a hendiadys between the two clauses in AH V,18,3:

> et secundum invisibilitatem continet quae facta sunt omnia

and

> et in universa conditione infixus.[25]

Here *continet* is probably a translation of *katechei,* which was an important Stoic term denoting the cohesion and union of all parts of the cosmos.[26] The causative, *quoniam*, is important in this phrase. It is *because* the Word of God governs and administers all things that the invisible Lord gives cohesion to all things and is imprinted in the form of a cross in all created things.[27] The same relationship is stressed in Proof 34. Orbe aptly discerns the symmetry in Irenaeus's thought: the sensible creation sustains the redemptive and visible cross of Christ, whereas the invisible Word, with his invisible cross, sustains and governs the sensible creation.[28] Predominant in Irenaeus's thought concerning the cross is the figure of the embrace. He sees the Word as a Being

---

persecución, Estudios Valentinianos (Romae: Apud Aedes Universitatis Gregorianae, 1956), 5:269.

[25]Orbe, 214.

[26]Ibid., 213, n. 1; cf. AH III,11,8.

[27]Ibid., 215.

[28]Ibid.

with his arms stretched out to gather the world together from one extreme to the other. He is invisibly imprinted upon the world because his embrace produces unity and stops the dispersion of its elements.[29] Furthermore, as Proof 34 indicates, this impression of the Logos in his immanence is participated in by all those beings that the Word preserves and governs. There is no being that does not participate in the cosmic cross.[30] Irenaeus thus taught the appropriateness (or even necessity[31]) of the incarnation and visible crucifixion of Christ, in order to manifest that all things participate in the invisible cross of Christ. he indicated that the efficacy of the Word's invisible crucifixion, namely, the universal power of cohesion peculiar to the Word (i.e. his government and administration of all things), is already experienced by all.[32]

What Irenaeus underlines, in his discussion of the cosmic cross, is its universal efficacy, with an emphasis on its extension rather than its intensity. Orbe discerns the influence of Paul, particularly of Ephesians 3:18,[33] but also identifies the theme of the heavenly places which was common in Stoic language.[34] Irenaeus thus explained the invisible cross according to the four dimensions that Paul cites, understanding them to be the universal diffusion of the Logos in the world. Stoicism spoke of a world that was full of the divine logos which penetrated it and gave it cohesion in the manner of a soul or living bond. Irenaeus applied the concept to the personal Word, the Son of God. Orbe rightly contends

---

[29]Ibid.
[30]Ibid., 217.
[31]As rendered by J. P. Smith, 70.
[32]Cf. Orbe, 217-18.
[33]Ibid., 218.
[34]Ibid., 220.

that the cross of Golgotha holds an independent reality in the order of redemption from sin. However, the cosmic theology of the Word interfaces with the soteriology because of the bivalence of the sensible cross, which corresponds, on the one hand, to the invisible cross, and, on the other hand, to the tree of Paradise, and through it to the disobedience committed there.[35]

Most significant to the particular focus of this study is the revelatory nature of this cosmic cross. Irenaeus speaks of it as "calling in all the dispersed from all sides to the knowledge of the Father" (Proof 34). On the basis of this statement, Orbe correctly indicates that the cosmic crucifixion is "oriented decidedly to the salvation of the dispersed elements."[36] The Logos is clearly not only a principle of physical cohesion, but also a principle of moral, and therefore of supernatural, unity, in the knowledge of the Father. The vertical arm of the cross symbolizes the influence of the Word in the illumination of the celestial beings, and also in his extension into the subterranean world. It is unclear what is the effect of his entrance into the latter, whether those contained there are being ruled and reprimanded or whether they are being embraced with an embrace which reconciles the inferior elements with the superior. Orbe is inclined to the latter view, because of a parallel in the *Acts of Andrew*, c. 14, and because the symbolism of the lateral arms confirms such an exegesis.[37] This second reason seems particularly significant, as the horizontal arms clearly signify the reconciliation of east and west, of Jew and Gentile, or of the inhabitants of the earth. The activity of the Word in every direction therefore leads to one end, the knowledge of the Father, the one

---

[35]Ibid., 222-23.
[36]Orbe, 228.
[37]Ibid., 223-24.

God. AH V,17,4 specifically refers the gathering accomplished by the outstretched arms to the two peoples scattered to the ends of the earth. There were two hands because there were two peoples, but there was only one head because there is only one God. Proof 34, however, is more general, taking in all elements dispersed in the universe.[38] AH V,18,3 likewise speaks more generally, relating this theme of the cosmic cross to that of the recapitulation of all things in the Word. More will be said on that subject in a moment.

The symbolism of Irenaeus, as described in these passages, may be represented in this manner:[39]

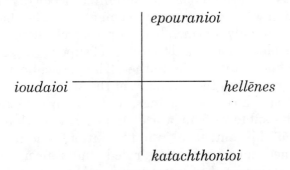

C. The Presence of the Word Prior to the Incarnation

Given the exclusive role of the Word as revealer of the Father, it is essential to Irenaeus that the action

---

[38]Orbe discerns a parallel to Jn 11:50,52 as well as *Acta Andrae, Evangelium Philippi* and other such works (226). Smith sees an allusion to Jn 12:32: "And I, if I be lifted up from the earth, will draw all things to myself," and Jn 11:51ff: "that Jesus should die for the nation and not only for the nation, but to gather together in one the children of God, that were dispersed" (173).

[39]As Orbe suggests, 225.

of the Word be recognized at every point of the divine self-communication.[40] Because of the Gnostic postulation that a different God was revealed in the Old Testament than in the New, it was also important to show that, while the Incarnation was the supreme step in the progressive divine self-disclosure, it was not the first time that the Word was revealed.

1. Theophanic appearances

The Word was present with the creature, from the beginning, not only by creation, but by theophanic appearances. He was present in Eden with Adam, who was himself the Word's creation (AH V,15,4). There he walked and talked with Adam, "prefiguring what was to come to pass in the future, how he would become man's fellow, and talk with him, and come among mankind, teaching them justice" (Proof 12). It was he who gave to Adam the prohibition concerning the eating of the fruit of the tree of the knowledge of good and evil (AH V,17,1, citing Gen 2:16,17; V,17,2). Then, when Adam had sinned and hidden himself from God, the Word sought him out, just as he seeks people in the last times, who are also hiding from him (Gen 3:8,9; AH V,15,4; IV,10,1).

The Word addressed Cain when Cain was angry with Abel, urging him not to commit violence, but Cain did not heed him (AH IV,18,3; cf V,14,1). Later, he spoke

---

[40]As seen in AH II,30,9, Irenaeus's emphasis on the *eternal* co-existence of the Word with the Father, *from the beginning*, is particularly with regard to his role as *always* revealing the Father. A. Harnack's comment is appropriate: "his very statement that the Logos has revealed the Father from the beginning shows that this relationship is always in the sphere of revelation. The Son then exists because he gives a revelation" (*History of Dogma*, trans. from the third German edition by Neil Buchanan [New York: Russell & Russell, 1958], 2:265).

with Noah and gave him the dimensions of the ark (AH
IV,10,1). Then he sent the flood upon the people of that
day, in judgment on their disobedience (AH IV,36,3), but
he made a covenant with Noah afterwards (AH III,11,8).
He spoke to Noah and his companions at that time and
gave the commandment regarding capital punishment for
the taking of human life (AH V,14,1; cf Gen 9:5,6).
Frequently, God manifested himself to the patriarchs,
"speaking to them according to his divinity and glory,"
through the Word (AH III,11,8). Interestingly, Irenaeus
describes Abraham as seeking God all over the earth and
on the point of giving up when God, in pity, revealed
himself to Abraham (Proof 24). J. P. Smith indicates that
this was founded on Jewish tradition.[41] The Word then
called Abraham out of Ur, and Abraham followed the
Word, as a pilgrim, until he settled in Judea, where God
gave him the promise of the land (Proof 25; AH IV,5,3).
The Word later appeared and spoke to Abraham about
the imminent judgment of Sodom (AH III,6,1; IV,7,4;
Proof 44), and Abraham pleaded with him for the city's
deliverance (Proof 44). In that experience, Abraham "saw
what was to come to pass in the future, the Son of God in
human form" who would speak and sit with men and
then bring down judgment from the Father (Proof 44). It
was in obedience to the command of the Word that
Abraham was prepared to offer up Isaac as a sacrifice
(AH IV,5,4). Abraham thus provides a splendid example
of the person of faith who believed the Word and followed
him obediently and gladly. Jesus specifically cites
Abraham for having seen him and rejoiced (AH IV,5,3,
citing Jn 8:56). Abraham knew both the Word and the
Father, of whom he learned from the Word (AH IV,5,5;
IV,7,1). It was specifically the Word who stood "circum-
scribed in space" and spoke with Abraham. It was he

---

[41]Smith, 161, n. 124.

"who was always with mankind, and foretold what was to come to pass in the future, and acquainted man with God" (Proof 45).

Jacob, heir to the covenant made with Abraham, saw the Word, in a dream, standing at a ladder which symbolized the cross, by means of which those who believe ascend to heaven (Proof 45). However, no one was more blessed with appearances of the Word than Moses, to whom the Word spoke as a friend (AH IV,20,9, citing Ex 33:11; cf. Proof 40). It was to Moses that the Word spoke in giving the Law (AH III,15,3; IV,9,1), having spoken to him earlier, out of the burning bush, when he declared himself as the God of the fathers and called Moses to lead Israel out of Egypt (AH III,6,2; IV,5,2; IV,10,1; IV,12,4; IV,29,2; Proof 2, 46). Nor was the Word's intervention in delivering Israel something unique, because the Word had been used to ascend and descend, in order to save those who are being afflicted, "from the beginning (*ab initio*)" (AH IV,12,4; III,6,2). Other incidents could be mentioned, such as the Word's presence with the three men in the furnace (AH IV,20,11), but the point of all these examples is to demonstrate, on the one hand, that no one ever knew the Father except through the Word, and, on the other hand, that the Word was definitely known by people in the Old Testament, prior to his incarnation.[42] Ochagavía aptly says:

---

[42] Jean Daniélou suggests that the passages that Irenaeus mentions "are in fact all traditional and constitute a commonplace of hellenistic theology in the early centuries, namely a group of *testimonia* on the manifestations of the Word." It is Daniélou's judgment, however, that Irenaeus's "characteristic, and original, contribution is his emphasis on the continuity between these earlier instances of the Word's presence among men and the Incarnation" (cf. AH IV,12,4). *A History of Early Christian Doctrine Before the Council of Nicaea*, vol. 2: *Gospel Message and Hellenistic Culture*, trans. and ed. John Austin Baker (New York: Westminster Press, 1973), 168.

Irenaeus . . . with his deep sense for the continuity and slow progressing growth of God's salvific plan, sees the fitness and also the necessity of many anticipations of the definitive event that took place in Jesus Christ. The Word was fit to carry out those missions since he possessed from the beginning the visibility required for this role.[43]

2. The Word speaks through the Law and the Prophets

Not only did the Word appear to people of the Old Testament and speak to them, but he spoke through them and in their writings. Thus, Irenaeus says that "the writings of Moses are the words of Christ" (AH IV,2,3), and cites John 5:46,47 as the ground of this statement. Likewise, the words of the other prophets were unmistakably the words of Christ (AH IV,2,3). By the Law and the Prophets, the Word preached himself and the Father (AH IV,6,6). For this very reason, Jesus did not expect that anyone who refused to obey Moses and the prophets would believe and obey his own words. The Lord himself spoke the words of the Decalogue to all alike and they remain permanently with us, not being abrogated by the incarnate coming of the Word, but rather being extended and augmented (AH IV,16,4).

The Marcionite teaching excluded all prophetic preparation because of an insistence on the novelty of the revelation made in Christ. Irenaeus urges his readers to read carefully the Gospel handed on by the apostles and also the prophets, because they will then find that all the work and doctrine and suffering of Christ were predicted by the prophets. The novelty which Christ brought was not in the content of revelation, but in the manner of his personal presence (AH IV,34,1). The patriarchs and prophets sowed the word concerning Christ, by their

---

[43]Ochagavía, 93-94.

prophetic announcement, and the Church has reaped the fruit (AH IV,25,3). The Son of God is therefore described as implanted or inseminated (*inseminatus est*) everywhere in the Scriptures, because the Old Testament so frequently and so clearly speaks of him (AH IV,10,1; IV,23,1). Furthermore, all who had known God from the beginning, and all those who, like the prophets, foretold the coming of Christ, received that revelation "from the Son himself" (AH IV,7,2).[44] This fact made conversion of the Gentiles more difficult than of the Jews, who already knew God from the Scriptures (AH IV,24,1-2). Thus, it was a relatively easy task for Philip to instruct the Ethiopian eunuch concerning the coming of Christ, because he was already instructed by the prophets, who had prepared him in the fear of God. The same preparation was evident in the conversion of three, four and five thousand people who were baptized in the early days of the Church as recorded in Acts (AH IV,23,2; Ac 2:41; 4:4; cf. AH III,12,8). Christ was like a treasure hidden in the Scriptures, in the form of types and parables, and brought to light by the events of his life (AH IV,26,1).

The experience of Cornelius, which has been of considerable interest to theologians of "anonymous Christianity," is explained in this light. He feared God, whom he knew through the Law and the Prophets, but he lacked knowledge of the Son of God. Peter therefore declared Christ to him, without rejecting the God whom Cornelius worshiped because of his knowledge of the Old Testament Scriptures (AH III,12,7). The Scriptures themselves are perfect, being spoken by the Word of God and his Spirit. It is a great impiety, therefore, to seek

---

[44]"Omnes qui ab initio cognitum habuerunt Deum et adventum Christi prophetaverunt revelationem acceperunt ab ipse Filio." Cf. IV,20,4: "prophetae, ab eodem Verbum propheticum accipientes charisma, praedicaverunt ejus secundum carnem adventum."

after some other God than the one who has been declared
by Scripture, simply because there are questions raised
by Scripture which we cannot understand (AH II,28,2).

The Law, spoken by the Word to Moses, was
certainly important to all those who lived afterwards.
Nevertheless, Irenaeus contends that the patriarchs had
not been shortchanged through lack of it. In answer to
the question why the Lord did not form the covenant
made at Horeb with the Fathers, Irenaeus quotes I
Timothy 1:9: "the law was not established for the righteous." The fathers had the virtue of the Decalogue
written in their hearts and souls,[45] since they loved the
God who had made them and abstained from injustice to
their neighbors. Having the righteousness of the Law
within themselves, it was not necessary that they should
be given the prohibitions of the Law. It was because that
righteousness and love toward God died out in Egypt that
God graciously spoke to Israel again through Moses and
taught them to love God and deal justly with their
neighbor. By means of the Decalogue, God therefore
prepared people for friendship with himself (AH IV,16,3).
It is interesting to note that Irenaeus does not appeal to
the theophanies, or to some form of pre-Mosaic supernatural revelation, in order to establish the sufficiency of
the patriarchs without the Law. His appeal is rather to
an innate knowledge of righteousness, "written in their
hearts and souls" (AH IV,16,3). However, due account
must be taken of the great emphasis Irenaeus has
elsewhere placed on the repeated appearances of the
Word to people, from the very beginning, as has already
been demonstrated. Abraham was justified without either

---

[45]Roberts suggests that by "in cordibus et animabus suis," Irenaeus
intends their "moral and mental natures." He cites this as a valuable
passage for arriving at a correct view of the patristic conceptions of
the Gentiles before the law" (ANF, 481, n. 11).

circumcision or the Law, but Irenaeus makes it clear that the righteousness of Abraham was on account of his belief in God, that is, his obedient response to the call, and to the promise, addressed to him by the Word (AH IV,16,2).

As William Loewe rightly discerns, Irenaeus "marshalls a thoroughly Christological reading of the Old Testament."[46] Irenaeus finds the Old Testament witness to Christ so ample that he can assert that for "those steeped in it, like the God-fearer Cornelius whose household Peter baptized (II,12,7) or the Ethiopian eunuch whom Philip converted (IV,23,2), only one thing was lacking which they did not already possess, knowledge of the incarnate Word himself."[47] Old Testament prophecy was clear only from hindsight; however, the treasure of Christ hidden in it comes to light only through a Christian reading, and specifically through the knowledge of the cross.[48]

D. Revelation in the Incarnation

1. Continuity with pre-incarnate revelation

Irenaeus did not consider the visible coming of the Word in human form to be his first manifestation of the Father, but it was, nonetheless, a significant step forward in the economy of God's self-revelation. The Incarnation itself was an important truth for Irenaeus to defend, because none of the heretics with whom he

---

[46]William P. Loewe, "Ireneaus' Soteriology: Transposing the Question," in *Religion and Culture: Essays in Honor of Bernard Lonergan S.J.*, ed. Timothy P. Fallon and Philip Boo Riley (Albany, New York: State University of New York Press, 1987), 169.

[47]Loewe, "Irenaeus's Soteriology," 169.

[48]Loewe, "Irenaeus's Soteriology," 170, referring to AH IV,20,1.

contended believed that the Word of God had been
incarnated, despite what Irenaeus saw as clear testimony
in John 1:14 (AH III,11,3). Much evidence has already
been cited of Irenaeus's concern for the unity of God's
economy and for the continuity in his self-manifestation
from stage to stage, within the pedagogic unfolding of the
divine self-revelation, leading people on to the maturity
of the ultimate vision of God which is life. It was in his
own person that the Lord spoke the words of the Decalogue, and, by his coming in the flesh, those words are
not abrogated, but are extended and augmented (AH
IV,16,4; cf. IV,12,4).[49] It was because the Word had
spoken through the prophets to foretell his coming that
Joseph was prepared to take Mary as his wife, the
Ethiopian eunuch was ready for Philip's message, and
the apostles were able to baptize, three, four and five
thousand people in a day, during the days after Pentecost
(AH IV,23,1-2).

   The novelty of revelation in the New Testament
is not in the intervention of a new revealer or the revelation of a different God, but in the superior form of
revelation made by the same Word, who has now come in
the flesh (AH III,10,2; IV,9,2). By his visible coming, he
has brought a greater privilege to those who believe in
him, and more severe judgment to those who do not.
However, that is not because he reveals a different
Father; it is because "by his coming he has poured out on
the human race a greater gift of the grace of the Father"
(AH IV,36,4). Instead of the earlier graces which were
figuratively represented, such as the reign of Christ
pictured in the reign of Solomon, and the resurrection

---

[49]Commenting on this passage, Daniélou states that "Irenaeus's
characteristic, and original, contribution is his emphasis on the
continuity between these earlier instances of the Word's presence
among men and the Incarnation" (*Gospel Message*, 168).

prefigured in Jonah, we now have the incarnate presence
of the King and the resurrection itself (AH IV,9,2). The
Word is the same steward of the house who produced
both covenants, who spoke with Abraham and Moses, and
who has now multiplied the grace which comes from
himself (AH IV,9,1).[50]

2. The invisible Father made known by the visible Son

A most important aspect of this new stage in the
Father's self-revelation through the Word is the Word's
visibility. The incarnate Son is the comprehensible and
visible one through whom the incomprehensible and
invisible Father worked, for example, at Cana and in the
feeding of the five thousand (AH III,11,5). Citing John
1:18, Irenaeus declares that the Son who is in the bosom
of the Father makes known to all the Father who is
invisible (AH III,11,6).

> The Father was manifested by the Word himself made visible
> and palpable . . . for the Father is the invisible [Reality, French
> trans.] of the Son and the Son is the visible [Reality] of the
> Father (AH IV,6,6).

In revealing God to people, the Son thus preserved the
invisibility of the Father, in order to protect people from
contempt for God, and so that they might always have
something toward which to progress (AH IV,20,7). Yet, he
provides a way of approach to the otherwise invisible and
inaccessible Father (Proof 47). The experience of Moses,

---

[50]See E. P. Meijering's fine discussion of the continuity between
the revelation of the Word in the Old and New Testaments (256-59);
also Ochagavía (80); and L. S. Thornton (*Revelation and the Modern
World, Being the First Part of a Treatise on the Form of the Servant*
[London: Dacre Press, 1950], 169-70).

in Numbers 12, had been a pre-figurative demonstration of the impossibility of seeing God, and yet of the fact that "in the last times people should see him on the pinnacle of the rock, that is to say, in his coming as a man." This promise was fulfilled at the Transfiguration (AH IV,20,9).

There is some difference of opinion among scholars as to the "novelty" of the Son's "visibility" in the New Testament in the thought of Irenaeus. Citing AH IV,6,6, Houssiau has contended that the Word was as invisible as the Father, before the Incarnation.[51] Ochagavía, following Orbe, demonstrates that this was not Irenaeus's conception of the situation.[52] Irenaeus uses the words "visible" and "invisible" in two different senses. Sometimes "visibility" designated a corporeal attribute, in which case the pre-incarnate Word was invisible and the incarnate Word was visible. Elsewhere, however, "visible" and "invisible" were simply synonyms for "knowable" and "unknowable" (e.g. AH IV,6,6).[53] Orbe thus contends that there is a "difference between the invisibility which is predicated of the Father (*invisibile Patri*) and that which is affirmed of the Word (*invisibile erat Verbum*)."[54] The fact that the human body, and not only the soul, was made after the image of the Word indicated, according to Irenaeus, that the Word had some sort of human form or shape even before the Incarnation (AH IV,16,2). The image is in the human frame (*plasma*) and the likeness is in the spirit. The image is the Son and the likeness is given by the

---

[51]*La christologie*, 87-91, 113.

[52]Ochagavía, 89-95; and citing Orbe, *Hacía la primera teología de la procesión del Verbo* (Roma, 1958), 655-56.

[53]As further examples of this distinction between the two senses, Orbe cites AH V,16,2; cf. also III,22,1; IV,33,4; IV,36,7; Proof 22.

[54]*Procesión del Verbo*, 656, cited by Ochagavía, 90.

Spirit.[55] Ochagavía thus concludes that "the pre-incarnate Word was in possession of a sort of visibility to the mind that was anterior to the visibility to the eyes of the flesh,"[56] and Orbe suggests that "the Word's visibility *according to the flesh* corresponds to his essential visibility or cognoscibility according to the mind."[57] Seen in the context of the controversy with the Valentinian Gnostics, this is an important perspective. The Valentinians accepted a visibility and comprehensibility of the incarnate Son, but Irenaeus was attempting to demonstrate that human knowledge of God in the New Testament is not fundamentally different from that of the Old Testament. The invisible Father was always known in and through the Son.[58]

---

[55]Ochagavía, 90, citing AH II,7,6-7; V,61; Proof 5,11,22,97.
[56]Ibid., 91.
[57]Orbe, *Procesión del Verbo*, 407, cited by Ochagavía, 91.
[58]Ochagavía, 94-95.

González-Faus gives a brief summary of the controversy between Houssiau and Ochagavía, and concludes aptly that it is important to retain the continuity (as Ochagavía does), but also to underline the progress (as Houssiau does). Indeed, he suggests that it may be precisely this double direction that accounts for the apparent vacillation in the language of Irenaeus. He also proposes that the positions taken by the various interpreters of Irenaeus are prejudiced by their opinion regarding the "personal properties" of the Trinity (156-59).

Jean Daniélou notes a difference between Justin and Irenaeus. In Justin's theology, "the Father is essentially invisible and the Son visible. For Irenaeus, the Father and the Son are equally inaccessible to human scope, and equally accessible, if they will to reveal themselves. What is involved, therefore, is not a difference of nature between the Son and the Father, but the reflection in their activity in the world of their inter-relation within the Trinity, by which the Son is the manifestation of the Father" (citing especially AH IV,20,6-7, *Gospel Message*, 359).

3. A saving revelation

Irenaeus makes it very clear that the purpose of the revelation in the incarnate Word was to further the salvific purpose of God. John the Baptist was therefore told that his role would be to "give knowledge of salvation" to God's people (AH III,10,3, citing Lk 1:76). The knowledge which people lacked was knowledge of the Son of God (AH III,10,3, citing Jn 1:29). Thus, the coming of the Word in the flesh gave people that necessary knowledge, of the Father and the Son, in order that they might be saved. More complex than this matter of saving proclamation, however, is Irenaeus's teaching concerning what was accomplished for human salvation by the Incarnation itself. It is this reality that makes the heretics' denial of the Incarnation so serious. Because they insist that Jesus Christ was simply a man, they do not receive the gift of eternal life. They are among those who "have not accepted the gift of adoption, but despise the incarnation of the pure generation of the Word of God, defraud humanity of its ascension toward God, and show ingratitude to the Word of God who was incarnated for them" (AH III,19,1). This is serious.

> For it was for this reason that the Word of God was made man, and that the Son of God was made the Son of man, in order that humankind, having been united to the Word of God [literally, "mixed together," *commixtus*] and receiving adoption, might become the Son of God. For we could not otherwise obtain incorruptibility and immortality if we had not been united to incorruptibility and immortality. But how could we be joined to incorruptibility and immortality if first incorruptibility and immortality had not been made what we are also, in order that what was corruptible might be absorbed by incorruptibility and what was mortal by immortality, in order that we might receive the adoption of sons (AH III,19,1).

This understanding of the Incarnation has produced much discussion of Irenaeus's soteriology. Is Irenaeus proposing efficacious salvation by the Incarnation of the Word? Is he presenting a "naturalistic" or "physical" doctrine of salvation, that is, a theory of salvation by bestowal of divinity or immortality on human nature? Harnack and Ritschl believed that he was, and Emil Brunner summarizes their line of argument as follows:

> The dogma of the Early Church is dominated by a "physical" (also "magical," "mystical," "naturalistic," "mechanical") conception of salvation. Salvation is a "redemption which is achieved in a psychomagical manner by means of the Incarnation;" the doctrine of salvation is "the idea of the deification of the children of Adam as a mechanical result of the Incarnation.[59]

Gustaf Aulén also describes this nineteenth-century Liberal Protestant perspective:

> The gift of immortality is regarded as dependent on the Incarnation as such; by entrance of the Divine into humanity, human nature is (as it were) automatically endued with Divine virtue and thereby saved from corruption. This is, then, a theology primarily of the Incarnation, not of the Atonement; the "work" of Christ holds a secondary place.[60]

However, Brunner points out that Harnack's thesis about the "physical" effect of salvation contradicts many of his other statements about Irenaeus. For example, salvation, which is created objectively through the Incarnation, is subjectively mediated. But, says

---

[59]Emil Brunner, *The Mediator: A Study of the Central Doctrine of the Christian Faith*, trans. Olive Wyon (London: Lutterworth Press, 1934), 250, citing especially Harnack, 1:545,562.

[60]*Christus Victor: An Historical Study of the Three Main Types of the Idea of the Atonement*, trans. E. G. Hebert (London: SPCK, 1953), 34.

Brunner, "If there really were a physical effect there could be no subjective mediation at all. Salvation would not be connected with faith, but it would become the portion of every human being quite naturally, 'mechanically' as Harnack says."[61] Yet, Harnack cites evidence that salvation is the portion of believers only (e.g. AH IV,2,7; IV,5).

The judgment one almost inevitably encounters in reading twentieth-century interpreters of Irenaeus's soteriology is that there is certainly an ambiguity in Irenaeus's teaching, but that the overall position of his work is definitely not a "physical" conception of salvation.[62] It is beyond the scope of this study to develop a comprehensive Irenaean soteriology,[63] but this particular

---

[61]Brunner, 255.

[62]See for e.g. Aulén, 34-36; Brunner, 25-59; A. J. Bandstra, "Paul and an Ancient Interpreter; a Comparison of the Teaching of Redemption in Paul and Irenaeus," *CTJ* 5 (1970):47-59; a very helpful study by Pierre Jossua, *Le Salut, incarnation ou mystère pascal chez les Pères de l'Eglise de saint Irénée à saint Léon le Grand* (Paris: Les Editions du Cerf, 1968), 57-135; Dai Sil Kim, "Irenaeus of Lyons and Teilhard de Chardin: A Comparative Study of 'Recapitulation' and 'Omega,'" *JEcSt* 13 (1976):86; John Lawson, *The Biblical Theology of St. Irenaeus* (London: Epworth Press, 1948), 14-15, 141-43, 154, 167-68.

[63]Bandstra, in a well-balanced treatment, discerns three related motifs in Irenaeus's doctrine of the atonement: 1) Victory over sin, death and Satan. This is the theme emphasized by Aulén and found in AH III,18,7; III,23,1 & 7; IV,24,1; V,21,1 & 3; Proof 31, 37, 38, etc. This is accomplished through his obedience (AH III,19,3; III,18,7; V,16,3). 2) Renewal into life and immortality (AH III,18,1; III,19,1; V,Pref.). With regard to this aspect, Bandstra insists that it is not a "physical" theory of the atonement but that, at most, the incarnation is the presupposition of redemption. Irenaeus insists on the importance of the death of Christ and the necessity of his obedience, and emphasizes the gift of the Spirit to humanity from Christ (cf. Proof 5-8). 3) Propitiatory and vicarious sacrifice for sin. Bandstra grants that this aspect is not as pronounced as 1) or 2), and that it is denied by

aspect is important to the situation of the unevangelized. Given the breadth and inclusiveness with which Irenaeus spoke of humanity as united to God in the incarnation, if Irenaeus had consistently put forward a "physical" or "incarnationist" doctrine of salvation, it would have resulted in universalism. It is clear, however, that Irenaeus did not reach that conclusion, as will be particularly evident in the later discussion of the necessary response to divine revelation (Chapter 8). While the Incarnation is the cornerstone of Irenaeus's theology, there is no cleavage between Incarnation and Atonement. "Incarnation is the necessary preliminary to the atoning work."[64] Irenaeus never speaks as if Christ's redeeming

---

Aulén (49ff.) and Lawson (193), while only guardedly accepted by Harnack (II:291ff.) and Wingren (117). AH V,17,1-3 is the central passage in this regard, with indication also in IV,8,2; V,2,2; V,16,3; and Proof 69.

[64]Aulén, *Christus Victor*, 36. Cf. J. P. Jossua's comment that nothing strikes the reader of Irenaeus more than his insistence on the line between incarnation and salvation, or on the incarnate condition of the economy of salvation (73, cf. AH V,17,1). Jossua points out that allusions to the saving value of the incarnation designate the effect of the whole of the economy, a permanent economy of carnal presence. This he corroborates by a study of parallel expressions, such as: an economy of humanity (AH V,33,7; V,18,2; V,19,2); an economy of corporality (Proof 32; AH IV,Pref. 4); an economy of the coming of the Son (AH III,10,5; III,16,3); an economy of the Son or of the Christ (AH III,13,1; III,17,4; IV,34,3); an economy of recapitulation (AH IV,20,8); and an economy by which humankind sees God (AH IV,20,10, etc.), 71-72.

González-Faus treats this aspect of Christ's redemptive work at length, in chapter 9, "La salvación en la muerte de Cristo en cruz" (215-53). Particularly significant are his discussions of "the cross as obedience" (231-36) and "the cross as satisfaction" (245-53). He suggests that Irenaeus spoke of two aspects of salvation: 1) consummation or fulfillment, i.e. participation in divinity, and 2) restoration, i.e. destruction of sin. The term "resurrection" expressed the fusion of the two aspects. For Irenaeus, no participation in the divinity is possible without the incarnation, and no restoration from sin is

death were a mere appendage to the Incarnation. *"Incarnatus* and *passus* are almost synonymous in such passages as I,9,3 and III,18,3."[65] In the economy of salvation, through which God is progressively preparing human beings for the vision of God, the Incarnation is important because, by means of it, the flesh is accustomed to live with the Spirit. The Word becomes human in order to accustom humans to see God, and to accustom God to live with human beings (AH III,20,2).[66]

4. Recapitulation

An important aspect of any consideration of Irenaeus's doctrine of the Incarnation is the theme of recapitulation. It can be treated only briefly here. However, our interest in the state of the unevangelized requires a brief look at this important topic. So important is it, in fact, that it has been considered the focal point around which Irenaeus constructs his entire theology.[67]

---

possible without Christ's work of obedience. The cross redeems and the incarnation divinizes (255).

[65]Lawson, 154.

[66]Cf. Benoit, 230; D. Unger, "Christ's Role in the Universe According to St. Irenaeus," *FranSt* NS 5 (1945):15. Unger suggests that the Word was going to become incarnate even apart from sin to "lead man gradually to the vision of God" (16).

Daniélou comments on this descent of God and ascent of human beings: "ascent consists in his education by the Word, who familiarizes men with his ways just as he himself becomes familiar with theirs (IV,5,4). Thus the Old Covenant, while preparing the divine nature to be united with that of Man, also prepares human nature for union with the divine (IV,14,2)" (*Gospel Message*, 169). The continuity between the Incarnation and the earlier stages of divine self-revelation is again evident, as the Old Testament is seen as a stage on the way to the Incarnation (cf. AH IV,9,1).

[67]Daniélou, *Gospel Message*, 167; Benoit, 225, 231; Johannes Quasten, *Patrology*, vol. 1: *The Beginnings of Patristic Literature*

a. Definition

Lexically, there are three senses in which "recapitulate" is used.[68] The classical Greek use of *anakephalaiōsis* was "the act of making a summary of the chapters of a work, a resumé of its principal ideas, a compendium."[69] In Ephesians 1:10, Paul uses the word to "refer to Christ as the one in whom all things find their unity."[70] By derivation from *kephalē*, it may mean "review" or "repetition," a sense that is captured in the Vulgate translation *instaurare*.[71] Irenaeus takes up all the above senses in his use of the term, which has, then, three basic elements: 1) restoration, in the sense of a bridge between creation and redemption; 2) summation; and 3) iteration, that is, Christ's going over the human process again, but being victorious where Adam failed.[72] Lawson summarizes many of the attempts that have been made to define "recapitulation," as Irenaeus uses it,[73] and reaches a helpful conclusion from his own study of Irenaeus, with the help of these other interpreters:

> The foundation of all would seem to be the conception of "going over the ground again," rather than that of "comprehension in unity," even though the latter springs so naturally from the derivation of the word. The fundamental fact in the work of Christ is that he went through all the experiences of Adam, but

---

(Westminster, Maryland: Newman Press, 1950), 295: "The heart of Irenaeus's Christology and indeed of his entire theology is his theory of recapitulation."

[68]Daniélou, *Gospel Message*, 172-73.

[69]Ibid., 172.

[70]Ibid., 173.

[71]Ibid.

[72]Turner, 63-64.

[73]Including Harnack, Wendt, Bonwetsch, Seeberg, Vernet, Loofs, Werner, Bousset and Beuzart. *Biblical Theology*, 141-42.

with the opposite result. The result of this process provides a secondary conception. The human race was given a new start. Last on the train of derived conceptions is that of collection under a single head, inasmuch as saved humanity is one in Christ.[74]

b. The consequences of recapitulation for salvation

From the standpoint of the focus of this study, the striking thing about Irenaeus's teaching concerning recapitulation is its universal scope. Christ recapitulated Adam in himself (Proof 32). As Adam had no father, so the Word was born of a virgin (AH III,21,10), thus "virginal disobedience" was destroyed by "virginal obedience" (Proof 33). As Adam committed sin through disobedience in regard to the tree, so Christ was obedient to God in being nailed to the tree, thereby "destroying the knowledge of evil, and bringing in and conferring the knowledge of good" (Proof 34).

Christ did more than simply recapitulate the first man. He recapitulated, in the shedding of his own blood, the shedding of the blood of all the righteous from Abel to Zechariah (AH V,14,1; cf. Mt 23:35ff; Lk 11:50). "He recapitulated the long history of humanity in himself and procured salvation for us in a concise way, so that what we lost in Adam, namely, to be according to the image and likeness of God, we recover in Christ Jesus" (AH III,18,1). "He passed through all the ages of life, restoring thereby all people to communion with God" (AH III,18,7; cf. II,22,4). He was what he appeared to be, "God, recapitulating in himself the old model (or form—*plasmationem*) of humankind, so that he might kill sin, and destroy death and make human beings alive" (AH III,18,7). He is the one who "has recapitulated in

---

[74]Ibid., 143.

himself all the nations dispersed from Adam onwards, and all the languages and generations of humankind, including Adam himself" (AH III,22,3). In his own person he saved, at the end, that which had perished in the beginning in Adam, presumably, the human race (AH V,14,1). Christ recapitulated all things, in heaven and earth, spiritual and physical (AH V,20,2, citing Eph 1:10; Proof 30, 34; cf. AH III,16,6).[75]

The doctrine of recapitulation, in later years, became a basis of salvific universalism, quite clearly in Origen, less so in Gregory of Nyssa. Irenaeus does not follow it to that conclusion. In AH I,10,1, he looks toward the return of Christ as the time when Christ's recapitulatory work will be manifested, when "all things" will be gathered together in unity (citing Eph 1:10) and every knee shall bow to him and confess him (citing Phil 2:10,11). However, it will not be a time of universal salvation, but one of just judgment upon apostate angels, and ungodly, unrighteous and wicked people, who will be assigned to eternal fire. It will also be a time when immortality is conferred upon the righteous, on those who have kept his commandments and persevered in love (AH I,10,1). It is frequently recognized, therefore, that although Irenaeus's doctrine of recapitulation might logically lead to universal salvation, for Irenaeus it does

---

[75]As José González-Faus has pointed out, in this latter passage two very important concepts of ancient theology were involved—the Pauline theme of headship and that of the second Adam. With regard to the first, Christ is presented as the head, not only of the "body of the Church," but, through the Church, of the "body of humanity." On this point, Irenaeus was preceded by Cyril of Alexandria (De Inc. Verbi 18,9,17). González-Faus thus sees in Irenaeus a certain continuity, as well as tension, between the two unions with Christ—that of humanity and that of the Christian (*Carne de Dios*, 175).

not conclude that way.[76] George Maloney sums it up as follows:

> Man's temporal life, by which Christ brings about the "new creation" determines whether he will possess the gift of incorruption. His deeds, informed by grace, decide his eternal destiny. No being is neglected by the eternal grace of Christ, by which he takes up all creatures and heals them. His work is one of renewing, of solidifying, of uniting.[77]

It is clear that Irenaeus was not implying that the Incarnation would automatically save the Gnostic heretics, but he is stressing the necessity of that incarnate work of recapitulation to the salvation of *anyone*. Jean Daniélou comments on AH III,16,6, where Irenaeus discusses the taking up of humankind into Christ and the summing up of all things in himself, that "it is the human race as a numerical whole which is substantially saved in him."[78] The emphasis here is on "objective" redemption, on the necessity and efficacy of Christ's redemptive recapitulatory work, and not on the subjective application of it to all individuals, regardless of their response to it.[79]

---

[76]See for example Adhémar d'Alès, "La doctrine de la récapitulation en saint Irénée," *RScRel* 6-7 (1916):199; Kim, 86.

[77]*The Cosmic Christ: From Paul to Teilhard* (New York: Sheed & Ward, 1968), 110.

[78]*Christ and Us* (New York: Sheed & Ward, 1961), 99.

[79]It is interesting to note the manner in which Irenaeus speaks of the anti-Christ as recapitulating in himself all the wickedness which had taken place during the history of humankind (AH V,29,2 [366-70]). There are two different heads of the different groups of humanity, with radically different destinies.

5. Proclamation in the subterranean regions

A significant aspect of the revelatory work of Christ during his incarnate existence is the account Irenaeus gives of the Lord's descent into the "regions under the earth," doubtless based on 1 Peter 3:19-20 (AH IV 27,2). There, the Lord declared the good news of his coming, namely, "the remission of sins for those who believe in him."

> And all those who had hoped in him believed in him, that is those who had announced beforehand his coming and had assisted in his economies, the righteous, the prophets and the patriarchs, to whom he remitted sins as he had done for us, which [sins] we ought not to impute to them, so that we might not show contempt for the grace of God. For as they did not impute our inconsistencies to us, which we committed before Christ was manifested to us, so also we should not blame those who sinned before the coming of Christ. For "all people have come short of God's glory," and they who direct their eyes towards his light are justified not by themselves but by the coming of the Lord (AH IV,27,2).[80]

In the context, Irenaeus is warning his readers against sin by reminding them of God's judgment upon people of the Old Testament who sinned against him, such as David and Solomon. If God punished those people "for whom the Son of God had not yet suffered," how

---

[80]"Crediderunt autem in eum omnes qui sperabant in eum, hoc est qui adventum ejus praenuntiaverunt et dispositionibus ejus servierunt justi et prophetae et patriarchae, quibus similiter ut nobis remisit peccata. . . . Quaemadmodum enim illi non imputant nobis incontinentias nostras quas operati sumus priusquam Christus in nobis manifestaretur, sic et nos non est justum imputare ante adventum Christi his qui peccaverunt. 'Omnes' enim homines 'egent gloria Dei', justificantur autem, non a semetipsis sed a Domini adventu, qui intendunt lumen ejus."

much more will he punish those who despise the Lord's coming and do not restrain their lustful desires (AH IV,27,2). The death of Christ became the means of the remission of sins to those people of the Old Testament, but no further provision will be made for those who now sin. When the Son of God comes next, it will be in the glory of the Father, to judge people according to their stewardship of God's gifts and according to the privileges which they have been given by God.

Clearly, the way of salvation for all, before and after the coming of Christ, was by his death. On the part of those who lived before Christ, Irenaeus required a specific anticipation of Christ. The Lord remitted the sins of those who believed in him, who had announced his coming beforehand. These were righteous people, like the prophets and the patriarchs who had directed their eyes toward the light of Christ.[81] This would no doubt include not only the patriarchs and prophets, but also a person like Noah with whom the Word spoke, and whose righteousness was the ground of his salvation from the judgment which the Word sent upon disobedient humankind. What remains somewhat unclear is what kind of Christological anticipation could be expected of all those to whom the Son revealed the Father, by his "presence with his own handiwork," that is, his providence (AH IV,6,7).

---

[81]Louis Capéran notes that Clement was less restrained in his interpretation of the Petrine passage. He viewed it as an invitation to salvation to all souls of good desire, without distinction, which removed from all the excuse that they had not heard. *Le problème du salut des infidèles; Essai historique* (Toulouse: Grand Séminaire, 1934), 64-66.

E. Revelation in the Millennium and in Eternity

1. Eternity

As we have seen earlier, the goal of God's self-revelation is that people should ultimately see the Father and live. The triune God is moving people toward that end, first showing God prophetically through the Spirit, and then adoptively through the Son and, finally, in a paternal fashion in the kingdom of heaven. The Spirit prepares people in the Son, and the Son leads them to the Father, who gives incorruption to those who see him (AH IV,20,5). Even in the next world, however, our love of God will continue to grow as we contemplate him (AH IV,12,2). There, we shall continue to make progress in our knowledge of the same Father, Son and Holy Spirit, seeing God face to face, and no longer as through a glass (AH IV,9,2). We shall "receive the Kingdom for ever and progress in it" (AH IV,28,2). It should not surprise us, therefore, if we do not understand everything concerning God's revelation in creation and in the Scriptures, because even in the world to come there will always be things for us to learn, and God will forever teach us (AH II,28,3).[82] Therefore, we can look forward to remaining with God in heaven and earth forever, and conversing with God in a manner that is always new (AH V,36,1).[83] Although we shall enter into a new phase in our

---

[82]Daniélou views this as a protection of the transcendence of God, and of the need of humanity to have always a goal toward which to advance. Because humans are creatures of becoming, and only God is Being, "progress is a constituent part of the nature of Man" (*Gospel Message*, 360; cf. AH IV,11,2).

[83]"Semper nove confabulans Deo," which Rousseau translates: "conversant avec Dieu d'une manière toujours nouvelle" (455).

knowledge of God, and a more direct vision of the Father, it would seem clear that the Word will continue to play his unique role as mediator, as he has done from the beginning. Irenaeus insists on the continuing incarnation of the Word, who shall return "in the same flesh in which he suffered" to reveal the glory of the Father (AH III,16,8).[84]

In regard to the eternal reward which is immortality, or the knowledge of God, Irenaeus draws some significant conclusions from the parable of the workmen in the vineyard, in Matthew 20:1-16 (AH IV,36,7). In the context, he is stressing the unity of the economy of salvation under the disposition of the one God. He points out that the same God called some "in the beginning of the formation of the world," and others at later times, including some at the end of time. However, there is only one vineyard because there is only one righteousness, and the Spirit of God is the one administrator who arranges all things. The reward is the same for all the workers in the vineyard, regardless of when they were called. Each of the workers in the parable received a penny with the royal image superscribed on it, and so each one who is called by God receives the knowledge of the Son of God, which is incorruptibility. The Incarnation, with its superior manifestation, is a giving of the reward first to those who were called at the end, but all will ultimately receive the same reward.

---

[84]Cf. AH IV,20,2, where Irenaeus emphasizes the unique position, in heaven, earth, and under the earth, of the "Lamb who was slain," to open the book of the Father and to see the Father. It is through his flesh that the paternal light comes to us and we see our King. Cf. Ochagavía: "The Word will continue forever his revelatory activity on behalf of men because in heaven there will be a constant growth in the vision of the Father. The Father will unceasingly unveil to his Son new aspects of his inexhaustible treasures, and our Revealer Jesus Christ will transmit them to his brothers" (114).

In a somewhat different vein, however, are the comments of Irenaeus on the three categories of fruitfulness, which Jesus describes in the parable of the soils (AH V,36,1-2, commenting on Mt 13:23). Jesus had predicted that when the seed of God's Word fell on fertile soil, some of it would produce a hundredfold, some sixtyfold and some only thirty. From this, Irenaeus predicts that there will be different degrees of blessedness for the just, according to their respective merits. The most worthy proceed directly to "heaven," the second group to "paradise" and the least worthy will "inhabit the city" (AH V,36,2). Noting this distinction of destinies, Brian Daley observes, however, that "Irenaeus seems to imply the possibility of growth and advancement toward closer union with God even after the judgment, until at last all distinctions disappear" (citing AH V,36,2 and II,28,3, where Irenaeus speaks of our eternal capacity to learn the things taught by God).[85] This reading of Jesus' distinction of levels of fruitfulness as levels of reward, through which the righteous will advance as they grow in their knowledge of God, raises an intriguing possibility in the context of this study. One might speculate that the difference between the soil producing thirtyfold and that producing sixtyfold could correspond to the differences that exist between those who have a clear revelation of the Son, through Scripture, and those who know him only through his presence in providence. A difficulty with this proposal is that it does not completely correspond to the features of the parable. On this hypothesis, the difference lies in the quantity or "quality" of the seed which is sown (gradations of revelation), whereas the parable assigns the difference to the varying fertility of

---

[85]Brian E. Daley, S.J. *The Hope of the Early Church. A Handbook of Patristic Eschatology* (Cambridge: University Press, 1991), 31.

the soil. The concept is still, perhaps, not without some prospect of positive development.

2. The millennium

Perhaps more significant to the concern of this study, however, is the place of the millennium in Irenaeus's scheme of progressive divine self-revelation. Houssiau draws our attention to the fact that Irenaeus's doctrine of the earthly reign of Christ plays a very important role in his scheme of salvation. It responds to two questions of his time: the salvation of the ancient righteous, and the salvation of the flesh.[86] Marcion had pushed his critique of the Old Testament so far that it excluded the salvation of the ancient righteous, avoided a judicial coming of Christ, and suppressed all promise of an earthly kingdom of Christ. In the Ptolemaean scheme, the psychics, including the ancient righteous (who were subjects of the Demiurge), could not attain to the Pleroma, but only to an intermediary order ruled by the Demiurge.[87] For Irenaeus, however, the righteous of both testaments will reign on earth with Christ before they enter the kingdom of heaven. In this way, they will prepare themselves, through the contemplation of the Son, for the immediate vision of the Father in heaven.[88]

Christ did not come only for those who believed in him during his earthly existence, but "for all people without exception, who from the beginning, according to their capacity, in their generation both feared and loved God, and practised justice and piety toward their neighbor, and desired to see Christ and to hear his voice"

---

[86]*La christologie*, 130.
[87]Ibid., 129; cf. AH I,7,1; I,8,3.
[88]Houssiau, 129.

(AH IV,22,2).[89] These people will be roused from their "sleep" first by Christ, when he returns, and shall be raised and given a place in his kingdom (AH IV,22,2). Just as the righteous of the Old Testament prefigured the Church, so now the Church prefigures the earthly reign of Christ, in which they will receive the reward for their labors (AH IV,22,2). Thus, the righteous of the Old Testament will have the opportunity also to see Christ. The earthly reign of Christ is the "beginning of incorruptibility" (AH V,32,1)[90] and the means by which "those who shall be judged worthy shall be accustomed little by little to comprehend God" (AH V,32,1).[91] They shall see God in the renewed world, receiving the reward for their suffering in the creation in which they suffered, and reigning in the creation in which they suffered, and reigning in the creation in which they experienced servitude. Abraham will then receive the land which was promised to him (AH V,32,2; cf. V,34,1-35,1).

Few, if any, proponents of "anonymous Christianity" will be enamored of Irenaeus's millennialism. However, within Irenaeus's own scheme of divine, salvific self-revelation, this is a doctrine of considerable importance in any analysis of the salvation of "non-Christians." At the end of Chapter 4, a question was raised with regard to the progress of divine self-revelation which Irenaeus portrays: How would the pagan who did not have the advantage of the threefold positive tradition progress toward vision of God? Can one move from knowledge of God through his providence to vision of the Father,

---

[89]See Latin text above, n. 15.

[90]"Principium incorruptelae" or as Rousseau suggests, the "prelude" of incorruptibility (397), translating, he believes, *prooimion* (SC 152, 337).

[91]"Qui digni fuerint paulatim assuescunt capere Deum."

without going through the stage of knowledge of the incarnate Word?

The answer to the difficulty posed there may be found here, in the doctrine of Christ's earthly reign. The righteous of the Old Testament will become accustomed gradually to the knowledge of God, through that time spent in the presence of the incarnate Word. One could postulate that, in the same manner, a pagan who responded properly to the revelation in the providence of the Father through the Word would, likewise, be raised at the return of Christ and would come to know the Father through the incarnate Christ and would be prepared, thereby, for the vision of the Father. Within the scheme of Irenaeus, such a "proper response" to providence would, of course, require a special illuminating work of the Word, and it is still unclear whether that possibility was envisioned by Irenaeus or not. In any case, it is clear that this doctrine of an earthly reign of Christ, following his second coming and prior to the eternal state, is a *very* important step in the progress of humans toward the vision of the Father. It has an important place in any attempt to find in Irenaeus an indication that those who remain without knowledge of Jesus Christ in this life may nonetheless eventually achieve eternal life (in Irenaeus's scheme, immortality and incorruptibility) with the Father.

F. Concluding Observations Concerning the Son and the Unevangelized

One thing, at least, has been firmly established in this chapter. Irenaeus firmly believed that there is no knowledge of God apart from the Word. He is the unique and indispensable mediator of all knowledge of the Father. However, his revealing operations are varied. From the very beginning, when he was the Father's agent in creation, he has been revealing the Creator, by means of his creation and of his providence. That revelation of the Father through creation and providence (the "presence" of the Word with man), though less valuable than that which is made through the incarnation of the Word, is nevertheless *life-giving, if believed.*

One interesting manner in which Irenaeus describes the revelatory significance of the Word's activity in creation is the symbolism of the cosmic cross. The invisible crucifixion of the Word in the cosmos is, as Orbe states, "oriented decidedly to the salvation of the dispersed elements."[92] Closely related to the symbol of the cosmic cross is the concept of recapitulation, which moves the economy on the incarnate stage of the Word's revelatory activity. Again the theme of reconciliation is dominant, and again the language is inclusive, to the point of being universalistic. However, Irenaeus draws back from the universalistic conclusion to which his concept tends, restrained possibly by his strong sense of the tradition of the Church, but particularly by the biblical witness to the twofold destiny of humankind and the division between those who believe and those who do not. Yet, the strong testimony to the objective accomplishment of a redemption which is universal in scope is clear, both in the image of the cosmic cross and in the recapitulation of all things in Christ. This universal thrust is further maintained in passages regarding the Incarnation, some of which are so strong that, taken alone, they might lead to a concept of "salvation by Incarnation."

Strange as the doctrine of the millennium is to many modern theologians, it plays a very important role in the preparation of people for the vision of God which is eternal life, within the scheme of Irenaeus. No hope

---

[92]*Los primeros herejes,* 228.

could be found, within Irenaeus's framework of divine self-revelation, for the "anonymous Christian" (that is, a person with "implicit faith" but without conscious knowledge of Christ), apart from the intermediate reign of Christ. It is then that the "anonymous Christian" would have the opportunity to know the Father through the incarnate Word and to be gradually prepared for the more direct vision of the Father.

Rahner has raised the question whether there may not be people, after the coming of Christ, who remain, as it were, in the pre-incarnate age. For them, the Incarnation has not yet taken place. They encounter the Word through creation and providence but, without the Scriptures or the proclamation of the Word in the Gospel, they do not know the incarnate Word. This is a significant question, and it gives great importance to an understanding of the condition of those who lived (chronologically, and not missiologically) before the coming of Christ. It is precisely at this point, however, that Irenaeus poses a difficulty to the theology of "anonymous Christianity." Because of the Marcionite devaluation of the Old Testament, Irenaeus is very conscious of the importance of clarifying the state of the salvation of the righteous ones of the Old Testament. He makes it clear that they too are redeemed by the obedience and death of the incarnate Word. They are included in his recapitulatory work, and they specifically had the opportunity of learning of Christ's advent, through his descent into the lower region to preach to them. Furthermore, they shall be raised first at Christ's return and will have the opportunity to become accustomed to the knowledge of God through the preparatory period of Christ's earthly reign, prior to the eternal state. Those who were called early will eventually receive the same reward as those who were called later in the economy of salvation.

If one were to grant a parallel between the Old Testament righteous and the "anonymous Christian," all of this would appear very positive. When one recalls that natural revelation provided a capacity for some sort of fear and love of God, and for the practice of justice toward one's neighbor, there is further cause for optimism. The critical problem is with regard to the anticipation of Christ that Irenaeus requires of those pre-incarnate righteous. Those "who from the beginning, according to their capacity, in their generation, both feared and loved God, and practised justice and piety toward their neighbor" (AH IV,22,2) are also described as having "desired to see Christ and to hear his voice" (AH IV,22,2). Those to whom Christ preached in the lower regions were "those who had hoped in him" and "who had announced beforehand his coming" (AH IV,27,2). Likewise, those who will be raised first at Christ's return and accustomed to the knowledge of God during the millennium are the ones who had "desired to see Christ and to hear his voice" (AH IV,22,2). In short, any attempt to find in Irenaeus a theology of "anonymous Christianity" will have to explain how the pagan who qualifies as an "anonymous Christian" can be said to anticipate Christ, to desire to see and hear him, and to hope in him. It would seem that, for Irenaeus, precisely their "anonymity," that is, their lack of conscious knowledge of Christ (which in this age could not be anticipatory, except in the sense proposed by Rahner), would eliminate them from the class of the righteous "before Christ" for whom Christ's life and death were effective to salvation.

6. THE SPIRIT: REVEALER OF THE SON

André Benoit, in his analysis of the doctrinal formulae of Irenaeus, suggests that the true Irenaean symbol would be "only one God, only one Christ, only one economy." These are the three dominant ideas that he discerns in Irenaeus's writing.[1] He does not deny that Irenaeus has a doctrine of the Spirit, but he contends that it was not an axis in his thought, and that it was related to the doctrine of Christ and was an aspect of the divine economy.[2] There is consequently much less to be said about the role of the Holy Spirit in divine revelation than was said concerning the Father or the Son, but Irenaeus has said enough to warrant this separate attention to the Spirit's role.[3]

---

[1]André Benoit, *Saint Irénée; introduction à l'étude de sa théologie*, Etudes d'histoire et de philosophie religieuses, no. 52 (Paris: Presses Universitaires de France, 1960), 224.

[2]Ibid., 224, n. 2. This leads Lindsay Dewar to the comment that Irenaeus's polemical work is "rather disappointing" from the point of view of the doctrine of the Holy Spirit (*The Holy Spirit and Modern Thought: An Inquiry into the Historical, Theological, and Psychological Aspects of the Christian Doctrine of the Holy Spirit* [London: A. R. Mowbray & Co., 1959], 100).

[3]Henry Barclay Swete points to Irenaeus as the first to give the doctrine of the Spirit a "place in an orderly scheme of Christian teaching." *The Holy Spirit in the Ancient Church: A Study of Christian Teaching in the Age of the Fathers* (London: Macmillan & Co., 1912), 86.

A. The Spirit in Creation and Providence

It has already been demonstrated that creation and providence play a significant revelatory role in the scheme of Irenaeus and it is, therefore, worthwhile to examine his concept of the Spirit's involvement. One notes first of all that the Spirit, like the Son, co-existed eternally with the Father, in proof of which Irenaeus cites Solomon's statements regarding Wisdom, whom Irenaeus identifies as the Spirit (AH IV,20,3, citing Prov 3:19-20).[4] The Spirit was present with the Father before creation and was instrumental in the Father's creation of earth and heaven (AH IV,20,3; IV,20,1; Proof 5). To describe this instrumentality of the Son and the Holy Spirit in the creative work of God, Irenaeus resorts to the image of the "hands of the Father" (*manus Patris* [AH IV, Pref. 4; IV,20,1; V,6,1; V,5,1; Proof 11]). Both the Son and the Spirit belong to the essential life of God. Although they are used as his ministers, they are not external instruments but are God himself at work.[5] This was important, in view of the Gnostic doctrine of emanation. Irenaeus distinguishes the modes of working of the three Persons—the Spirit operates (*operante*), the Son administers (*administrante*), and the Father approves (*comprobante*)—but it is difficult to ascertain the exact connotation of these different operations (AH IV,20,6).

The Holy Spirit was vitally involved in the creation of humankind in the image and likeness of God (AH IV, Pref. 4; V,6,1). Indeed, it was specifically through the Spirit that the likeness (*homoiōsis*) was given which

---

[4]As J. N. D. Kelly notes, Irenaeus follows Theophilus rather than Justin in this identification of the Spirit with Wisdom (*Early Christian Doctrines*, 2nd ed. [New York: Harper & Row, 1960], 106). Cf. AH IV,20,1; IV,7,4.

[5]Cf. Swete, 88.

was necessary to make humans perfect, capable of understanding God (AH V,6,1; cf. V,1,3; Proof 5).[6] There is a
certain ambiguity in Irenaeus's discussion of the "image"
and "likeness." Generally, Irenaeus distinguishes between
the two and indicates that the likeness was lost in the
fall, whereas the image was not.[7] The image is most
frequently described with an emphasis on the body and
is particularly oriented toward the incarnate Son. It is in
his image that humankind was created (AH V,6,1; V,16,2;
Proof 22).[8] It is the human spirit that bears the

---

[6]John Hick comments on V,6,1: "The 'imago' which resides in
man's bodily form apparently represents his nature as an intelligent
creature capable of fellowship with his Maker, whilst the 'likeness'
represents man's final perfecting by the Holy Spirit" (*Evil and the God
of Love* [London: Macmillan, 1966], 217).

[7]Cf. David Cairns, *The Image of God in Man* (London: Collins,
1973), 80. Cairns agrees with Ernest Klebba "that the confusion of the
debate about Irenaeus's views on image and likeness is due not only
to his careless use of the terms, but also to the fact that critics have
not noticed that the references are sometimes to the fallen Adam,
sometimes to his state of integrity, sometimes to mankind in the
various stages of its history from sin to redemption" (citing *Die
Anthropologie des Hl. Irenaeus* [Munster, 1894], 22).

[8]Cf. José Ignacio González-Faus, *Carne de Dios: significado
salvador de la Encarnación en la teología de san Ireneo* (Barcelona:
Herder, 1969), 65-66, 84-87. There is a difference of opinion among
scholars as to whether the image also includes human freedom and
rationality. As noted above (n. 6), Hick includes human intelligence in
the image. Cairns cites AH IV,4,3 to demonstrate that "at least a
dominant part of the image of God which cannot be lost by sin" is
human freedom and rationality (*The Image of God*, 81-83). He
recognizes this as a part of the human soul, but views the image as
"linked in its two aspects to the psycho-physical nature, body and
soul" (ibid., 84). A similar interpretation is made by J. N. D. Kelly
(171) and Emil Brunner (*Man in Revolt: A Christian Anthropology*
[London: Collins, 1939], 93, 503-5).

Antonio Orbe, on the other hand, contends that the image
includes only the body. He understands the soul to be a necessary
medium between spirit and flesh which is not part of either the image

"likeness," and it is in this aspect of human creation (and renewal) that the Spirit is especially active.

Mention was made in the previous chapter of the Hellenistic reference to God's presence with humankind as a description of divine providence. It was noticed that Irenaeus also used this language in speaking of the Son's providential activity as his presence with humankind. He also describes the Spirit of God as having been "from the beginning, in all the economies of God, present with humankind" (AH IV,33,1).[9] It is true that no reference is made to a revelatory activity of the Spirit in creation and providence. However, we have seen that Irenaeus taught a knowledge of God the Creator, apprehended by human reason through observation of creation and providence, and a knowledge of God mediated by the Son and the Spirit, the Word and Wisdom, the two hands of God; and given their reciprocal activity in revelation, which will be discussed later, it must be assumed that the Spirit's activity in creation and providence also has revelatory significance.

B. The Spirit and Old Testament Revelation

We have seen that the Word spoke through the prophets, but it is the Holy Spirit whose activity is most stressed by Irenaeus, when speaking of prophetic revelation in the Old Testament. The Spirit of God "signified (or pointed out) the future by the prophets" (AH IV,20,8),

---

or the likeness ("La definición del hombre en la teología del S. II°," *Greg* 48 [1967]:575). The soul is the organ by which the Spirit of God mediates the "likeness" (*Antropología de San Ireneo* [Madrid: Biblioteca de Autores Cristianos, 1969], 131).

[9]"Spiritum Dei, qui ab initio in universis dispositionibus Dei, adfuit hominibis (i.e. *sumparon tois anthrōpois*)." Cf. AH V,33,15.

and also revealed things present and past (AH IV,33,1; Proof 67). He "proclaimed, by the prophets, the economies, the coming, the birth of the Virgin, the passion, the resurrection from the dead, the ascension into heaven, in the flesh, of our beloved Lord Jesus Christ and his coming from heaven in the glory of the Father to recapitulate all things . . ." (AH I,10,1).[10]

Irenaeus thus describes the Old Testament as the stage in the progress of divine revelation in which God was seen "according to a prophetic mode by means of the Spirit" (AH IV,20,5; cf. V,1,2). He later suggests that some of those people in the Old Testament "saw the prophetic Spirit and his work in view of the outpouring of all kinds of gifts," for the Father was manifested through the working of the Holy Spirit, as he was through the ministry of the Son (AH IV,20,6). It was through the Holy Spirit that "the prophets prophesied and the patriarchs were taught about God and the just were led in the path of justice" (Proof 6).

It is not clear exactly what Irenaeus means when he says that "the Spirit of God, taking form and shape in the likeness of the person concerned, spoke in the prophets; sometimes he spoke on the part of Christ sometimes on that of the Father" (Proof 49). It is difficult to know whether "the person concerned" is the prophet through whom the Spirit spoke or another Person of the Trinity and, "in either case," as J. P. Smith says, "'taking form and shape . . .' is difficult to account for."[11] What is clear is that the Holy Spirit was speaking when the prophets spoke. Sometimes, he spoke through the prophet as though it were the Father who was speaking and,

---

[10]H. B. Swete notes that the faith which Irenaeus had received "laid chief stress on the Holy Spirit as the Spirit of prophecy, i.e. of Old Testament Christological prophecy" (86).

[11]Proof, 188, n. 235.

sometimes, as though it were the Son.[12] The important thing is that, when people prophesied, they did not do so in their own name. It was not they but the Spirit who spoke (Proof 49).

C. The Spirit and the Son

Ochagavía has found the Son and the Spirit to be so closely related in Irenaeus's thought that it is often difficult to distinguish the function of one from the other.[13] However, there is a difference usually apparent in their relationship to one another, within the self-revealing of the triune God. Irenaeus finds a general statement of the economic relationship of the Trinity to the creature in the apostle Paul's words in Ephesians 4:6:

> Hence too his apostle Paul well says: "one God, the Father, who is above all and with all and in us all;" for "above all" is the Father, but "with all" is the Word, since it is through him that everything was made by the Father, and "in us all" is the Spirit "who cries: Abba, Father" and has formed man to the likeness of God (Proof 5).

In general, the Spirit is seen to relate to the Son in much the same manner as the Son relates to the Father. The Word reveals the Father and the Spirit reveals the Word (Proof 7).[14] So close is the working of the Son and the Spirit, however, that Irenaeus declares:

> the Spirit manifests the Word, and therefore the prophets announced the Son of God, but the Word articulates the Spirit,

---

[12]Justin describes the same sort of thing, I Apol., 36-38.

[13]Juan Ochagavía, *Visibile Patris Filius; A Study of Irenaeus's Teaching on Revelation and Tradition*, Orientalia Christiana Analecta, no. 171 (Rome: Pont. Institutum Orientalium Studiorum, 1964), 61.

[14]Cf. Jules Lebreton, "La connaissance de Dieu chez Saint Irénée," *RechSR* 16 (1926):400.

and therefore it is himself who gives their message to the prophets, and takes up man and brings him to the Father (Proof 5).

Thus it is actually the Son who speaks through the prophets, although it is correct to say that the Spirit does so.

The Spirit leads people to the Word, and the Son "takes them and presents them to the Father" who confers incorruptibility upon them (Proof 7).[15] As Ochagavía recognizes, the Spirit's action is not consecutive with faith. Although simultaneous, it is in a different order; "not in the order of revealing new contents of faith, but in the order of empowering man to accept that faith and thus come to the Son."[16]

> So without the Spirit there is no seeing the Word of God, and without the Son there is no approaching the Father; for the Son is knowledge of the Father, and knowledge of the Son is through the Holy Spirit. But the Son, according to the Father's good pleasure, administers the Spirit charismatically as the Father will, to those to whom he will (Proof 7).

Irenaeus taught that the Spirit descended upon the Son, empowering him for his ministry, and that the Son, after his ascension, sent the Spirit upon his disciples to empower them for the evangelization of the Gentiles and to effect reconciliation and communion between God and

---

[15]Cf. AH IV,20,5, where the Spirit prepares people for the Son, and the Son leads them to the Father and the Father gives eternal life to those who see him; and AH V,36,2, where the arrangement is that those who are saved "ascend through the Spirit to the Son, and through the Son to the Father." Cf. also V,18,2.

[16]Ochagavía, 134. Cf. 61-62: "While the Son is *the manifestation* of the Father, the Spirit *empowers* man to recognize the Son as *Patris* or the *Manifestatio Patris* or the *visibile Patris*, the Spirit confers the interior force that man needs to believe in the Son, follow his teachings and imitate him."

humankind (AH III,9,3; III,17,1; III,18,3; V,1,1; Proof 41).[17] The Spirit of God anointed Jesus for the preaching of the Gospel and then the Son poured the Spirit on the disciples for the same purpose (AH III,9,3; III,17,3). In the last days, the Spirit was "poured forth in a new manner upon humanity over all the earth renewing man to God" (Proof 6).

The pattern is clear. The Father initiates a self-manifestation according to his own good pleasure. The Son mediates this revelation to those whom the Father wills, and he does so by giving them the Spirit. The Spirit leads them back to the Word, who presents them to the Father, who gives them eternal life, and the circle is complete.

D. The Spirit and Scripture

Evidence has been cited that Irenaeus believed that it was the Holy Spirit who spoke through the prophets of the Old Testament. That work of the Spirit was not restricted to the speech of the prophets; it extended to their writings. Thus Irenaeus speaks of what the prophets *wrote* as being *said* by the Holy Spirit. He cites Psalm 110:1: "The Lord says to my Lord, 'Sit at my right hand . . . '" and says, concerning it, that "since the Father is truly Lord and the Son is truly Lord, it is right that the *Holy Spirit designated* them by the title 'Lord'"

---

[17]John Lawson suggests an apparent contradiction between two ways of working in divine revelation. These he defines as the ascent through the Spirit to the Son (cf. n. 15, above) and the ascent to the Spirit through the Son. Here he cites III,17,1; Proof 9,41 (*The Biblical Theology of Irenaeus* [London: Epworth Press, 1948], 127-28). However, it is difficult to see why these references to the descent of the Spirit upon the Son should be interpreted as teaching an ascent of humans to the Spirit through the Son. Lawson is attempting to resolve a difficulty of his own making.

(AH III,6,1, italics supplied). Again, Irenaeus writes: "And the Father is *called by the Spirit* 'Most High' and 'Almighty' and 'Lord of Hosts,'" describing thus the words of Scripture (Proof 8).[18] Specifically, Irenaeus refers to what the Old Testament Scriptures said as what the Holy Spirit now *says*: "the Spirit of Christ, who also spoke in the other prophets about him, now also, through David, says: 'I have slumbered and slept. . . .'" (Proof 73). He also describes New Testament Scriptures as a speaking of the Holy Spirit. The Spirit had testified through many people concerning the righteousness imputed to Abraham on account of faith and now, by Paul, "gives testimony" in that regard (AH IV,8,1).

E. The Spirit in the Church and in the Believer

Irenaeus emphasizes the importance of the sending of the Holy Spirit at Pentecost for the universalizing of the economy of salvation, which had centered primarily in the Jewish people prior to that time. The Spirit introduced the nations into life and opened up the New Testament for them. He united distant tribes and offered to the Father the first-fruits of all nations (AH III,17,2). This was the reason why the Lord promised to send the Spirit, to join people to God. Thus, he sent the Holy Spirit upon all the earth (AH III,17,2). To the Spirit

---

[18]Cf. also the citation of Psa. 1:1 as "the Holy Spirit says through David" (Proof 2); reference to Gen. 15:6, as cited in Rom. 4:3, as "saying through the Holy Spirit in the Scriptures," (Proof 24); Moses is "spoken about by the Spirit" in Num. 12:6 and Heb. 3:5 (AH III,6,5). It is important for the Christian to be nourished by the Scriptures and therefore the Holy Spirit *says*, in Gen. 2:16: "'You may freely eat from every tree in paradise,' that is to say, 'Eat all the Scriptures of the Lord.'" (AH V,20,2).

is therefore entrusted the work of renewing humanity in the image and likeness of God, which was revealed in the Incarnate Son (AH III,17,3). This is a gradual work, in which the Holy Spirit gradually accustoms people to know and to bear God (AH V,8,1).

An essential, life-giving relationship exists between the Spirit of God and the individual Christian.

> Where the Spirit of the Father is, there is a living person. . . . Therefore, since without the Spirit of God we cannot be saved, the Apostle exhorts us to preserve the Spirit of God through faith and a chaste life, lest, by not having participation in the Holy Spirit, we lose the kingdom of heaven, . . . (AH V,9,3).[19]

However, the Spirit is given to the Body of Christ, and through the Church to individuals, because "where the Church is, there also is the Spirit of God; and where the Spirit of God is, there is the Church and all grace" (AH III,24,1).[20]

The Holy Spirit, who is the earnest of incorruptibility, the confirmation of our faith and the ladder of

---

[19]"Quoniam igitur sine Spiritu Dei salvari non possimus, adhortatur Apostolus nos per fidem et castam conversationem conservare Spiritum Dei, ut non sine participatione sancti Spiritus facti amittamus regnum caelorum, . . ."

[20]"Ubi enim Ecclesia, ibi et Spiritus Dei; et ubi Spiritus Dei, illic Ecclesia et omnis gratia." (Cf. Swete, 92.) Dewar bemoans the fact that "by inverting the proposition 'Where the Church is there is the Spirit of God,' at one stroke of the pen he wipes out the doctrine of the Holy Spirit, the Life-giver" (101). Dewar concludes that "taken as a whole, Irenaeus's theology has little grasp if any, of the doctrine of the working of the Holy Spirit at two levels" (the natural and the supernatural) (ibid.). In view of our discussion above, of the Spirit's role in creation and providence, Dewar's judgment perhaps needs to be softened. However, it is true that the preponderance of Irenaeus's references to the Holy Spirit are to a supernatural and salvific operation and that this work is carried out within the bounds of the institutional Church.

ascent to God, is the communion with Christ which has been "deposited" in the Church, because it is in the Church that God has put the apostles, prophets and teachers and all the other means by which the Spirit works. Consequently, those who do not join the Church do not participate in the Holy Spirit (AH III,24,1).[21] The Spirit continually renews the tradition which God has entrusted to the Church for the enlivening of its members, and therefore renews also the Church which contains that precious deposit (*depositum juvenescens*) (AH III,24,1). Indeed, so valuable is the working of the Spirit in regard to the tradition of the faith that "many nations of barbarians" believe in Christ, without having had the benefit of the Scriptures, simply through the testimony of the Church. Such people are described by Irenaeus as "having salvation written in their hearts by the Spirit, without paper and ink" (AH III,4,2). In the context, this would not appear to be referring to an inner saving work of the Holy Spirit, but to the working of the Holy Spirit in the proclamation of faith by the Church. Those who hear the Gospel proclaimed and believe it have, as it were, had the Spirit write on their hearts directly rather than on paper with ink.

The Holy Spirit plays a vital role in the preparation of human beings for the sight of God (AH IV,20,5), and, as the prophets declared figuratively, those people who will eventually see God are those "who bear his Spirit" and always wait for his coming (AH IV,20,6). The error of the heretics lies in their formulation of opinions on matters beyond the limits of their understanding, but

---

[21]"Et in eo [i.e., Ecclesia] deposita est communicatio Christi, id est Spiritus sanctus, . . . 'In Ecclesia' enim, inquit, 'posuit Deus apostolos, prophetas, doctores', et universam reliquam operationem Spiritus, cuius non sunt participes omnes qui non concurrunt ad Ecclesiam, . . ."

when Christ causes the Spirit to live in people they are able, through the Spirit, to "see, hear and speak" (AH V,20,2). Knowledge of the truth requires a working of the Spirit in the hearer but it is also acquired through the Church in which the Holy Spirit works.

> Therefore the message of the Church is true and firm, since it is in her that one and the same way of salvation is manifested in the whole world. For the light of God is entrusted to her, and this is why the "wisdom" of God, by which she saves people, "is celebrated in its going out. It acts confidently in the streets, is proclaimed on the tops of the walls, and speaks with assurance in the gates of the city." For the Church proclaims the truth everywhere; she is the seven branched candlestick which bears the light of Christ (AH V,20,1).[22]

No doubt, because of Irenaeus's identification of Wisdom with the Spirit, Rousseau capitalizes Wisdom (*la Sagesse*) in his translation, in this citation from Proverbs 1:21.[23] Read in that way, the close conjunction of the Spirit and the Church in the proclamation of truth is again underlined.

F. Concluding Observations Concerning the Spirit and the Unevangelized

Although no attempt has been made to develop at any length the role of the Spirit of God in the salvation of humankind, sufficient evidence has been cited to show that, for Irenaeus, the work of the Spirit is indispensable to salvation. No one can obtain salvation without vision

---

[22]"Ecclesiae igitur praedicatio vera et firma, apud quam una et eadem salutis via in universo mundo ostenditur. Huic enim creditum est lumen Dei, et propter hoc 'sapientia' Dei, per quam salvat homines, 'in exitu canitur'. . . Ubique enim Ecclesia praedicat veritatem: et haec est *heptamuxos* lucerna, Christi bajulans lumen."

[23]SC 293, 257; cf. also Dewar, 101.

of the Father; no one can know the Father unless the Son reveal him; and no one knows the Son except through the Holy Spirit, whom the Son administers according to the good-pleasure of the Father.

Given the mysterious invisibility of the working of the Holy Spirit (cf. Jn 3:8), this would provide no limitation upon the possibility of the Spirit's working in the life of the non-Christian. However, Irenaeus goes on to tie the Spirit expressly to the Church; to the Church as an institution which is visible in its catholicity because of the unity of its profession of faith and the succession of its bishops from the apostles. Not to have the Spirit is to be without life. But, not to be a part of the Church, to which the Spirit gave apostles, prophets and teachers, and in and through which the Spirit does all his work, is not to have a part in the Spirit. It is possible that one could believe without the Scriptures, as many did in Irenaeus's day. However, they were able to do so because the Spirit spoke to them through the oral proclamation of the Church. Henri de Lubac believes that the Christian cannot deny that there may be "anonymous Christians in divers milieux where the light of the Gospel has penetrated in one way or another, perhaps even by some secret operation of the Spirit of Christ."[24] Irenaeus does not speak of secret operations of the Spirit apart, perhaps, from the universal revelation in creation and providence. However, the previous chapter took note of Irenaeus's perception of the life-giving quality of that revelation. The Spirit certainly plays an important role in the believing response to this revelation.

The next chapter will deal at greater length with the role of the Church. Then we will be able to see more definitely what, if any, possibility Irenaeus may have

---

[24]*The Church: Paradox and Mystery*, trans. James R. Dunne (Staten Island, New York: Alba House, 1969), 87.

held out of salvation apart from association with the institutional Church.

7. THE CHURCH: RECIPIENT, PRESERVER, AND PROCLAIMER OF DIVINE REVELATION

A. The Challenge of the Gnostic Claim to a "Living Voice"

In the final chapter of Book II of *Adversus Haereses*, and in the Preface of Book III, Irenaeus declares his intention to prove from "the Scriptures of the Lord" (AH II,35,4) the arguments he has brought against the errors of his opponents (AH II,35,4; III, Pref.). As he begins his third book, however, his attention is immediately drawn to the problem of oral tradition. It disturbed Irenaeus that, while his Scriptural proofs may have been of help to the orthodox who were troubled by Gnostic teaching, they would be of little value to the Gnostics, who did not place the same value on Scripture. Irenaeus was appealing to the truth which the apostles had first proclaimed publicly and then handed down in the Scriptures to be the foundation and pillar of the faith of the Church (AH III,1,1).[1] However, when the heretics were confronted with Scripture, they denounced the Scriptures as incorrect and without authority. They claimed that the language of Scripture was equivocal and that it was impossible to find truth in the Scriptures, if one were

---

[1]Roberts notes that in I Tim 3:15 "these terms are used in reference to the Church" (ANF, 414, n. 2); cf. also AH III,11,8, where the Gospel is the column and foundation of the Church.

ignorant of the tradition (AH III,2,1). The Gnostics contended that the truth was not handed on by means of scriptures, but rather by means of a "living voice" (*vivam vocem*, AH III,2,1). They themselves were, therefore, wiser not only than the elders of the Church but also than the apostles. For the apostles, they contended, mixed up the teachings of the law with the words of the Savior; and even the Lord spoke words coming sometimes from the Demiurge, sometimes from the intermediate place and sometimes from the Pleroma. Therefore, only the Gnostics had pure knowledge of the "secret or hidden mystery" (*absconditum scire mysterium* or *apokryphon mystērion*, AH III,2,2). Pheme Perkins has demonstrated that even the Gnostic writings made no claim to being textually authoritative. Truth was "not definitively embodied in any inspired text."[2]

> Gnostic interpretation is still the hermeneutic of an oral tradition. It does not provide the formalized interpretation of a text that would sponsor a systematized and rational account of Christian theology such as that proposed by Irenaeus or Origen.[3]

This challenge from the Gnostics is the context that underlies Irenaeus's doctrine of the Church as a faithful preserver of the faith handed down from the apostles through a succession of bishops, whose lineage can be traced back to the apostles. As Henry Chadwick indicates, it was also this claim to secret unwritten tradition that brought Irenaeus to the realization that Marcion was right in at least one thing, the necessity of a canon of authoritative writings of the New Testament.

---

[2]Pheme Perkins, *The Gnostic Dialogue: The Early Church and the Crisis of Gnosticism* (New York: Paulist Press, 1980), 202.

[3]Ibid.

Hitherto the dividing line between books accorded the status of being read in the Church lectionary and books that were of approved orthodoxy had not been decisively drawn. Irenaeus drew the line, and is the first writer whose New Testament virtually corresponds to the canon that became accepted as traditional.[4]

B. The Handing on of the Apostolic Faith to the Church

1. The Church and the apostolic tradition

In his contention with the Gnostics and their secret living tradition, Irenaeus found that it was inadequate to simply appeal to the writings of the apostles, which the Gnostics did not accept as authoritative. He therefore developed a concept of apostolic tradition which would serve as a response to the Gnostic position and which would show that the tradition they claimed to possess was not genuinely "apostolic."

First, Irenaeus had to defend the apostles, since some of the Gnostics contended that the apostles preached before they had "perfect knowledge" themselves. On the contrary, insisted Irenaeus, when the Holy Spirit descended upon the apostles he empowered them from above and "they were filled with a certitude concerning all things and had perfect knowledge" (AH III,1,1).[5] The

---

[4]Henry Chadwick, *The Early Church* (Baltimore, Maryland: Penguin Books, 1967), 81. Chadwick also notes, however, that "Irenaeus never quotes from III Jn., Jas., or II Pet." (ibid., n. 1).

[5]"Et induti sunt superveniente Spiritu sancto virtutem ex alto, de omnibus adimpleti sunt et habuerunt perfectam agnitionem." The phrase "de omnibus adimpleti" is a bit obscure. Roberts translates it: "were filled from all [His gifts]" (ANF, 414). In the context, Rousseau's translation seems much better: "ils furent remplis de certitude au sujet de tout" (23). He suggests a Greek retroversion as *peri pantōn plēphorēthentes*, and he develops at some length a parallel between

Church, in turn, received "the only true and life-giving faith" and distributed it to her children (AH III, Pref.).[6] Although the Church is scattered throughout the world, it carefully preserves the faith which it has received from the apostles and their disciples, and it "proclaims, teaches and hands it on" (*tradit* or *paradidōsin*) as though speaking with only one voice (AH I,10,2). Although the languages spoken by members of the Church around the world differ greatly, the meaning or content (AH I,10,2)[7] of the tradition to which they hold is "one and the same." This is true of churches in Germany, Spain, and Gaul, in the East, in Egypt, in Libya and in Palestine (literally: *in medio mundi*) (AH I,10,2; cf. III,12,7; III,24,1; IV,33,8; V, Pref.; V,20,1).

To the secrecy of the Gnostic traditions, and to the great diversity of teachings among the Gnostics, Irenaeus therefore opposes the public proclamation of the Church all over the world, and the unity and consistency that characterizes its preaching and teaching. The role of the Church is to receive the Gospel handed on to it by the apostles, and to faithfully pass it on to "her sons," to those who will heed her message. Generally, Irenaeus uses the term *tradere* (*paradidonai*) of the apostles,[8]

---

this text and I Clem. 42,3 (SC 211, 213-17, n. 1).

[6]"Sola vera et vivifica fide, quam ab apostolis Ecclesia percepit et distribuit filius suis."

[7]The Latin here is *virtus*, translating *dynamis*. Rousseau notes that, when attached to things, *dynamis* has a variety of senses, such as the "value" of money, or the "meaning" of a word. In this context he suggests *contenu* as a translation, paralleling V,16,3, where Irenaeus speaks of *tēn dynamin tēs dekalogou, le contenu du décalogue*. Roberts translates it "import" (ANF, 331).

[8]Jean Daniélou counts 15 out of 21 times in Book III. *A History of Early Christian Doctrine Before the Council of Nicaea*, vol. 2: *Gospel Message and Hellenistic Culture*, trans. and ed. John Austin Baker (New York: Westminster Press, 1973), 145, citing AH I,27,2; III,14,2; and IV,37,7.

whereas with regard to the *paradosis* "it is never the
Apostles, but only the Church which does the receiving."[9]
Tradition thus comes from the apostles and is received by
the Church, which preserves it (like a "precious deposit
in an excellent vessel" [AH III,24,1; cf. III,2,2], or like
money deposited in a bank [AH III,4,1]), and passes it on
(AH V, Pref; I,10,2).[10] In this passing on of the apostolic
tradition,   which   the   Church   does   through   its
evangelization (the preaching of the good news concerning the one God, Father of all, and the one Word who is
Savior and Lord), there is a living tradition which is in
principle independent of written documents. As Kelly
remarks, it was Irenaeus's contest with the Gnostics
"which led him to apply the word 'tradition' in a novel
and restricted sense, specifically to the Church's oral
teaching as distinct from that contained in Scripture."[11]
He uses the term sixteen times in this way in AH III,2-
5.[12] To the "living voice" of the Gnostics, Irenaeus
opposed the tradition which was alive in the Church's
proclamation of that which had been received from the
apostles. For those who had no access to the Scriptures,
it was sufficient for faith that they hear the Gospel
proclaimed by the Church, in other words, an oral

----

[9]Daniélou, 145, citing AH II,9,1; III,2,2; III,3,2; III,3,3; III,5,1.

[10]Daniélou seems somewhat hesitant to admit this role of the
Church as transmitter of tradition. Although he grants that *tradere*
is not exclusively used of the apostles, when he sums up he avoids
ascribing to the Church a role of transmitter; e.g. "The tradition is
apostolic as regards its source, ecclesiastical as regards its destination;
it is a tradition *ab apostolis ad ecclesiam*" (146); and "Christ teaches,
the apostles transmit, the Church preserves" (ibid.). This formula
misses the dynamic role of the Church with regard to tradition, which
Irenaeus describes as "*praedicat* et *docet* et *tradit* quasi unum
possidens os" (AH I,10,2, italics supplied).

[11]J. N. D. Kelly, *Early Christian Doctrines*, 2nd ed. (New York:
Harper and Row, 1960), 37.

[12]Ibid.

handing on of the tradition (AH III,4,2). By the same token, if the apostles had not left writings to the churches, they would have had to rely on the account of the apostolic faith which was given by those to whom the apostles entrusted the churches (AH III,4,1).

2. The reliable transmission of the apostolic tradition

From the view obtained thus far, it might appear that Irenaeus and the Gnostics were headed for a great "shouting match." The Gnostics claimed a "living voice" which gave them a unique access to the truth, and Irenaeus counterclaimed a living tradition which went back to the "perfect knowledge" of the apostles. Having moved away from the battlefield of written tradition handed down by the apostles, though needing interpretation, who is to say which "living voice" is an accurate representation of the truth? To bolster Irenaeus's claim, he appeals to the line of presbyterial succession from the apostles.

The tradition which originates from the apostles (*ab apostolis*) is preserved by means of the succession of the elders in the Church (*per successiones presbyterorum in Ecclesiis custoditur,* AH III,2,2). The theory is that, if the apostles had in fact known of some "hidden mysteries" which they wished to impart to an elite group (as the Gnostics averred), they would have chosen the ones into whose care they entrusted the churches as the recipients of those secrets (AH III,3,1). The apostles had, in fact, put into the hands of the Church everything which pertained to the truth, as a rich person would deposit money in the bank. One does not need to go outside of the Church and its teaching, in order to discover the secret truths from the apostles (AH III,4,1). If there is a dispute concerning some important matter, the

logical recourse is the Church, whose relationship to the
apostles can be demonstrated (AH III,4,1). Specifically,
one should have recourse to the elders of the Church
because they have received "the sure gift of truth according to the good pleasure of the Father" (AH IV,26,2; cf.
IV,26,4).[13] If there is a question concerning the

---

[13]The meaning of this *charisma veritatis certum* is disputed. Yves
M.-J. Congar has noted three different interpretations of the phrase
(*Je crois en l'Esprit Saint* [Paris: Cerf, 1979], 2:62, n. 22).

1) Some have taken the phrase to refer to a grace of infallibility
or orthodoxy, that is, a power of teaching infallibly, which was
received in the ordination with the succession. (Jerome Quinn is one
who has understood the phrase in this way. He takes the term *veritas*
as, "for all practical purposes, equivalent to revelation or the faith as
a deposit and trust that can be transmitted or abandoned." The
presbyter-bishops have the power from God to do the former; the
heretics have done the latter. "In the Irenaean phrase," Quinn
proposes, "the genitive *veritatis* specifies the object of the *charisma*."
Presbyteral ordination has given the prophetic task of transmitting
and teaching the divine revelation. That presbyteral prophetic gift
then qualified as *certum*, "i.e. exact, secure, sure, in its communicating
that truth" ["'Charisma Veritatis Certum': Irenaeus, *Adversus
Haereses* 4,26,2," *TS* 39 (1978):524]). Congar notes, in favor of this
first interpretation, its harmony with a broad context, the relation
that the text seems to indicate between the consecration and a grace
which would be its effect. However, he sees three difficulties: a) there
are no parallels to so formal a statement; b) this would suppose a kind
of mechanical manner of acting, an automatism, that other passages
exclude (e.g., AH III,3,1; IV,26,5); and c) Irenaeus's theology of
tradition calls for an objective meaning for *veritas*.

2) For such reasons as these, many have understood *charisma
veritatis* to be the spiritual gift of truth, that is, the tradition in the
objective sense, e.g., D. van den Eynde; H. von Campenhausen.

3) A third approach studies the use of *charisma* in Irenaeus and
later writers and understands it as a reference to personal spiritual
gifts. The sense would then be that one ought to obey the presbyters
that God has called to the episcopacy because of the evidence of that
calling in the spiritual gifts which preceded and accompanied their
ordination. In particular, the reference is to their fidelity to the
tradition of the apostles, their gift for expounding truth (cf. AH

interpretation of Scripture, such as a difficulty in understanding the unity of the two Testaments, then one should seek the help of those who are the preservers of apostolic doctrine. People can, therefore, understand such a matter, if they read the Scripture with an attentiveness to the elders in the Church (AH IV,32,1).[14] They need, therefore, to avoid the doctrines of those who depart from the preaching of the Church and who question the knowledge of the elders. They should, rather, flee to the Church and there be nourished by the Scriptures of the Lord (AH V,20,2).

It was Irenaeus's contention, therefore, that the true tradition, coming down from the apostles in oral and

---

IV,26,5. E.g., E. Flesseman-Van Leer, *Tradition and Scripture in the Early Church* [Assen, 1954], 119-22; R. P. C. Hanson, *Tradition in the Early Church* [Philadelphia: Westminster, 1962], 159-61).

These three interpretations are perhaps not completely exclusive of one another, if the first one is not stated too strongly. Irenaeus may have intended to indicate something of all three ideas. His argument would then be that the presbyters should be obeyed because they, as successors to the apostles, have received the truth, i.e. the revelation or the tradition handed down from the apostles (2); they have demonstrated their reliability, through their personal fidelity to the tradition received (3); and they are enabled by God to faithfully hand on that truth to those who come after them (1). These leaders of the Church are themselves gifts to the Church, and one can expect to learn the truth where God has placed his gifts, particularly when the conduct and speech of those people is of a righteous character (AH IV,26,5). However, Irenaeus recognizes the possibility that these leaders could fall away, bringing great calamity upon the Church (III,3,1). Congar's warning against understanding this gift in too mechanical or automatic a fashion is therefore in order.

[14]"Post deinde et omnis sermo ei constabit, si et Scripturas diligenter legerit apud eos qui in Ecclesia sunt presbyteri, apud quos est Apostolica doctrina" (cf. AH IV,33,8). Roberts translates: "read the Scriptures in company with those who are presbyters" (ANF, 506). Rousseau: "qu'il lise aussi les Ecritures d'une manière attentive auprès des presbytères" (799).

written forms, was to be found in the care of the elders of the Church who faithfully preserve and proclaim it. Given the possibilities of error and schism within the Church, how then is one to know *which* elders of which churches are the genuine heirs of the apostolic tradition? Irenaeus's answer to that question is the line of succession, which could be traced back from the contemporary episcopate to the apostles. Since it would be too tiresome to the reader for Irenaeus to list the succession in all the churches, he cites only the case of "the very great and very ancient and universally known church which the two very glorious apostles Peter and Paul founded and established at Rome" (AH III,3,2).[15] That church was committed by the apostles into the care of the bishop Linus who passed it on to Anacletus and on down the line to Clement, Evaristus, Alexander, Sixtus, Telephorus, Hyginus, Pius, Anicetus, Soter, and finally Eleutherius, who held the episcopate at the time of Irenaeus's writing. By that succession, the tradition of the Church and the preaching of the truth came down to Irenaeus's contemporaries from the apostles (AH III,3).[16]

---

[15]"Ad hanc enim Ecclesiam propter potentiorem principalitatem necesse est omnem convenire Ecclesiam, hoc est eos qui sunt undique fideles, in qua semper ab his qui sunt undique conservata est ea quae est ab apostolis traditio."

[16]Irenaeus was not the first to compile a list of bishops "as a mark of the authenticity of the churches. Hegesippus was probably the pioneer" in that regard (Lawson, 90). Eusebius reports that he wrote: *genomenos de en Rhōmē diadochēn epoiēsamēn mechris Anikētou* (H. E. IV,22,3). Lawson suggests that while the meaning of the sentence is obscure and disputed, "the opinion of many scholars, including Lightfoot is that the only possible rendering is: 'Being in Rome, I composed a catalogue of Bishops down to Anicetus'" (90, n. 2).

It is worthwhile to note that Irenaeus is not propounding a *sacramental* episcopal succession in this passage. His purpose is simply to show the continuity of Christian tradition. This is particularly clear from the excursus regarding Clement and the letter

Exactly why Irenaeus chose the Church of Rome as the norm for the tradition is a matter of some controversy. In the discussion of the historical grounds for a primacy of the Roman church, this is obviously a passage of great interest. Two major interpretations have been proposed: 1) Irenaeus cited Rome because it had a place of pre-eminent authority among the Christian churches,[17] or 2) Rome was the ideal example because

---

dispatched from Rome to Corinth declaring the tradition received from the apostles, in order to renew the faith of the Church in Corinth which was threatened by dissension (cf. Ochagavía, 196-97). As Lawson says, Irenaeus stressed

the succession of Bishops and Presbyters as possessors of the gift of truth, as the givers of the Creed, and as organs of doctrinal authority. He had, however, little to say of them as channels of sacramental grace. The power of Baptismal Regeneration was indeed given by the Lord to the Apostles (III,17,1), who, having received the Holy Spirit, were granted the power to impart him in Baptism to those who believed (Dem. 41). . . . Irenaeus does not discuss whether these functions were passed on in the Succession (254).

[17]Anglican translator Alexander Roberts renders the passage in a way that testifies to such Roman primacy: "For it is a matter of necessity that every Church should agree with this Church, on account of its pre-eminent authority, that is, the faithful everywhere, inasmuch as the apostolical tradition has been preserved continuously by those [faithful men] who exist everywhere" (ANF, 415-16). He admits, in a footnote, that "it is impossible to say with certainty of what words in the Greek original 'potiorem principalitatem' may be the translation. We are far from sure that the rendering given above is correct, but we have been unable to think of anything better" (415, n. 3).

Rousseau has translated "propter potentiorem principalitatem" as "en raison de son origine plus excellente" (33), a rendering of *dia tēn hikanōteran archēn* (SC 210, 229). He suggests that what constituted the place of privilege of the Church at Rome, in particular, is therefore based on the great excellence of its origin. The exceptional dignity possessed by the Church of Rome is attributed to the fact that, in the person of Eleutherius, its twelfth bishop, the voice of the

it was a commercial and political center. As such, it was
a place to which Christians from all over the Empire
traveled, and it was therefore the church in which could
be found the widest consensus, or the best representation, of what was believed by Christians all over the
world.[18]

---

apostles Peter and Paul continues to be heard (SC 210, 230). With
regard to the point of reference of "ab his qui sunt undique," Rousseau
believes that the Latin is an incorrect translation of *tois pantachothen*
as a dative of interest rather than a dative of agent (SC 210, 223). He
therefore translates "en qui toujours, *au bénéfice* de ces gens de
partout" (33), that is: "in which always, *for the benefit* of these people
everywhere" [italics supplied].

We might translate Rousseau's paraphrase of the passage as
follows: "For with this Church (of Rome), by reason of its more
excellent origin (of which I have just spoken), it is necessary that the
whole Church should agree, that is to say the faithful everywhere
(with this Church, I say), in which always, for the benefit of these
people everywhere, has been (effectively) preserved the Tradition
which comes from the apostles" (SC 210, 234).

To those who may protest that Rousseau has minimized the
"authority or power" of the Church of Rome expressed by *potentiorem*
by considering it a reference only to "origin," he suggests that the
"idea of origin, as Irenaeus understood it, included already in fact that
of authority" (SC 210, 235). The normative value of the tradition of
the Church of Rome goes back, then, to the authority of the two great
apostles whose voice continues to be heard in a special way in the
Church at Rome.

[18]A. Cleveland Coxe protests Roberts' rendering and cites, as
"better and more literal," a translation "from a candid Roman
Catholic": "For to the Church, on account of more potent principality,
it is necessary that every Church (that is, those who are on every side
faithful) *resort*; in which Church ever, *by those who are on every side*,
has been preserved that tradition which is from the apostles" (ANF,
415, n. 3, citing Berington and Kirk). Coxe considers it obvious that
the faith was preserved at Rome "*by those who resort there from* all
quarters. She was a mirror of the Catholic world, owing her orthodoxy
to them; not the Sun dispensing her own light to others, but the glass
bringing their rays into focus" (ibid; see further comment, 460-61).

James Bethune-Baker takes a similar view to that of Coxe. Since

It is unnecessary to resolve the question here, as it is not essential to the present discussion.[19] It is sufficient to recognize that, whatever may have been the precise role of the Church at Rome relative to the Church in other localities, it provides an excellent example of the

---

Christians from all lands were continually coming and going, any departure from the tradition would be easily detected. "The tradition preserved at Rome might therefore be regarded as having the tacit sanction of all the other Churches, and by reference to it anyone in doubt might easily convince himself of the oneness of the apostolic tradition of the whole Church" (*An Introduction to the Early History of Christian Doctrine to the Time of the Council of Chalcedon* [London: Methuen & Co., 1903], 56-57).

More recently, Luise Abramowski has objected to Rousseau's translation ("Irenaeus, Adv. Haer. III,3,2: Ecclesia Romana and Omnis Ecclesia; and Ibid. 3,3: Anacletus of Rome," *JTS* 28 [April 1977]: 101-4). Abramowski contends that *in qua semper . . . unique* belongs to *omnem ecclesiam,* not to *hanc ecclesiam* as Rousseau believes. Therefore, "the meaning of Irenaeus is that every Church (i.e., all believers everywhere) in which the apostolic tradition is kept is necessarily in agreement with Rome by reason of the very high age of the Roman Church" (102). "Irenaeus begins the paragraph by saying that it would take too much room '*omnium* ecclesiorum enumerare successiones;' therefore he will give the succession of the very great, very old and very famous Roman Church" (103). The paragraph then ends with the quoted lines "which revert to '*omnis* ecclesia' in which the apostolic tradition is kept" (103). Abramowski disagrees with Rousseau's argument for a conditional rendering of the sentence. The meaning of Irenaeus, Abramowski suggests, is not that *if* the churches keep the apostolic tradition they are under moral obligation to agree with Rome, but rather: "there are *in fact* other apostolic churches, and by reason of this they *cannot have any* other kind of relationship with the apostolic church of Rome than agreement" (103).

[19]The reader wishing to pursue this question further may see also: Lawson, 275; James F. McCue, "The Roman Primacy in the Second Century and the Problem of the Development of Dogma," *TS* 25 (1964):161-96, especially the conclusions on pages 178-79; and journal articles listed by Rousseau (SC 210, 235-36). Rousseau's own recommendation, as the "best study of this passage," is D. van Den Eynde, *Les Normes de l'Enseignement Chrétien . . .*, 171-79.

faithful preservation of the apostolic tradition through a line of episcopal succession that goes back to the apostles themselves. Furthermore, the tradition preserved and proclaimed in the Church at Rome could be considered normative. This was clearly Irenaeus's belief, whether derived from a conviction of Rome's intrinsic hierarchical authority or from its position as a meeting point for Christians from all over the world, who testified to the same truth. Any so-called "living voice" which presumed to speak authoritatively for the apostles must, therefore, be compared with the tradition proclaimed in the Church at Rome. "Ad hanc enim Ecclesiam . . . necesse est omnem convenire Ecclesiam" (AH III,3,2).

In addition to the witness of the Church in Rome, Irenaeus appealed to the unanimous testimony of "all the churches in Asia" (AH III,3,4). In that case, a significant link with the apostles themselves was found in Polycarp, who was taught by the apostles themselves, spoke with many who had seen Christ, and was appointed Bishop of the Church in Smyrna by apostles in Asia. He was influential in turning back to the Church of God, in Rome, many people who had been led astray by the heretics Valentinus and Marcion.[20] He did this by preaching the truth which he received from the apostles and which the Church handed down. His Epistle to the Philippians remained a permanent record of the truth that he had preached (AH III,3,4). Additional witness to the truth which Irenaeus was defending was to be found in the Church in Ephesus. This too had excellent origin, having been founded by Paul, and having the presence of

---

[20]Paul Aubin finds Irenaeus to be the first to use this expression "convertir à l'Eglise de Dieu," which, in this context, involves a return to the Church by those who had left it; cf. AH I,6,3; I,13,5; *Le problème de la "conversion." Etude sur un terme commun à l'Hellénisme et au Christianisme des trois premiers siècles,* Théologique historique, no. 1 (Paris: Beauchesne et ses fils, 1962), 105.

John until the time of Trajan. Its teaching in Irenaeus's day was therefore a good representation of the truth that had come down from the apostles (AH III,3,4).

In contrast to the clear line of succession going back to the apostles, Irenaeus demonstrates a different line among the Gnostics, which goes back through Menander to Simon Magus (AH I,23,2; I,24,1; I,25,1; III,4,3). In the case of Valentinus and Marcion, Irenaeus stresses the novelty of their views. Prior to them, no one taught the things which they propounded (AH III,4,3). This novelty is condemning, because it is a departure from that truth which was perfectly revealed to the apostles and handed down by them.

3. The "rule of truth"

Much reference has been made to the tradition of the Church, which it had received from the apostles and then faithfully preserved and proclaimed. That tradition was not only the writings of the apostles but was the "faith" which they handed on, which the Church then announced, and from which the heretics were departing. Rousseau notes that Irenaeus frequently uses the terms *paradosis*, *kērygma* and *pistis* to refer to the same reality, namely the truth which Christ has brought to humanity from God. "This truth is 'transmitted' by the apostles (*paradosis*), 'preached' by the Church (*kerygma*), 'believed' by the faithful (*pistis*)."[21] In Book III, this truth tends to crystallize in two major affirmations: one God, Creator of

---

[21]SC 210, 227; cf. also T. F. Torrance, "The Deposit of Faith," *SJT* 36 (1983):6: "'the tradition,' 'the *kerygma* of the truth' and 'the canon of truth' were all treated as operative equivalents with only differing emphases."

the universe, and one Christ, the Son of God incarnated
to save humankind (AH III,1,2; III,1,1).[22]

Irenaeus referred to this core of truth as the "rule
of truth" (*ton kanona tēs alētheias*, AH I,9,4),[23] or the
"rule of faith" (Proof 3). Ochagavía points out that
"practically every time the expression *regula veritatis*
appears, it refers either explicitly or implicitly to the
Scriptures."[24] It is broader in content than the statements of every symbol that Irenaeus mentions and is
sometimes synonymous with the Church's preaching.[25]
In short, it appears to be a synonym for the tradition of
the apostles, in condensed form, preserved and proclaimed in the Church.[26] The explicit formulations of
belief, which eventually became the early Creeds,
emerged as the Church was "engaged in clarifying its
grasp of the doctrinal substance of the Faith . . . in the
light of its objectively grounded structure."[27] It was this

---

[22]Cf. also I,10,1; V,20,1; Proof 6; Rousseau, SC 210, 220.

[23]Cf. also I,22,1; II,27,1; II,28,1; III,2,1; III,11,1; III,12,6; III,15,1;
IV,35,4; cf. Daniélou: "the rule of truth is the principal content of the
tradition received from the Apostles by their successors" (*Gospel
Message*, 153); Ochagavía: "the 'rule of truth' embraces the whole
Christian faith as found in the Scriptures and in the preaching of the
Church" (204); and Rousseau (SC 210, 220-21).

[24]Ochagavía, 203.

[25]Ibid., 203-4; cf. AH I,9,5 (152); Proof 3 (49).

[26]Cf. J. N. D. Kelly: "For practical purposes, this tradition could be
regarded as finding expression in what he called the 'canon of the
truth'" (*Early Christian Doctrines* [New York: Harper & Row, 1960],
37). As Irenaeus used the term, this "canon of truth" was "a condensed
summary, fluid in its wording but fixed in its content, setting out the
key points of the Christian revelation in the form of a rule" (ibid.).

[27]Torrance, 6. As Torrance points out, the creedal statements are,
therefore, "not statements which are connected with one another
through some logico-deductive system, but statements which are
ordered and integrated from beyond themselves by their common
ground in the Apostolic Deposit of Faith, and in the final analysis in
the objective self-revelation of God in Jesus Christ" (7). Torrance

"rule" which provided the essential key to the interpretation of Scripture. The problem with the heretics was that they took isolated passages of Scripture and rearranged them to serve their own ends (AH I,8,1; I,9,1-4). Irenaeus insisted that Scripture can only be understood correctly if it is read in the light of the basic core of truth which is identical with the original revelation and which has been faithfully preserved in the Church (AH I,9,4).[28] Correct

---

contrasts Irenaeus's "evangelical and Christocentric approach and Tertullian's rather legalist and anthropocentric approach to the Faith" (15). While, for Irenaeus, the canon of truth was in fact the Truth itself (AH II,28,1), "for Tertullian the rule of faith was consistently regarded as a fixed formula of truth for belief, which he claimed had been instituted by Christ himself and had been handed down entire and unchanged from the Apostles (De praescriptione haeriticorum, 13,20-28, 31-32)" (15). Torrance regrets that there were far-reaching effects, in the Western Church, of a "legalizing movement of thought which tended to impose Tertullian-like ways of thought upon the basic contributions of Irenaeus" (16). He is pleased, therefore, that Vatican II tackled these problems, "with a very remarkable recovery of the Irenaean approach to the Gospel, that is, with a radically Christocentric orientation regarding the doctrine of the Church, Divine Revelation and the Liturgy" (17). In this new orientation, "the concept of Faith once for all delivered to the Church was identified in the last analysis with the saving Event of Christ Himself, with a central place accorded to the Holy Scripture" (18).

[28]Cf. the discussion of this passage by Robert L. Wilken, "The Homeric Cento in Irenaeus, *Adversus Haereses* I,9,4," *VigChr* 21 (1967):25-33.

T. F. Torrance notes the importance to Irenaeus of "the fact that 'the body of truth' which constituted the theological content of the Deposit was characterized by an intrinsic order or structure reflecting the economic design of God's redemptive action in Jesus Christ and the essential pattern of the self-revelation of God the Father through the Son and in the Holy Spirit" (6). He suggests that "it is by uncovering this internal structure of the Faith and bringing into clear relief the essential arrangement of 'the body of truth and the harmonious adaptation of its members,' that the Deposit of Faith can be utilized" as a canon of truth enabling the Church to offer a clear demonstration

exegesis was therefore the prerogative of the Church (AH IV,26,5; IV,32,1; V,20,2).

This concept of the "rule of truth" or faith is important to an understanding of the relative roles of Scripture and tradition within Irenaeus's doctrine of revelation and authority. However, there is still a great difference of opinion among the interpreters of Irenaeus as to where the locus of authority actually lay in his thought.[29] Our conclusion is that it would be wrong to pose Irenaeus's position in terms of a two-source theory—Scripture and oral tradition as independent and supplementary—or to describe one as subordinate to the other. Irenaeus's concern was with divine revelation. The Father had manifested himself in the Son, who declared the Father to the apostles and endued them with a gift of certainty in the truth by the Holy Spirit. The apostles handed on the divine revelation through their preaching and their writings. Those to whom the apostles entrusted the churches—the bishops—preserved the "truth" or "faith" received from the apostles and handed it down faithfully. That truth is certainly contained in the Scriptures, and Irenaeus appealed to the "rule of truth," the tradition which was to be found in the consistent testimony of the apostolic successors, particularly in the Church of Rome, but also in the consensus of all the faithful all over the world. That rule, or tradition, was not something independent of Scripture, nor additional to

---

of the Apostolic *kerygma* whereby it can be distinguished from all heretical deviations and distortions and shine forth in its own self-evidence" (ibid.).

[29]See the review of various approaches (van den Eynde, Lawson, Benoit, Flesseman-van Leer) in Philip Hefner ("Theological Methodology and St. Irenaeus," *JR* 44 [1964]:294-95). Hefner himself concludes that "the one highest authority for Irenaeus is the system, framework, or 'hypothesis' of the Faith whose substance is comprised in God's redemptive dispensation on man's behalf" (295).

it. It expressed the essentials of divine revelation as found in Scripture and as preserved in the faithful proclamation of the Church. Thus the tradition itself was confirmed by Scripture, yet Scripture could be properly understood only if read in the light of tradition, itself a condensation of the message of Scripture. J. N. D. Kelly well summarizes the position as we understand it:

> The whole point of his teaching was, in fact, that Scripture and the Church's unwritten tradition are identical in content, both being vehicles of the revelation. If tradition as conveyed in the 'canon' is a more trustworthy guide, this is not because it comprises truths other than those revealed in Scripture, but because the true tenor of the apostolic message is there unambiguously set out.[30]

---

[30]*Early Christian Doctrines*, 39. Cf. Hefner: "Irenaeus seems to say that the function of tradition is to assure continuity with the revelation which comprises the 'hypothesis' or system of truth which can alone serve as the hermeneutical principle for the exegesis of Scripture" (303). He contends that Irenaeus did not subordinate Scripture to tradition, because "tradition as such possesses whatever interpretive authority it has by virtue of the Faith or 'hypothesis' which it transmits" (306). It is therefore better "to speak of both tradition and Scripture as sources or instruments which make the exposition of the normative Christian faith possible in any given situation" (ibid.).

Similarly, Ochagavía contends that "in Irenaeus's view, tradition is not necessarily orally handed down, nor does it constitute a body of teaching separate from the Scriptures" (194). Tradition is in the Scriptures and in the oral preaching of the apostles. "The manner of transmission does not occupy the center of his attention. For him, the tradition is primarily an objective reality" (194).

He holds that the whole *Evangelium Dei* is contained in the oral preaching of the apostles and in the Scriptures. Consequently, there is no room to affirm that a part of the faith (or of the "apostolic tradition," if we want to stick to Irenaeus's terminology) went into the Scriptures, while the rest was orally handed down. . . . The content of tradition—except for some matters of cult and discipline—is merely a declaration and further explication of things already taught by the Scriptures (204-5).

C. The Church as the Way of Truth and of Life

Truth was the issue between Irenaeus and the Gnostics, as it is in the relationship between Christianity and other religions. To Irenaeus, it was clear that truth was to be found in the Church, which was spread all over the world, but which had a unity of faith (AH I,10,2). The Church had *received* that faith from the apostles and it then preached the truth, like a great sun, shining everywhere and "illuminating all who will to come to the knowledge of the truth" (AH I,10,2). The truth is not to be found anywhere else but in the Church where the apostles deposited it, and thus the Church is the "entrance to life" (AH III,4,1). The Church stands firmly on four pillars, the Gospels, which "breathe out immortality in all directions and give life to people" (AH III,11,8).[31] Indeed, what the Church preaches is a faith ordered to the salvation of human beings. The gift of God, which is tradition delivered to the Church, was given for the purpose of bringing life to the members of the Church. To the Church, God has given the Holy Spirit, who is the communion with Christ and the way of ascent to God. The Spirit is so identified with the Church that to be cut off from the Church is to be cut off from the life-giving Spirit (AH III,24,1). The Gnostics, by rejecting the truth proclaimed in the Church, have cut themselves off

---

Cf. George Tavard, *Holy Writ or Holy Church: The Crisis of the Protestant Reformation* (New York: Harper & Bros., 1959), 9; and Yves M.-J. Congar, *Tradition and Traditions: An Historical and Theological Essay* (New York: Macmillan Co., 1967), 33-35.

[31]As Emile Mersch puts it: "the Church is considered as a means established for salvation; we have an ecclesiology that is at the same time soteriology" (*The Whole Christ. The Historical Development of the Doctrine of the Mystical Body in Scripture and Tradition,* trans. John R. Kelly [London: Dennis Dobson, 1938], 240).

from the light of God (III,24,2). Therefore, those who
have been led astray by the heretics must be converted
back to the Church in order to be rescued from their
dangerous situation outside the truth (AH I,6,3; I,13,5;
III,3,4).

Here the observation of Lawson is correct:

> The interest, then, for St. Irenaeus in the Church centres in the
> doctrine which she preaches and guarantees. The call he makes
> is never for submission to the Church on the ground that loyalty
> to the body is a salutary moral exercise. Always it is that men
> should accept the Apostolic doctrine from the Church, because
> this, and this alone is God's saving truth.[32]

The assumption of Irenaeus seems to be that all who
accept the truth of the apostolic teaching, as proclaimed
by the Church, are a part of the Church, and all who
reject that teaching are cut off from the Church.[33] The
truth-proclaiming and life-giving characteristics of the

---

[32]Lawson, 255.

[33]Describing the sociology of the early Church, Henry Green
comments: "Attacks by individuals like Irenaeus, for example, against
heretical movements such as Gnosticism, can be interpreted as a
calculated attempt on the part of the Church Fathers' behalf to abuse
the Gnostic's fragmented ideology, and by so doing to reinforce
Christian beliefs and values. Thus the Church Fathers reacted to
Gnosticism in the way that Rabbinic Judaism reacted to Christianity;
they made their religion exclusive and defined their membership by
ideology" ("Suggested Sociological Themes in the Study of Gnosticism,"
VigChr 31 [1977]:175).

Gerard Vallée suggests that Irenaeus's "part in the rejection of
gnosis in favor of *pistis* contributes to the choice of an authoritarian
structure in Christianity" ("Theological and Non-Theological Motives
in Irenaeus's Refutation of the Gnostics," in *Jewish and Christian
Self-Definition*, vol. 1: *The Shaping of Christianity in the Second and
Third Centuries*, ed. E. P. Sanders [Philadelphia: Fortress Press,
1980], 185). This pattern, devised to meet heretical challenges,
appealed particularly to antiquity (apostolicity) and consent (majority)
(ibid.).

Church are inextricably related, by virtue of the working of the Word and the Spirit in the Church.

It would appear that, in the view of Irenaeus, an acceptance of heresy (and hence a rejection of the apostolic tradition) automatically cut one off from the Church and from the life of the Spirit, whether formal excommunication had taken place or not. Those who distinguished Jesus from the Christ, or the only-begotten One from the Word, were "outside of the economy." Although their public pronouncements appeared to be the same as those of Irenaeus and other presbyters, they were in fact false prophets. They looked like sheep, but they were actually wolves whose doctrine was deadly (AH III,16,8). Irenaeus did not conceive of the possibility that someone could be a member of the Church of God and not a part of the institution which is cared for by the bishops or presbyters, who function in their pastoral role as successors of the apostles. Heretics or false prophets, who departed from the rule of truth, were outside of the Church and of the saving economy of God. Yet, one can not be unmoved by the graciousness of Irenaeus's attitude toward these heretics. Although he took their error very seriously, he did not have a vengeful or vindictive spirit. He desired and prayed for their conversion. He expressed a love for them which was intended to draw them back to the Church for the sake of their own salvation. His apologetic writing was thus intended not only to guard the orthodox from error, but to convince the heretics of their error and bring them back into the Church as children of God (AH III,25,7).

Irenaeus was very firm concerning the wrongfulness of schism.[34] The spiritual disciple (that is, one who

---

[34]Jaroslav Pelikan notes that "in its earliest Christian use, the term 'heresy' was not sharply distinguished from 'schism;' both referred to factiousness. . . . At least as early as Irenaeus, therefore,

has received the Spirit of God, not the "spiritual" one of the Gnostic scheme) shall judge those who have divided the Church, which is the "great and glorious body of Christ," for insignificant personal reasons (AH IV,33,7). Irenaeus was convinced that no reformation could be of such value that it would compensate for the damage done by schism. Benoit notes that the expression *una ecclesia* is not found in Irenaeus, and the expression *unitas ecclesiae* is used only rarely. However, Irenaeus was still very much a theologian of the unity of the Church. Its unity is grounded in the oneness of the faith which goes back to the apostles. The Church is one, because it is founded on the apostolic tradition which is one.[35] The spiritual person will therefore judge all who are outside the Church, that is to say, who are outside the truth (AH IV,33,7).

The Church was characterized by great fruitfulness. It was much larger than the Synagogue was, and through it large numbers were saved. That was because salvation is accomplished through it by the Lord himself, and not by means of a human intercessor (Proof 94).[36] In fact, the Church follows on, from the Incarnation, as the next step in the ongoing of the divine economy. Christ himself is fulfilling the new covenant *in the Church*, moving forward to the consummation of all things (AH IV,34,2).[37] Christ carries out the

---

'heresy' came to be the term for a deviation from the standard of sound doctrine" (*The Christian Tradition. A History of the Development of Doctrine*, vol. 1: *The Emergence of the Catholic Tradition [100-600]* [Chicago: University of Chicago Press, 1971], 69; cf. AH IV,26,2).

[35]*Saint Irénée*, 215-16; cf. AH I,10,2; V,20,1.

[36]J. P. Smith notes that this argument "seemed to have been a feature of the Catena against the Jews which may well have been the source of much of the Proof" (215, citing Rendel Harris, *Expositor* 7 [1906]:406-7). The argument was also used by Clement of Rome (Ep. 2.2).

[37]Cf. Ochagavía, 125.

recapitulation in himself, by uniting humanity to the
Spirit and causing the Spirit to dwell in human beings.
In this repetition, the Church becomes the counterpart of
paradise in the original creation, a garden planted in the
world by God, within which people may eat from the
trees, that is, from Scripture. To eat of the "knowledge"
of the heretics, who claim a knowledge of good and evil
greater than that which God has given within the Church
through the presbyters, would result in being cast out of
the "paradise of life" (AH V,20,2).[38] It is through the
Church that humankind will reach its destiny.[39] The
instrumentality of the Church, both in revelation and
salvation, is important to a right understanding of the
effects of Christ's recapitulation, as demonstrated in
Chapter 5. As Henri de Lubac points out, "by virtue of
the assumption of all human nature by the Word incarnate, a primordial, essential and inalienable bond unites
all men to Christ," but this does not automatically entail
membership in the mystical body.[40] Acceptance of the
rule of faith is critical.

D. Concluding Observations on the
Church and the Unevangelized

In the examination of Irenaeus's teaching concerning the role of the Church in regard to divine saving
revelation, we find a very different picture from the one
presented by a theology of "anonymous Christianity." As

---

[38]Cf. Kim: "Logically, the perfection of creation means that the
Church embraces the entire creation. By being called into the Church,
we are saved, because it is in the Church that Christ recapitulates us,
uniting us with the Spirit" (83).

[39]Cf. Henri de Lubac, *The Church: Paradox and Mystery*, trans.
James R. Dunne (Staten Island, New York: Alba House, 1969), 78.

[40]Ibid., 73.

the third chapter of this study demonstrated, Irenaeus conceived of a world that had contact with the Church through its missionary ventures. That is not to say that the Church was in a majority around the world, or that there were not large numbers of pagans. Nevertheless, he seems to have pictured most of those people as having some contact with the proclamation of the Church. In a sense, that made it "easier" for him to take a view very similar to that of Cyprian in later years. He viewed the Church as the exclusive means to salvation. It was the "glorious body of Christ" indwelt by the Spirit, whose operations in the world were co-extensive with the Church. It was the body in which Christ continued to fulfill the prophecies of the Old Testament. It was the fellowship of all those who believed the "rule of truth." That rule had been entrusted by the apostles to their successors, into whose hands they placed the care of the churches, and had been faithfully preserved and handed down to the time of Irenaeus. At that time, it was faithfully proclaimed by the bishops and elders throughout the world, with a unity and unanimity that were in marked contrast to the fragmentation of the Gnostic teaching. Nowhere was the unity of the tradition more evident than in the old and renowned Church in Rome, which became a norm by virtue of its relationship to the apostles and of its character as a meeting place for Christians coming and going from all parts of the world.

In the whole world, as Irenaeus saw it, there was therefore no other way of ascent to God than through the Church. No teaching could be accepted as truth which did not conform to the unanimous witness to the apostolic faith which was borne by the bishops and presbyters in the Church around the world. No claim to a "living voice," and no interpretation of Scripture, had any claim to truth if it differed from the teaching of the presbyters who were successors of the apostles. Those aspects of

Christ's incarnate and recapitulatory work which appeared to have a direction that tended toward universalism are now harnessed within the work of Christ and the Spirit in and through the Church. To know truth and to have life, to be part of the ongoing of the divine economy which was leading humankind toward the vision of the Father, one had to be part of the *institutional* Church.

8. THE HUMAN RESPONSE TO DIVINE REVELATION

In the preceding chapters, a careful study has been made of Irenaeus's teaching concerning divine revelation, and special attention has been paid to the significance of each aspect of the study to the question of the state of the unevangelized. It has been evident at a number of points in the study that a critical factor in this regard is the role which Irenaeus attributes to the personal response to divine revelation. The purpose of this chapter is to examine that subject in more detail.

A. The Twofold Destiny of Humankind

1. Irenaeus versus the Gnostic threefold division of humankind

In Chapter 2, it was seen that the Gnostics divided humanity into three classes: 1) The "spiritual" were those who possessed perfect knowledge of God and had been initiated into the mysteries of Achamoth (AH I,6,1). When they have completed their course of instruction in this world, they will be perfected and married to the angels of the Savior (AH I,7,5). The Gnostics, of course, were in this class. Being by nature spiritual, they had grace from above, by an indescribable relationship, and their conduct had no bearing on their salvation (AH I,6,4). 2) The "physical" included Irenaeus and a large part of the Church. Their destiny is still undetermined and depends upon the choice they make. They have been given grace to use, but cannot be saved without good works and faith (AH I,6,2). 3) The "material," however, are destined for corruption because of an intrinsic impossibility that material substance should experience salvation (AH I,6,2). The key to salvation for the first two classes lay in the achievement of *gnosis*, which was virtually synonymous with salvation.

Irenaeus was firmly opposed to the fatalism of the Gnostic position, which began with a presupposition of the salvation of some people and the damnation of others. He insisted, rather, on the inclusion of all human-kind in sin, which alienated it from God and incorrupti-bility, and on the liberty of all people to choose their own destiny. That destiny was ultimately one of two choices: life with God in an ever-expanding vision of the Father, or alienation from God in eternal fire, which was death. This possibility of two different destinies is based upon the character of the one God who is both good and just and who "saves those whom he ought to save and judges those who ought to be judged," as opposed to the division made by Marcion between one God who is good and one who is "merciful and good and patient" (AH III,25,3). His justice, however, is not cruel, for his goodness precedes it (AH III,25,3).

2. The universality of sin

Lawson contends that Irenaeus did not believe in original sin in the proper sense of the word. He repre-sented the inherent defect of the human race "as a grievous disability, but not as involving man in guilt or constituting him the object of God's wrath."[1] Lawson

---

[1]John Lawson, *The Biblical Theology of St. Irenaeus* (London: Epworth Press, 1948), 216. André Benoit has suggested that Irenaeus tended to see the fall as an unfortunate accident which introduced

cites AH IV,28,3 as evidence of this. There Irenaeus speaks of "innocent children who have had no thought of evil" (AH IV,28,3). However, it is possible that Lawson is making too much of a reference to an Old Testament type of salvation. Irenaeus asks who are the ones who will be saved and receive the inheritance, and the idea of "inheritance" seems to take his mind back to Israel's entry into the land of Canaan. He therefore cites, as examples of the kind of person who will be saved, Caleb and Joshua, whose entry into the land was promised by God in Numbers 14:30. In the next verse, God promised that the children would also enter the land, presumably because they had not been of an age when they could responsibly side with the faith of Caleb and Joshua or with the unbelief of the other ten spies. Irenaeus's comment regarding the innocent children is clearly a reference to Numbers 14:31. Rousseau's translation gives a force that is a little different from the Latin text[2]: "les enfants innocents *qui ne parlèrent pas contre Dieu* et n'eurent pas la pensée du mal" [emphasis supplied]. He gives a Greek retroversion which supports this rendering[3] and which is apparently justified by the Armenian translation.[4] Furthermore, Irenaeus finds a New

---

some disorder into the plan but did not modify it as a whole. It just retarded its realization. Benoit emphasizes the immaturity of Adam when first created and of his need to develop and progress to the state of spiritual maturity to which God wished to conduct him. The remission of sin, in that perspective, is just a preparatory step in the course of the grand progression which leads humanity to perfection (*Saint Irénée; introduction à l'étude de sa théologie*. Etudes d'histoire et de philosophie religieuses, no. 52 [Paris: Presses Universitaires de France, 1960], 230).

[2]"Pueri innocentes qui neque malitiae sensum habuerunt."

[3]"ta paidia ta anamartēta *mēte tō theō anteirēkota mēte kakias dianoian eschēkota.*"

[4]Cf. Rousseau's textual note on AH IV,28,3 (764).

Testament counterpart in I Corinthians 14:20, in people
who are like children in their lack of malice (AH IV,28,3).

There is indication that Irenaeus did consider
infants in need of saving grace. It was important to him
that Christ passed through every age of human matura-
tion, thereby "sanctifying every age" (AH II,22,4; cf.
IV,38,2). All are therefore saved who are regenerated
through him, namely, *infants*, children, boys, youths, and
old men. Christ became an infant and thereby sanctified
infants,[5] just as he became an old man for the sanctification of old people, and died at the age of fifty (Cf. AH
II,22,6). This is to be understood within the Irenaean
concept of recapitulation. In that regard, it is significant
to note that Irenaeus did not say that Christ came to
save *all* without exception, but qualifies the "all" as those
who are born again to God.[6]

In other instances, Irenaeus gives further indication that he was conscious of an implication of the human
race in sin, through Adam. He describes the war of
Christ against our enemy who "in the beginning, in
Adam, had made us his captives" (AH V,21,1). He speaks
of Christ's passion as destroying that human disobedience which had taken place at the beginning, since *we*

---

[5]Roberts cites this passage as "a valuable fact as to the baptism of
infants in the primitive Church," taking *renascuntur in Deum* to be a
reference to baptism; cf. AH III,17,1, where Christ gave the disciples
the *potestatem regenerationis in Deum* when he commanded them to
teach the nations and baptize them (ANF, 391). Rousseau concurs that
the new birth of which Irenaeus speaks is incontestably baptism (SC
293, 287).

It may be worth noting, however, that many Christians who do
not believe in baptismal regeneration (e.g. Presbyterians and Baptists)
believe in an "age of accountability" prior to which children who die
are saved through the efficacy of Christ's atonement, apart from a
personal act of faith. Such a salvation is seen as an aspect of God's
grace and mercy in redemption, and not as a denial of original sin.

[6]A point stressed also by Rousseau (SC 293, 287).

had offended God in the first Adam and *we* had become debtors to God through the covenant which *we* transgressed at the beginning (AH V,16,3). He speaks of sin and death as entering through one man, in obvious reference to Romans 5:19 (AH III,21,10). Likewise, he says that "being all implicated in the first formation of Adam, we were bound to death through disobedience, the bonds of death had necessarily to be loosed through the obedience of him who was made man for us" (Proof 31).[7]

Therefore, contrary to the Gnostics, who described a class of people who were by nature perfect through relationship to the Aeons, Irenaeus views the entire human race as implicated in Adam's sin and needing to have the consequences of its disobedience undone.[8] It is also apparent that the obedience of Christ

---

[7]Cf. Proof 37 (71), which speaks of "primal disobedience," and says that "we were in the bonds of sin, and were to be born through sinfulness and to live with death"; cf. also AH IV,22,1.

[8]Gustaf Aulen notes that the assertion has been made that Irenaeus "placed relatively little emphasis on sin, because he regards salvation as a bestowal of life rather than of forgiveness, and as a victory over mortality rather than over sin" (*Christus Victor: An Historical Study of the Three Main Types of the Idea of Atonement*, trans. A. G. Hebert [London: SPCK, 1953], 38). However, Aulen labels the assertion misleading because it fails to grasp that, for Irenaeus, sin and death were closely associated and sin was not of secondary importance (39). Irenaeus constantly emphasized salvation as a bestowal of life, because life is fellowship with God, partaking of the life of God, and therefore deliverance from sin (41). "Disobedience to God is essentially death" (41, citing AH V,27,2).

Emil Brunner also protests the idea that Irenaeus had a minimal view of sin, particularly objecting to Harnack's suggestion that "Irenaeus does not possess a perception of sin sufficient for an adequate presupposition for a doctrine of the atonement" (*The Mediator: A Study of the Central Doctrine of the Christian Faith*, trans. Olive Wyon [London: Lutterworth Press, 1934], 257-58). Brunner contends that none of the doctors of the Early Church, not even Augustine, had so deep a sense of "the fact that the sin of Adam

was objectively effective to the undoing of that original disobedience so that there is no class of people whose situation is hopeless or whose condemnation is certain. All share an equally fallen beginning and an equally hopeful future. Whether, in fact, their destiny is salvation or condemnation will depend upon the free exercise of their will, not upon a metaphysical distinction outside of their control.

3. The human free choice of personal destiny

It was in response to the fatalistic determinism implicit in the threefold division of the Gnostics that Irenaeus stressed human freedom to choose between two possible destinies. In the Gnostic scheme, only the psychical had any choice. For Irenaeus, the justice of God's condemnation of people rests on the fact that they have been endowed with reason and free will. Although the Lord used the separation of wheat and chaff at harvest time as an illustration of judgment, there is an important difference between the illustration and reality. The wheat and the chaff are inanimate and irrational, and were by nature what they were. Human beings, on the other hand, have the power to decide whether they will become "wheat" or "chaff." Should they choose to be chaff, their condemnation would be just, because they made a free choice, even though it was an irrational one (AH IV,4,3).[9]

---

is the real sin of us all" (258). For Irenaeus, the Fall was real sin, and that sin was disobedience against God (IV,39,3-4).

See also the discussion by Henri Rondet (*Original Sin: The Patristic and Theological Background*, trans. Cajetan Finnegan [Shannon, Ireland: Ecclesia Press, 1972], 37-50).

[9]Cf. Antonio Orbe, *Antropología de San Ireneo* (Madrid: Biblioteca de Autores Cristianos, 1969), 174-75.

From the beginning, humans were created free, with power over their own souls, so that they could obey God's precepts of their own volition, and not by any compulsion from God. God's will or purpose toward humanity is always good and he gives good counsel (*consilium bonum* or *gnōmēn agathēn*) to all, but people must give obedience to God and preserve that good which is given to them by God. They have the power to do good and will be justly condemned if they do not do it (AH IV,37,1). Lawson has remarked that Irenaeus was so dominated by the interest in human personal moral choice "that his statements on free will sometimes sound almost Pelagian."[10] He rightly notices, however, that, in the preceding context of this statement regarding human ability to do the good, the grace of God (his good will or counsel) precedes human working. "That 'working of good' which is within human power would therefore appear to be nothing other than a steadfast holding on to the grace of God."[11]

While Irenaeus clearly affirmed the necessity of God's grace prior to human choice of the good and the decision of faith in God, he did not consider that grace efficacious in a predestinarian sense. God's foreknowledge of all things includes a knowledge of who will and who will not believe, but it is not elective or reprobationary (AH IV,29,2; cf. AH IV,37,2; IV,39,4). How people respond to God's grace is left in the power of their own freedom. Faith in God is within human power, and they choose to believe or not to do so, of their own free will (AH

---

[10]*Biblical Theology*, 73.

[11]Ibid. As further indication of the priority of God's grace in human salvation, Lawson cites AH III,20,3, which clearly attests to humans' inability to save themselves, since there is no good in them (citing Rom. 7:18). The "good" of human salvation comes from God. Cf. also III,18,2, which states the impossibility of human attainment of salvation because of the subjection to the power of sin.

IV,37,5). When people do not believe, the cause does not lie in a deficiency in God's call. God's light continues to shine but some people blind themselves to it. That they live in darkness is therefore their own fault and no fault of God's light (AH IV,39,3-4). However, God does judicially blind these unbelievers, giving them up to the darkness which they have chosen for themselves (AH IV,29,1; IV,39,4; III,7,1; V,27,2).

It needs to be noted again that this stress which Irenaeus places on human freedom to choose personal destiny is in a context of optimism regarding the opportunity provided for choice of the good. From the beginning, the Son has been present with his handiwork, revealing the Father to all whom the Father wills (AH IV,6,7). This included the revelation in creation, the preaching through the law and the prophets, the visibility of the Word in the incarnation, and then the continuing working of the Word through the Church's proclamation and the inspired Scriptures. Irenaeus had no room in his experience for a category of people who have had no *opportunity* to believe. God's just judgment of people rests on their free response to his gracious self-revelation, and there does not seem to have been anyone, in Irenaeus's frame of reference, who did not have sufficient revelation to make an adequate moral response.[12]

---

[12]Gustav Wingren has tended to make Irenaeus in the image of Karl Barth. However, keeping that in mind, his comments are worth pondering:

Man is free and responsible [IV,37,1-7]. He may receive Christ's word in faith, or reject it in unbelief. But in neither case does his freedom contradict Christ's Lordship. Freedom is a reflection of Christ's government in its present form, a government exercised through the preaching of the Word [Proof 55]. Free man is implicated in preaching, in the *kerygma*, as subject, as recipient; were it not for man, vacillating between faith and unbelief, the *kerygma* would not be the *kerygma*. . . . In Irenaeus, the whole movement is towards resurrection and the Last Judgment. There is no one alive, and there never will be any, who is free to resist Christ for all time to come, for no one has freedom independently of Christ, who has power to judge men with a final annihilating judgment. Our present freedom is grounded on the fact that Christ has not yet begun the Final Judgment, and for the present he addresses us in his *kerygma*, which is the means of his appeal to us. . . . Man's freedom for Irenaeus is, therefore, an expression of God's power. Divine sovereignty and human freedom are not in opposition to one another, but belong together and are mutually dependent. Man's freedom is a sign of Christ's dominion: *all* men can be raised from the condition in which they are, and the Gospel, which is now spreading apace throughout the world, is proclaimed to all (*Man and the Incarnation: A Study in the Biblical Theology of Irenaeus*, trans. Ross Mackenzie [London: Oliver & Boyd, 1959], 139-40).

Wingren presents Irenaeus in typically Barthian terms, emphasizing the universal effect of Christ's recapitulatory work, and stressing the irrationality of unbelief, which does not, however, thereby thwart God's elective purpose in Christ:

In the judgment it will be seen that some men are in the Serpent's power and are doomed to an end which completely reverses their destiny. They will . . . suffer death and punishment. Despite this, Irenaeus clings to his concept of recapitulation, and repeatedly states that Christ recapitulates *all things*, and that he gives life to mankind as a whole. In the same way he says of God the Creator that he has created and is creating *all things*, and that nothing can come into being apart from God, and yet he is not responsible for creating evil. Evil is something incomprehensible both when it enters Creation through the Devil and when it is condemned by God in the Last Judgment.

. . . God deals with all men equally in his divine nature. Those who are condemned "gather up" the same work of God as the saved, but the way of gathering up and receiving are different. God's dealings are not changed or suspended by any difference in the reception of them—God is what he is, and he acts according to his inner divine will, everywhere and in everything. The light shines on, even though one blinds oneself to it (197-98).

Wingren thus sees in Irenaeus's doctrine of recapitulation a parallel to Barth's doctrine of universal election in Christ. "In Christ this salvation for the whole of mankind is achieved without restriction. The Incarnate One's *recapitulatio* of Adam encompasses the

4. The hierarchy among non-Christians

It has become clear, in the two preceding chapters, that Irenaeus did not conceive of the salvation of people in his own day outside of the institutional Church, within which the Spirit's saving operations are performed. However, it is interesting to notice that he does not view all non-Christians as equally guilty in their failure to appropriate, or share in, the salvation which is mediated through the Church. Within the absoluteness of their judgment, there are degrees of evil, and hence of punishment, related to the degree to which people receive divine revelation. Thus Irenaeus cites the statement of the Lord that, in the general judgment, the people of Sodom will be less severely punished than will those who saw the incarnate Word doing wonders and heard him preach, and still did not believe.

> For as he has given, by his advent, greater grace to those who believed on him and did his will, so also he indicated that those who did not believe on him would have a more severe punishment in the judgment, for he is equally just toward all, and from those to whom he has given more he will require more (AH IV,36,4).[13]

---

whole of human life to all eternity" (200). Yet, some people reject and reverse their destiny (cf. 197). Cf. Karl Barth, *Church Dogmatics* (Edinburgh: T. & T. Clark, 1957), II/2, IV/1.

For an interesting discussion of Irenaeus's discussion of evil in God's purpose for humanity, as contrasted with that of Augustine, see John Hick, *Evil and the God of Love* (London: Macmillan, 1966), 217-21, 239-91.

[13]"Quaemadmodum enim majorem dedit gratiam per suum adventum his qui crediderunt ei et faciunt ejus voluntatem, sic et majorem in judicio habere poenam eos qui non crediderunt ei significavit, justus existens super omnes aequaliter, et quibus plus dedit, plus ab eis exacturus."

We can safely say, therefore, that if Irenaeus did not positively conceive of the salvation of any who are outside the Church's saving proclamation and life, yet he would not consider all people to be equally guilty before God, nor equally punished by God. In God's justice, he will deal with people according to the privilege of revelation which he has given them.

There are gradations in the evil of human religious error. Irenaeus therefore makes the judgment that the Gnostics and their followers were *more* evil (*peiores*) than the pagans. The pagans "serve the creature rather than the Creator" and worship "those which are not gods," but at least they attribute first rank in divinity to the God who is Creator of the universe (AH II,9,2, citing Rom 1:25; Gal 4:8). The Gnostics, on the other hand, describe the Creator as the product of a defect in the Aeons and attribute evil to him. They thus show themselves to be more evil than the pagans (AH II,9,2). Later, Irenaeus makes another judgment concerning the relativity of the error of non-Christians. Plato is pronounced "more religious" (*religiosior*) than the Marcionites because he attributed both goodness and justice to God, and acknowledged God's providence over all things (AH III,25,5).[14]

---

[14]Gérard Vallée cites this as the only passage in which Irenaeus commends a philosopher, but notes that the judgment of Plato as superior to Marcion was "very faint praise" ("Theological and Non-Theological Motives in Irenaeus's Refutation of the Gnostics," in *Jewish and Christian Self-Definition*, vol. 2: *The Shaping of Christianity in the Second and Third Centuries*, ed. E. P. Sanders [Philadelphia: Fortress Press, 1980], 177).

André Méhat has pointed out that the major objection of both Tertullian and Irenaeus against the philosophers was that they were responsible for the heresies. About 225, the *Refutation*, generally attributed to Hippolytus of Rome, took up that thesis and showed that each heresy corresponded to a school of philosophy. Clement of Alexandria, on the other hand, was aware of Christian hostility to the

Irenaeus discerned a graduation of evil in Psalm 1:1. The "ungodly" are "the peoples that know not God" (Proof 2). These are presumably the pagans. "Sinners," on the other hand, are those "who have knowledge of God, and do not keep his commandments; that is, scornful, disdainful folk" (Proof 2). J.P. Smith wonders if this might be "a reference to the arrogance of the Gnostic view that good works were unnecessary for the initiate."[15] In any case, these are people who have a knowledge of divine revelation but who do not obey God. More serious still are the "pestilential," who corrupt not only themselves but others with "wicked and perverse doctrine" (Proof 2). These are the heretical teachers.

Another form of classification is made by reference to the Old Testament distinction between ceremonially clean and unclean animals (AH V,8,3). These are the two classes of people: those who are proceeding toward God and those who are not. However, the class of unclean animals is again divided into three groups. First are the *Gentiles,* or the pagans, who (like the animals that neither chew the cud nor have a cloven hoof) neither have faith in God nor meditate upon his words. The second class is the *Jews.* They have the words of God (i.e., chew the cud), but are not fixed firmly in the Father and the Son (i.e., do not have the surefootedness of the divided hoof). The third class is the *heretics.* They claim to believe in the Father and the Son (i.e., have a divided hoof), but they do not meditate on God's words with a view to growing in obedience and righteousness. In this case, Irenaeus does not explicitly pass judgment on the relative seriousness of the condition of the three

---

Greek philosophers, but did not share it ("La philosophie troisième testament? La pensée grecque et la foi selon Clément d'Alexandrie," *LV* 32 [January-March 1983]:17).

[15]*Proof,* 134, n. 15.

"unclean" classes, but there seems to be an order of progression in his treatment. In keeping with the concept of culpability according to the degree of revelation, the Gentiles are the least guilty and the heretics the most so, because the latter have a knowledge of both Father and Son but have distorted it. Ignorance is less pernicious than perversion of the truth.

5. The futility of pagan worship

Irenaeus drew a very strong contrast between the gods which the heathen worshiped and the true God, citing the message both of the Old Testament prophets (AH III,6,3) and of the apostle Paul (AH III,6,5). There is no suggestion made that one might in fact be worshiping the one true God through sincere, though ignorant, worship of idols. These were, in fact, "idols of demons" (AH III,6,3). The evangelization of the pagans was more difficult than that of the Jews because there was no Old Testament Scripture to which appeal could be made as witness to Christ. (Irenaeus makes no suggestion that other scriptures—religious or philosophical—might serve a parallel, preparatory function for those who did not have the Old Testament.) Nonetheless, the missionaries to the Gentiles declared the same message concerning the one God and his Word who was incarnated and suffered death on the cross for human salvation (AH IV,24,2). The apostles therefore called upon the Gentiles to leave the gods of their own making and worship the true God (AH III,5,3).

It was clear to Irenaeus, therefore, that the apostles were not guilty of any form of syncretism in their missionary preaching. They did not accommodate their message to the idea of the pagans (Gentiles), but boldly told them that their gods were not gods at all but were "idols of demons," and pointed them toward the true

God (AH III,12,6; cf. III,12,13). This defense of the
apostles against the charge of syncretism was of vital
importance to Irenaeus's apology for the apostolic tradition. The Gnostics were contending that the apostles had
accommodated their preaching among the Jews to the
opinions that the Jews already had. The same was said
to be true of the Lord himself. Thus the teachings of
Christ and the apostles regarding God, which Irenaeus
was defending as divine truth, were dismissed by the
Gnostics as syncretism and accommodation. The doctrine
of God that Irenaeus was presenting was simply the
Jewish view adopted by the apostles, the Gnostics
claimed, and not a distinct truth of revelation from God
through his Word. To this, Irenaeus objected strenuously,
because his whole argument depended on the assumption
that what the apostles declared to the Jews and to the
Gentiles was divine truth, unadulterated by accommodation to the errors of the hearers. Had Irenaeus conceded
the point to the Gnostics, there would have been no way
to avoid relativism and pluralism.

B. Faith: The Saving Response
to Divine Revelation

1. The necessity of faith

There is a repeated and insistent testimony, in
Books IV and V of *Adversus Haereses*, that salvation is by
faith and only to those who believe, and that the unbeliever will be condemned. The human possession of the
power to believe is important precisely because it is by
faith that eternal life is received (AH IV,37,5, citing Jn
3:36). Through the one God, the Father, the one Son and
the one Spirit, there is therefore "one salvation to all who
believe in him" (AH IV,6,7). Faith has thus been essential
at every stage of the divine self-revelation. At the very

basic level of revelation, namely, creation, which addresses all people equally, there is the problem that not all believe (AH IV,6,6).

Abraham was accounted a righteous man because of his faith in God, believing the Word spoken to him by God. In the Spirit, he saw prophetically the Lord's coming, and suffering, through whom he and all who followed his example of faith would be saved. That gave Abraham great joy, and provided an early example of the fact that "it is faith in God which justifies a person" (AH IV,5,3-5). It was evident from the experience of Abraham, and also of Lot, Noah and Enoch, that justification was not dependent on the ceremony of circumcision and the keeping of the law (AH IV,16,2; IV,25,1; cf. Proof 87).

The Old Testament law served as a schoolmaster to lead people to Christ, so that no one could blame the law for hindering anyone from faith. Indeed, the law declared that "people could not be saved from the old wound of the serpent," except by believing in him who, in the likeness of sinful flesh, was lifted up above the earth on the tree of a martyr, and draws all things to himself, and gives life to the dead (AH IV,2,7).

John the Baptist was commissioned to go before the Lord and prepare the way for him, giving the "knowledge of salvation to his people, for the remission of their sins" (AH III,10,3). This "knowledge of salvation was knowledge of the Son of God" (AH III,10,3), and was communicated by John to "those who repent and believe in the Lamb of God who takes away the sin of the world" (AH III,10,3).

The Father revealed himself through the Son expressly so that those who believe in him might be brought into incorruption (AH IV,6,5). This is because the Son of God is "Lord of all men, and Saviour of those who believe in him, Jews and others" (Proof 51, cf. 52; 53). Although, in the sense of creation, all people are children of God, in a more significant sense only those who believe in him and do his will are God's children, and those who do not are children and angels of the devil (AH IV,41,2). Those who receive the Spirit of adoption are "those who believe in the one true God and in Jesus Christ the Son of God" (AH IV,1,1).[16]

When the Lord descended into the regions beneath the earth and preached his advent, those who received the remission of sins were those who believed in him. These are further described as those who had "hoped in him, that is to say, those who had announced his coming in advance and had cooperated with his economies." They were the righteous, the prophets, and the patriarchs (AH IV,27,2). Later, the apostles preached among the Gentiles the good news that those who believe in Christ shall be incorruptible and shall receive the kingdom of heaven (AH IV,24,2). The final judgment, therefore, will be made on the basis of faith or unbelief in Christ (AH V,27,1; cf. IV,22,2; IV,27,2). Thus it would appear that faith in God, and specifically in Christ, is the *sine qua non* of salvation, for Irenaeus.

1. The nature of faith

a. In the time of Irenaeus

There seems to be no room in the teaching of Irenaeus regarding the conditions for salvation, in his day, for a concept of "implicit faith." The saving faith which he defines as the necessary response to divine revelation is very explicit. It is, for one thing, a holding to the unadulterated "rule of truth" (AH III,15,1; cf. IV,1,1; Proof 3-4, 98). This involves a firm commitment to

---

[16]Interestingly, III,6,1 says, of those who received the adoption, that "these are the Church."

the faith or tradition of the Church, which is ordained to human salvation (AH III,24,1; cf. III,25,7). In this regard, the barbarians who did not have the Scriptures were particularly to be commended, because they believed the "faith" simply through the proclamation of the Church (AH III,4,2). The faith which is saving is thus one that has a certain content, minimally defined in the trinitarian confession of the Church (Cf. AH I,3,6; I,10,1-2; IV,24,2; IV,33,7). As was evident in the Lord's training of his disciples, a certain amount of knowledge was necessary to lead them to salvation (AH III,5,2). The disciples, in turn, preached Christ daily, because that was a "knowledge of salvation" which would make perfect those who "knew" the coming of the Son (AH III,12,5). This faith "maintains our salvation" and causes us to remember that we have received baptism for the remission of our sins in the name of the Father, Son and Holy Spirit, and that this "baptism is the seal of eternal life and is rebirth unto God," making us children of God (Proof 3).

Abraham provided a great pattern of saving faith which was specifically Christological. He believed in the one God who made the world, but he also accepted as truth the revelation of God to him with regard to the promise of a great nation, and he followed the Word of God wherever he led (AH IV,5,3). This same faithful following of the Word characterized the disciples whom Christ called, and it will characterize all those who have the faith that Abraham had (AH IV,5,4; IV,21,1; cf. V,32,2; IV,7,2).[17] Faith is seen to be almost synonymous,

---

[17]Wingren comments:
In believing in the promise Abraham actually possessed Christ as he then was, thereby grasping the Incarnation. Abraham had essentially the same kind of faith as we have (IV,21,1). Every phase of Christ's redemptive work means that something completely new occurs, but provided men live completely in the conditions of faith, the terms faith are the same (IV,32,2). The basis of faith is always

on occasion, with doing the will of God (AH IV,6,5).[18] It
is no mere verbal profession, no mere intellectual assent
to doctrines, but is an obedient response to God's com-
mands. Here Irenaeus was in disagreement with the
Gnostic view of a class of people, the spiritual, who did
not have to do righteous deeds. Christ demanded a
righteousness greater than that of the scribes and
pharisees. Therefore, it is necessary not only to believe in
the Father and the Son, but to do works of righteousness,
in keeping with the Law (AH IV,13,1). Thus it is those
who "have obeyed and have believed on him" who will
receive immortality (AH IV,15,2). God demanded "faith
and obedience and righteousness" for salvation (AH
IV,17,4; Cf. Proof 2,3), and those who are called the
children of God are "those who believe in him and do his
will" (AH IV,41,2). Likewise, salvation depends on the
possession of the Spirit of God, and his presence must
therefore be preserved by "faith and a chaste life" (AH
V,9,3).[19] The resurrection to life at the return of Christ
will therefore be for those who believe and who will do
the will of the Father (AH V,27,1).[20] It is not that one is
justified by the works of the law. Abraham is the prime
example that such was not the case. Nonetheless, true
faith increases our love for God, and love is the fulfillment of the law. "So he [the Lord] has increased, through
our faith in him, our love towards God and our neighbour, rendering us godly and just and good" (Proof 87).

---

the promise of God's Word, which relates to Christ (IV,22,2) (74-75).

[18]"Credere autem ei est facere ejus voluntatem." Cf. AH IV,39,1.

[19]Cf. AH IV,36,6, where the wedding garment is identified as both
the Spirit of God and deeds of righteousness.

[20]Note that those who shall be raised first at Christ's return are
those who, in their generation "feared and loved God, practised justice
and goodness to their neighbour," and had a desire to see Christ (AH
IV,22,2).

b. Faith, obedience and natural revelation

1) Naturalia legis. It is important to consider Irenaeus's comments on the precepts of natural law (*naturalia legis*), particularly since he speaks of people being justified by them before the giving of the Law of Moses (AH V,9,3; cf. IV,13,1).[21] In the context, Irenaeus is demonstrating the unity of the testaments against the Marcionites. He therefore shows that there is a continuity from the natural law—the law of God as people knew it before Sinai—through the Mosaic code, to the Lord's commandments which did not abrogate the Old Testament law but extended and fulfilled it. As John Hochban points out, "the context seems clearly to indicate that the verb *justificare* is here used in a rather loose sense, . . . since in the phrase that immediately follows justification is ascribed to 'faith.'"[22] Nevertheless, Irenaeus does describe a period during which God was content to leave humanity with natural precepts which he had given to them from the beginning, by implanting them within human nature. These precepts were the same as those which were eventually written in the decalogue (AH IV,15,1).[23] Irenaeus describes the patriarchal period as one in which Abraham and others were justified by

---

[21]"Et quia Dominus naturalia legis, per quae homo justificator, quae etiam ante legis dationem custodiebant qui fide justificabantur et placebant Deo, non dissolvit, sed et extendit et implevit . . . ."

[22]"St. Irenaeus on the Atonement," *TS* 7 (December 1946):536. Hochban draws a parallel to Tertullian's "naturalia legis justitia" (Adv. Judaeos, 2), and cites other passages which clearly refer Abraham's justification to faith, and ground his righteousness on the redemption accomplished by Christ (cf. AH IV,5,5; IV,8,1-2; IV,22,2).

[23]The importance of a "clear conscience" in the worship of God and in the offering of an acceptable sacrifice is borne out in the case of Cain, whose heart was full of envy and ill-will to his brother. It is the pure conscience that sanctifies the sacrifice (IV,18,3).

faith without the Mosaic law, having the law written on their hearts and souls. It was only when that inner conformity to God's law, and love for God, degenerated in Egypt, that it was necessary for God to reveal himself more externally through Moses (AH IV,16,2-3).

In order to allow of salvation apart from explicit faith in Christ, it is generally necessary to place heavy emphasis on the natural law as salvific. The theory is that people who now live without the written law are dependent on the law of God written on their hearts, as Adam and the patriarchs were. In such a context, Irenaeus's somewhat obscure mention of justification by the natural precepts would appear to give some hope. However, to attribute such hopefulness to Irenaeus himself would be improper. The context must be kept in mind, including the aforementioned passages regarding the salvation of the patriarchs.

A further difficulty lies, however, in the analogy between "hidden peoples" of the twentieth century and the patriarchs. In Irenaeus's thought, there is a linear movement, from the creation and fall of the immature Adam, through the patriarchal period, to the giving of the law and onwards to Christ. Can we postulate that there are people in the position of the patriarchs, still following the precepts of God written on their hearts and not needing the written law? Even if we were to take so optimistic a view of the religious state of pagans as to describe them in such a fashion, a problem remains in imputing this optimism to Irenaeus. The patriarchs had encounters with the pre-incarnate Word, in theophanic appearances, and had various typical revelations which created a Christological anticipation. To expect to find an "anonymous Christian" within the Irenaean structure, it would be necessary, therefore, to have not only the *naturalia legis*, but also some kind of manifestation of the Word.

2) Creation and providence. Finally, one would not want to forget the revelation of God the Creator, by the Word, in his creation. This, too, Irenaeus describes as necessitating a response of faith (AH IV,6,6). Furthermore, his statement that not *all* believe would imply that at least some do. Yet, fundamental as is that belief in the one God who created the world and formed humanity, is it sufficient to give the kind of knowledge of the Father which Irenaeus describes as salvific? This may have to remain an open question because of the limitations of Irenaeus's own frame of reference. He did not have in mind people who had *only* revelation in creation and providence, because he assumed that everyone had further modes of revelation, even in Old Testament times. His emphasis in this context is that there are some who reject revelation even at that first basic level. Yet, in AH IV,20,7, Irenaeus makes what José González-Faus labels a "surprising parallelism."[24]

> If the revelation of God by creation already gives life to all who live in the earth, much more does the manifestation of the Father by the Word give life to those who see God.[25]

González-Faus appears to be right when he states that Irenaeus indicates here that revelation in creation is already salvific, at least in germinal form.[26] This would assume, of course, that there was a Word-illumined response, but the revelation itself seems adequate to salvation (i.e., it gives life). While Irenaeus does not appear to have conceived of people who were restricted to

---

[24]*Carne de Dios: significado salvador de la Encarnación en la teología de san Ireneo* (Barcelona: Herder, 1969), 52.

[25]"Si enim quae est per conditionem ostensio Dei vitam praestat omnibus in terra viventibus, multo magis ea quae est per Verbum manifestatio Patris vitam praestat his qui vident Deum."

[26]González-Faus, 52.

that revelation (and might have spoken more cautiously if he had had such people in mind), this is a very significant point in our own context, where we are acutely aware of such people. This will have to be considered further, in the discussion of unbelief below.

c. The "hope in Christ" of the righteous of the Old Testament

The theology of "anonymous Christianity" has had considerable interest in the salvation of the righteous of the Old Testament, prior to the Law and the prophets. Analogy has been made between their situation and that of pagans without the gospel, after the Incarnation. Notice has already been taken, however, of Irenaeus's statements that those Old Testament righteous ones had hoped in Christ (AH IV,27,2; IV,22,2). There are many nameless people of Old Testament times whom Irenaeus must have included in that category, and we cannot be sure what kind of anticipation of Christ he attributed to them. It is interesting, however, to study the cases of a few whose names are known.

1) Abel. Abel was clearly one of those of the Old Testament who was saved. Interestingly, Marcion did not think so. He declared that Abel, along with Enoch and Noah, the righteous descendants of Abraham, the prophets, and "those who were pleasing to God" were not saved. He contended that when Jesus went down to Hades, these people did not go to him or believe in him because of their previous experiences of God as one who had tempted them. Consequently, their souls remained in Hades. On the other hand, Cain, the Sodomites, the Egyptians, and others like them were saved because they ran to Jesus, received him and welcomed him (AH I,27,3). The Valentinians referred to Abel as the forerunner or type of the psychics, in their three-class scheme

(AH I,7,5). Irenaeus, however, had no doubt about the righteousness of Abel.

God accepted Abel's offering because it was given with simplicity and righteousness (AH IV,18,3). In that regard, Abel served as an illustration that it is the pure conscience that sanctifies a sacrifice and causes God to accept the offering as from a friend (AH IV,18,3). It is not difficult to account for Abel's "hope" in Christ. Although Irenaeus says nothing of this, the very fact of Abel's sacrifice is significant. His mother and father doubtless told him of the promise of the Savior, and his sacrifice had value in the light of his simple acceptance of that promise. Although Irenaeus tells us nothing about the nature of Abel's faith, he emphasizes the typical significance of Abel's death as a prefigurement of the death of Christ.

The passion of the Just One "was prefigured from the beginning in Abel, described by the prophets and accomplished in the last times in the Son of God" (AH IV,25,2). Isaiah predicted the death of a righteous man about which people did not care. This was prefigured also in Abel, and finally accomplished in the Lord (AH IV,34,4). Abel's death at the hands of an unrighteous man was also "a sign for the future, that some would be persecuted and straitened and slain, but the unjust would slay and persecute the just" (Proof 17). In this way, what began in Abel and was accomplished in the Lord is carried on in believers, as in the body following the example of the Head (AH IV,34,4). In Abel, the gathering in of a righteous race was prefigured (AH IV,34,4). When the Lord said that he would demand an account of the blood of the righteous from Abel to Zachariah, he meant that he would recapitulate it all in the shedding of his own blood (AH V,14,1, referring to

Mt 23:35-36; Lk 11:50-51).[27] Abel's "announcement [of
the Lord] beforehand" was thus an unconscious one but,
in Irenaeus's scheme, his death served that purpose. As
a righteous person, however, Abel had too much contact
with the revelation of the Word to be a model of the
"anonymous Christian."

 2) Enoch. In AH IV,16,2, Irenaeus speaks of
Enoch, Noah and Lot as examples, in addition to
Abraham, of men who were accounted righteous by God,
without circumcision or the law of Moses. Of the three,
Irenaeus tells us least about Enoch. He says that Enoch
"pleased God" without circumcision, that he was sent as
an ambassador to the angels, and that he was "translated
in salvation" (*translatus est in salutem*). Enoch serves as
a witness to the just judgment of God in that the angels
who had transgressed were judged, whereas the person
who pleased God was saved. Enoch therefore prefigured
the translation or the taking up of the just (AH V,5,1).
Again, the nature of Enoch's hope or faith is undefined.
He "anticipates" the Lord in the sense that he illustrated
the just judgment of God and prefigured the taking up of
the just. Interestingly, as with Abel, this prefigurement
was not a deliberate action on Enoch's part. We have
very little idea, therefore, of the nature of Enoch's part.
What mattered to Irenaeus was that Enoch was a man
who pleased God, though he was not circumcised and
though he did not have the law of Moses. He was part of
the one economy of salvation that the Word was carrying
out from the beginning.

 3) Noah. The least likely example of all these

---

[27]José González-Faus points out that the idea of Christ, the
recapitulator, as the true reality of all things provides the foundation
for the necessity of a type-antitype scheme impressed upon creation.
The typological mode of exegesis is therefore a consequence of the very
structure of things (180).

people to be an "anonymous Christian" was Noah, for the
Son of God spoke with him, and gave him the dimensions
of the ark (AH IV,10,1; IV,16,1). His history served as an
example of the Son of God's implantations in the Old
Testament Scriptures (AH IV,10,1). He also prefigures
the last judgment, when the people will carry on as
usual, not expecting judgment of their sins but experi-
encing the Lord's punishment, as did the wicked of
Noah's day upon whom the Lord sent the flood (AH
IV,36,3). After the flood, the Word again spoke to Noah
and to his companions, giving them directions regarding
the punishment of those who take human life which is
valuable because of man's being created in the image of
God, that is, of the Son of God (AH V,14,1).

The covenant made with Noah is of interest
because of its universality.[28] Irenaeus describes it as a
"covenant for the whole world, and for all living beasts,
and for men, that he would no more destroy with a flood
all the new life of the earth" (Proof 22). Irenaeus
describes this, in the Proof, as a natural or physical
covenant rather than a salvific one. However, he includes
the covenant with Noah as one of the four testaments
that God made with humankind, culminating in the
recapitulating work of the Gospel (AH III,11,8). This
places the covenant with Noah in the line of the progress

---

[28]Hans Urs von Balthasar suggests that Irenaeus finds the totality
of the fulfillment in Christ promised not only in Abraham, but also in
the preceding Noahic covenant (*Herrlichkeit. Eine theologische
Asthetik* [Einsideln: Johannes Verlag, 1962], 83). Cf. also Walbert
Buhlmann:

The covenant with Noah can be considered the formalization and
conclusion of the history of creation. All peoples stand within the
salvation order of God. It is inconceivable that there ever be, or
ever has been a time when any people of this world had no
salvation history (*God's Chosen Peoples*, trans. Robert R. Barr
[Maryknoll, New York: Orbis Books, 1982], 19).

of the one economy of salvation. However, Irenaeus does not attribute to it any specific salvific significance in the ongoing of that economy.[29]

More significant in this regard is the blessing of Shem and Japheth by Noah. Hans Urs von Balthasar includes this in the covenant of God with Noah, but that does not seem valid. However, it explains in part the salvific significance which he attributes to the Noahic covenant in Irenaeus's theology.[30] Irenaeus describes the blessing of Shem as indicating that God was to be a "peculiar possession of worship" for him. Shem's blessing was carried over to Abraham (Proof 21; cf. 24). More significant, however, is the blessing of Japheth, which is understood as having its fulfillment in the end of the age, "in the manifestation of the Lord, to the Gentiles of the calling" (Proof 21). The enlargement of Japheth, and his dwelling in the house of Shem, are a prediction of the calling of the Church and its coming into "the heritage of the patriarchs, in Christ Jesus receiving the birthright" (Proof 21; cf. 42; AH III,5,3). Thus Noah and his sons play an extremely important predictive role with regard to the outworking of the economy of salvation through Christ, the "son" of Abraham, the "son" of Shem, and then on through the Church, which comes into the

---

[29]Gustave Thils has seen the scheme as progressing to an absolutely universal perspective (*Propos et problèmes de la théologie des religions non-chrétiennes* [Paris: Casterman, 1966], 67), but we have already demonstrated that Irenaeus does not in fact follow through to that point. Auguste Luneau calls the first basic step in the pedagogy the "natural law," a period from Adam to the double gift of circumcision and the Law. His estimation appears correct that, although Irenaeus distinguishes between the testament of Adam and that of Noah, the second adds little to the first (*L'histoire de Salut chez les Pères de l'Eglise: La doctrine des âges du monde*, Théologie historique, no. 2 [Paris: Beauchesne et ses fils, 1964], 97).

[30]*Herrlichkeit*, 83.

inheritance of Christ, as Japheth dwelt in the tents of Shem. It does not seem valid, however, to make this predictive blessing by Noah a part of God's covenant with Noah, and thereby to stretch it to universal salvific scope. In fact, the curse of Ham specifically points to the fact that there will be those who are not included within the economy of salvation. Noah, Shem and Japheth all had very specific encounters with the Word and are, therefore, also not models of "anonymous Christianity."[31]

4) Lot. The last one to be considered, of those who were declared righteous without circumcision or the Law, is Lot. He is interesting because, like Abel and Enoch, he unconsciously served a prefigurative role. In an attempt to respond to moral censure of Lot by

---

[31]Bühlmann has drawn conclusions from Noah that seem quite alien to Irenaeus. He suggests that Noah was "not a member of the people of Israel—still less of Christianity—but one of those religions that would be labelled 'pagan' and disparaged" (20). Yet he "'found grace in the Lord's eyes', was 'a just man and perfect among his contemporaries', and 'walked with God'" (ibid.). Consequently, Bühlmann discerns in Noah

a legitimation of all non-Israelite religion that goes back to God himself. . . . Both the peoples of the covenant with Noah—the pagans—and the peoples of the covenant with Abraham—Israel—come within the scope of God's salvific will, albeit in different fashions. In both, God has acknowledged all peoples as "His"—and even to our own day makes the rainbow rise over them all as a sign of ever new hope after the storm (ibid.).

Given Irenaeus's view of the unity of the covenant of salvation, and his perspective on the distinct contact which Noah had with the Logos, he would not have considered Noah a model of the "pagans," nor have seen in him a legitimation of non-Israelite religion. In Irenaeus's perspective, the pagans were the ones who perished in the flood. It is also important to note that Irenaeus understood the Noahic covenant in strictly physical terms, so that the sign of the rainbow gives no particular hope with regard to the salvation of the world, unless one abstracts from its demonstration of God's providential concern for his creation.

Irenaeus's opponents, Irenaeus urges his readers to examine the typical significance of Lot's incestual relationship with his daughters. Irenaeus absolves Lot of guilt because he was unaware of what was going on, and he absolves Lot's daughters because they thought that the rest of the human race had been destroyed, and felt an obligation to perpetuate it. However, the more significant point is that the seed of the Father of all, that is to say, the Spirit of God, was united with flesh (His own workmanship) and through that union the two synagogues (i.e., Israel and the Church) were produced as living sons of the living God. Lot's wife also had typical significance. Being left behind as a pillar of salt, and no longer corruptible flesh, she typifies the Church, the salt of the earth which is left on the earth and endures through time and persecution (AH IV,31,1-3; cf. IV,33,9).

Lot's story also has prefigurative significance because of the Son of God's activity in judgment of Sodom (AH IV,36,3-4; Proof 44). This record is another example of the Son of God being "implanted" in the Old Testament Scriptures (AH IV,10,1). In these unconscious ways, Lot might thus be described as "announcing the Son of God beforehand." However, Irenaeus says nothing more specific about Lot's faith in Christ. He was not addressed by the Word in theophanic form, as Abraham was. The Lord left after talking to Abraham, and only the two angels visited Lot (AH III,6,1). However, Lot was clearly a very privileged person in regard to revelation. Having accompanied Abraham from Mesopotamia, after the Word called Abraham out, he knew what the Word had said and was a willing companion of Abraham in his obedient following of the Word. Lot too, while a good example of a righteous person of the Old Testament before the Law or the prophets, was certainly privileged with regard to divine revelation.

5) A concluding note. Not surprisingly, the ones whose names we know were not "anonymous Christians." None of them serves as a ground of appeal to Old Testament models of the modern-day pagan, whose salvation without conscious knowledge of Christ is an object of hope by modern theologians. Irenaeus does not help us by speaking of those who lived in that day who are anonymous to us, but who may have "anonymously," that is, unconsciously, hoped for Christ. The ones of whom he speaks had more privileged revelation.

Brief attention may be drawn, however, to the case of Abel, Enoch and Lot, who prefigured Christ and who cooperated in the economy, but who did so in an unconscious manner. It raises the question whether there might be others in our own day who are part of the economy of salvation, but who are not conscious of that fact. However, it is impossible to respond with any validity to such a question from this material presented by Irenaeus. It is important to recognize that, while their particular prefigurement of future salvation was not conscious, they were already people accounted righteous because of their deliberate and voluntary response to God, and not simply on account of their unintentional, typical role.

Before leaving this subject, it may be interesting to notice the manner in which Irenaeus uses the metaphor of the Body of Christ with regard to the righteous of the Old Testament. Whereas Paul speaks of himself as filling up "what is still lacking in regard to Christ's afflictions" (Col 1:24), Irenaeus refers to the Old Testament prophets as members of the Body of Christ, prefiguring the suffering of Christ (AH IV,33,10).[32]

---

[32]Cf. F. W. Dillistone, *The Structure of the Divine Society* (London: Lutterworth Press, 1949), 88-89.

3. The Judgment of the unbeliever

Irenaeus clearly stated the converse of the salvation of the obedient believer, namely, the judgment of the unbeliever. This he describes as a righteous act on God's part, shutting out in darkness those who have chosen darkness rather than God's light, that is, those who do not believe (AH IV,6,5). The just grounds of God's judgment of the unbeliever are therefore twofold: the universality of divine revelation and the freedom of human beings in response to God's revelation (Cf. AH V,27,1; IV,6,5-6). This raises an important question, however. While God has revealed himself to all humankind through the Word, not all have had that revelation in equal measure. Irenaeus states that God had addressed all people in the same way (*similiter*), by means of the creation of the world and the formation of human nature (AH IV,6,6). That is not a problem. However, he goes on to say that "all the people (*universus populus*) likewise heard" the Word speak through the Law and the Prophets, and *all* saw the Father in the Son (AH IV,6,6). Did Irenaeus think that all the peoples of the Old Testament times had heard the Law and the Prophets, or does he mean by *populus* the people of Israel? The latter would seem to be the case. Likewise, there were many people in Jesus' day who did not see the incarnate Son. Irenaeus recognized that even in his own day there were barbarians who had not had the Scriptures, but they did have the oral proclamation of the Church (AH IV,24,2; cf. III,4,2). It would appear that these statements must be considered in the context of the earlier discussion of judgment according to opportunity. No one is without some form of revelation, and all will be judged according to the degree of revelation which they have received (AH IV,28,1-2). It would seem, then, that the "all" who are addressed by the revelation in creation are a larger group than "all the people" who were addressed by the Law and the Prophets, and the "all" who saw the incarnate Son. The important point that Irenaeus is stressing is that *not all* believed the revelation at any of these levels. From the beginning, the Son has been present with his creation, revealing the Father to all, *in some manner or mode,* and all who do not "believe" are justly judged. Specifically, Irenaeus speaks of the judgment of those who experience God's providence in the sending of the sun and rain, which he distributes with equal kindness upon all, but who do not live in keeping with the bounty of God. These are people who have lived in luxury, but have blasphemed the God who provided for them, through a failure to attribute their blessing to him (AH III,25,4).

At least Plato was more religious than these deniers of divine providence (AH III,25,5), and some of the heathen Gentiles were moved by God's providence to call the Maker of the universe the Father (AH III,25,1). Rejection of God's providence, which all people experience, is clearly condemning (Cf. AH IV,26,6; Proof 8). Is it possible, then, that a grateful recognition of God's providence by those who do not know of Christ would be saving? (If so, would this be a parallel to accepting one's "own limited transcendence," or accepting oneself "in freedom as he is," in "unreserved faithfulness to his own moral conscience," in the scheme of Rahner?) Irenaeus's statements elsewhere, regarding the co-extensiveness of the saving work of the Holy Spirit with the institutional Church, and his emphasis on faith in Christ, seem to address the situation of those who had these means of revelation available. Because of his assumptions regarding the evangelization of the world, he does not specifically address the condition of those who may have been beyond the reach of the Church (or of Israel, in the Old Testament) or without knowledge of Christ. He neither

assumes nor explicitly denies the salvation of Plato.
However, it seems highly improbable that he is intending
to indicate a salvation of the aforementioned "Gentiles."
Again, however, those were people who had rejected
further revelation. What if they had had no revelation
beyond creation and providence?

Irenaeus is clear regarding the judgment of those
who have revelation of the Son and who do not believe in
him. This includes those who hold to untrue doctrine
regarding the nature of Christ Jesus, denying his divinity. Such people cut themselves off from incorruptibility
and immortality, which could come to people only
through the incarnation of the Word, uniting humanity
to God (AH III,19,1; cf. III,21,9). To deny the "rule of
truth," that core of revealed truth expressed in the belief
in one God, Creator of heaven and earth, and one Christ,
the Son of God, is to be "self-condemned" and to resist
and oppose one's own salvation (AH III,1,2; Cf. III,17,4).
Those who oppose the truth and who lead others away
from the Church shall be punished to hell (AH IV,26,2;
cf. III,4,2; IV, Pref. 4). The coming of the Son therefore
had a twofold effect: it results in the resurrection of those
who believe in him and in the condemnation of those who
do not believe. The Son comes in the same manner for all
people, but his coming effects the separation of the
believing from the unbelieving (AH V,27,1). An aspect of
the judgment of the unbelieving is God's judicial blinding
of those who reject his light. Those who do not believe,
choosing darkness rather than light, are abandoned by
God to their darkness (AH IV,29,1-2).

C. Concluding Observations

It is clear that Irenaeus was not a universalist.
Whatever tendencies to universalism may be found in his
Christology are firmly denied when he discusses the

destiny of humankind. There are two destinies between which all people must choose: life, incorruptibility, and the vision of God; or eternal death and separation from God. God's justice in the judgment of some people is grounded in the universality of his self-revelation and on the freedom with which all people choose to believe in God or not to do so. Salvation is the end of those who believe, that is, who accept the rule of truth, the apostolic tradition proclaimed by the Church, and who do God's will. They participate in all the benefits of the redemptive work of the incarnate Son, particularly the adoptive knowledge of God which leads to vision of the Father.

On the other hand, the lot of unbelievers is judgment. Their condemnation is proportionate to the revelation they have received and the blessing of God that they have experienced. However, no one is without some revelation and experience of God. All have had revelation of God the Creator, by the Word, in his creation of the world and of humans themselves. All have experienced the goodness of God in his providential care for his creatures, which is designed to lead them to repentance (Proof 8). Saving faith is defined in very explicit terms, and with Christ clearly its object, on the assumption, however, that all have received sufficient revelation to make such a response, if they choose. Irenaeus does not discuss the justice of God's judgment of people who did not believe in Christ because they did not know him. This may have been because of an assumption that there were no such people (cf. Chapter 3). However, it is even more readily explained by the context of Irenaeus's polemic. He was contending with heretics, people who distorted the truth and led others astray. His concern was to demonstrate that no one can reject Christ with impunity. His discussion of natural revelation and the experience of divine providence seems directed toward showing that people can reject God at every level of revelation, and that some rejected even the most basic revelation of God's creatorship and of the benevolence of his providence. However, in Irenaeus's view, these were people who also had more specific Christological revelation, and therefore Irenaeus did not discuss the destiny of people who had only natural revelation.

Irenaeus describes saving faith as explicit and Christological. He describes rejection of Christ as definitely damnable. He recognizes degrees of judgment appropriate to one's experience of God. He attributes people's just judgment to their own rejection of revelation. It does not seem that one can clearly conclude from all of this what Irenaeus would have to say about the justice of the condemnation of people who had no knowledge of Christ. He does indicate, however, that "to those who believe and follow him he [God] gives a fuller and greater illumination of the mind" (AH IV,29,1). One can only conclude that there is a responsiveness on God's part to human response to the divine initiative in revelation. Those who reject God's light are blinded and those who accept it are given a greater capacity to look upon it. One can infer that, if pagans were to believe in the one God, the Creator, through the Word's revelation in creation, and were not to blind themselves to that revelation, their capacity for the knowledge of God would be graciously expanded. Irenaeus gives no indication, however, that such response would elicit further revelation such as special theophanies, deathbed encounters with Christ, or opportunities to "meet" Christ after death. These questions are simply beyond Irenaeus's frame of reference.[33]

---

[33]"Anonymous Christianity" needs none of these special opportunities to know Christ, but theologians who demand explicit faith sometimes speak in these terms. Karl-Heinz Weger, discussing the

dogma that *extra ecclesiam nulla salus,* suggests that:
> This dogmatic pronouncement was made when the one Christian faith was universally accepted by all men in what was geographically a very small world. It was known that other people existed elsewhere, but the people were, as it were, "curiosities", and did not present the Church with any real problem of missionary work. It was possible for the salvation of these people to be regarded as taking place *in a miraculous way* [italics supplied] *Karl Rahner: An Introduction to His Theology* [New York: Seabury Press, 1980], 96).

However, Rahner writes:
> In order to bring divine revelation to a non-Christian who is not reached by Christian preaching, there have indeed been suggested private revelations or extraordinary illumination, especially at the hour of death, and such things as this. But prescinding from the fact that these are arbitrary and impossible postulates, and that it is impossible to see why they may only be allowed to play a role in special and extraordinary cases, such means as this contradict the basic character of Christian revelation as well as man's nature (*Foundations of Christian Faith. An Introduction to the Idea of Christianity,* trans. William V. Dych [New York: Seabury Press, 1978], 314).

In Rahner's discussion of death, he seems to suggest that death itself might be an act of faith and that, by the grace of Christ, the pagan may be able to die such a death. When a person "positively accepts the comprehensive sense of his existence even in the face of the dark appearance of senseless death," this "can and must necessarily be called an act of faith." It could be performed only by virtue of the grace of Christ (*On the Theology of Death,* trans. Charles H. Henkey [London: Nelson, 1961], 96). Rahner claims that the "offer of a concrete opportunity for men to secure supernatural salvation through their own acts has to be conceived ... in such a way that one should be able to comprehend it without relying on miraculous events" (ibid., 100). He asks whether a "good death" may occur, "as an historical demonstrable reality, in the actual, spiritual history of humanity, elsewhere than in Christianity," and answers in the negative (ibid., 120). "Other than a Christian, nobody can do this (naturally, those who are Christian in spirit though not in name should be included here, provided they do not die for anything opposed to Christianity)" (ibid.). Presumably, these are the "anonymous Christians," and Rahner therefore seems to say that "anonymous Christians" can die a "Christian death" which is an act of faith, just

A. Luneau generalizes from his study of the early Fathers that "the Fathers believed in the salvation of all men of good will, at least implicitly."[34] On the other hand, Gustave Martelet is convinced that no Father, however optimistic he had been in regard to Gospel preparation, would have been prepared to dispense the pagans from an explicit conversion to the Lord. They would have to convert to be saved.[35] Regarding those who had explicit contact with Christianity, Martelet's

---

as they can make an act of faith, in life, by accepting their absolute transcendence.

J. A. di Noia has proposed the concept of "prospective affiliation" with the Church as better than Rahner's idea of a "hidden member-ship." He suggests:

Rather than attributing an implausible implicit faith in Christ to the members of other religious communities, a theology of religions employing the concept of prospective affiliation could assert that non-Christians will have opportunity to acknowledge Christ in the future. This opportunity may come to them in the course of their lives here on earth or in the course of their entrance into the life to come. Recent discussions of the theology of death and purgatory suggest that the postulation of such an opportunity is more compatible with central Catholic doctrines than has sometimes been thought in the past ("Implicit Faith, General Revelation and the State of Non-Christians," *Thom* 47 [April 1983]:240).

On the possibility of attaining salvation at the moment of death, see also Joseph Segers ("The True Religion and Religions," *CTTW* 28 [January-April 1983]:76-78); and Robert M. Pelagia ("The Theory of the Moment of Full Vision at Death," *CTTW* 28 [January-April 1983]:79-81). Cf. also George Lindbeck on confrontation with Christ at death and the eschatological understanding of salvation ("*Fides ex auditu* and the Salvation of Non-Christians: Contemporary Catholic and Protestant Positions," in *The Gospel and the Ambiguity of the Church*, ed. Vilmos Vashta [Philadelphia: Fortress Press, 1974], 115-16).

[34]A. Luneau, "Pour aider au dialogue: Les Pères et les religions non-chrétiennes," *NRT* 89 (November 1967):923.

[35]Gustave Martelet, *Les idées maîtresses de Vatican II. Introduction à l'esprit du Concile* (Desclée de Brouwer, 1966), 47-48.

generalization is certainly true of Irenaeus. It is not clear, however, what Irenaeus would have said about those without knowledge of the incarnate Word. His whole scheme of the economy of salvation describes a line of progressive revelation moving humanity towards vision of the Father, and he does not really address the situation of the person who is limited to revelation at the level of creation and providence. He speaks with some favor of pagans who are moved by God's providence to recognize their Creator, but the only ones whose salvation he specifically discusses are those who believe on account of the preaching of the Church. His whole focus in regard to divine judgment is on those who have known Christ and have rejected him.

9. CONCLUSION

It is possible now to draw together the results of the investigation that has been made of the salvation of the unevangelized, in the theology of Irenaeus. The question of the state of the non-Christian, particularly of the individual who has not had opportunity to learn of God as revealed in Christ, is of great importance. In the face of the apparent failure of Christian missions to reach larger groups of people with the Gospel, various theories have been developed to describe the situation of the non-Christian in relationship to divine revelation, and to divine grace in general. In the quest for a proper perspective on the non-Christian, and on non-Christian religions, there has been a considerable amount of interest in the writings of the early Church Fathers. Frequently, one encounters the suggestion that a more positive view is found in those early centuries than in more recent Christian theology.

One theory that has received a great deal of attention, and that still has many ardent proponents, is the concept of "anonymous Christianity," which has been most thoroughly expounded by Karl Rahner. There are writers who have claimed seeds of this idea in the second- and third-centuries, citing particularly Justin, Irenaeus, and Clement of Alexandria. It has been the purpose of this study, therefore, to examine the views of Irenaeus regarding divine revelation, particularly as it affects the unevangelized. Given the attempts to claim Irenaeus as an antecedent of the theology of "anonymous Christianity," special attention has been devoted to a comparison of Irenaeus's theology with that modern view of divine revelation and the non-Christian. However, the study made of Irenaeus could easily be compared with other theories now being proposed. This will be done only to a very limited extent in these final pages.

In this concluding chapter, a summary will be made of Irenaeus's doctrine of divine revelation and the non-Christian. Then a specific comparison will be made of Irenaeus's view with the theology of "anonymous Christianity" as one modern example of a perspective that has specifically been claimed by some writers (though not by Rahner himself) as having antecedence in Irenaeus.

A. A Summary of Irenaeus's Doctrine of Divine Revelation and the Salvation of the Unevangelized

1. The context

In order to do justice to Irenaeus's theological formulation, it is important to understand the context within which Irenaeus was thinking and working. This will help to keep us from imposing upon Irenaeus a framework which was alien to his own context.

a. The struggle with Gnosticism

The primary reference point of Irenaeus's theological work was his apologetic against the Gnostic heretics. Their doctrine of divine revelation and the non-Christian is the foil for Irenaeus's perspective. The Gnostic view against which Irenaeus contended was, as its very name indicates, a claim to special knowledge. They described themselves as a privileged class (the "spiritual") who possessed perfect knowledge of God and

had been initiated into the mysteries by Achamoth.[1]
They appealed to the Scriptures to support their system
of truth but also claimed secret traditions (a "living
voice") handed down to them from Christ and the
apostles. In this way, they represented themselves as
having a knowledge of truth which was superior to that
of Irenaeus and the Church which he represented.

The Gnostic doctrine of salvation was largely one
of salvation by knowledge. In fact, knowledge was not
only the major instrument of salvation; it was itself the
form in which the goal of salvation is possessed. The
situation was complicated, however, by an anthropology
that distinguished between three kinds of people. Salvation was impossible for the lowest level—the hylic or
material—by reason of their materiality. The metaphysical dualism of the Gnostics assumed the inherent evil of
matter. The class in which Irenaeus, and most of the
Church, was placed was the psychical. These are people
whose destiny was not already determined. They do not
have perfect knowledge but they may be saved through
good works and faith. The spiritual are those who possess
grace by virtue of their relationship to the Aeons, and
whose salvation is ensured by their nature, apart from
good works on their part, but on the assumption that
they possess perfect knowledge.

The Gnostics had little to say about paganism,
but they did not consider pagan religions to have
attained the truth about God. The primary target of
Gnosticism was not the pagan religions but the larger
Christian community. It was probably assumed that the
pagan was in the class of the material, and hence in a
hopeless condition. Those in the Church were psychical

---

[1]Since this is largely a summary of material documented in
previous chapters, references for summary statements will not be
cited.

and therefore worth the efforts made to bring them to knowledge of the truth.

b. The success of the Christian mission

It has been demonstrated that Irenaeus believed that in the time of the apostles, the world had been evangelized, in fulfillment of Old Testament prophecy and in obedience to the commission of Christ. Irenaeus viewed the Church in his own day as spread throughout the whole world with a unity of faith that was preached everywhere. This assumption on the part of Irenaeus is extremely important to this study. Because Irenaeus was wrong in this perception, the reader may be tempted to dismiss his statements on the extent of evangelization as hyperbole, and to suggest that this was not really the perspective from which Irenaeus viewed the unevangelized. However, it has been demonstrated that the assumption clearly underlay Irenaeus's understanding of the just judgment of the unbeliever. Those who are condemned are justly punished because they personally rejected the Gospel. Clearly, Irenaeus assumed that all people had salvific revelation. Yet he taught that salvation was restricted only to the Church in its institutional form. No one could be saved apart from the Church, but it was assumed that everyone had the opportunity to be saved, and those who did not believe were therefore culpable. Thus, his belief in the success of the Christian mission is evident, not only from his explicit statements regarding the spread of the Church, but even more significantly from his theology of salvation and judgment.

We have shown that Irenaeus's view was inaccurate, but what matters for this study is that he thought it was correct. Jean Daniélou therefore observes correctly that "Irenaeus's ecclesiastical frontiers are identical with

those of the known world in his day."[2] The difference
between Irenaeus's view of the success of the Christian
mission and the situation as we see it in our own day is
definitely a limiting factor in any comparison between
Irenaeus's view of divine revelation and the non-Christian and modern theories on the subject.

2. The gracious self-revelation of the transcendent Father

Irenaeus stressed the transcendence of God no
less than the Gnostics did, but he denied the Father's
complete unknowability. Though God is incomprehensible
in his essence and greatness, he has graciously made
himself known to humankind in his love and great
goodness. This is particularly important because the
knowledge or vision of God is life-giving. It is, in fact, the
ultimate goal of human life. To see God is to live, to have
immortality and incorruptibility. This is why it is so
important that God chose to reveal himself to human
beings, and that he does so out of a continual good will
toward humanity. Consequently, the Father has revealed
himself, in some way, to *all* people.

Most basically, God has revealed himself through
his creative work and through his continual providence
over the affairs of the world which he created. In particular, God has demonstrated his power, wisdom and
goodness by these means. It is possible for people, by
their natural reasoning capacity, to attain knowledge of
God the Creator by means of creation. However, Irenaeus
distinguishes between the knowledge achieved in this

---

[2]Jean Daniélou, *Gospel Message and Hellenistic Culture: A History
of Early Christian Doctrine Before the Council of Nicaea*, trans. and
ed. John Austin Baker (Philadelphia: Westminster, 1973), 2:150.

way, and the saving knowledge, which is the experience
only of those who are inwardly illumined by the Word.

3. The exclusive mediation by the Son

To know the Father, in the full and salvific sense,
the Son's work as mediator is essential. There is no way
for people to know the Father except as the Son reveals
him. So interrelated are the Father and the Son that any
manifestation of the Son gives knowledge of both the
Father and the Son. Thus, there has been a progressive
self-manifestation of God to humanity, with the Son
involved as exclusive mediator at every stage of that
revelation. The Son was involved in the divine work of
creation and continues active in providence. He is
continually present with his creatures, revealing the
Father to them from the beginning, and not only in his
incarnation. Nowhere is this work of the Son more
intriguingly described than in the passages that describe
the "cosmic cross." The Word is invisibly imprinted upon
the world, in the form of a cross, with his arms stretched
out to gather the world together from one extreme to the
other. He gives cohesion to all created things by his
immanence in the creation. All beings participate in the
cosmic cross. Furthermore, the cosmic cross has an
orientation to the salvation of the dispersed elements.
This activity of the Word leads to the knowledge of the
Father, being the principle not only of a physical cohesion, but also of a moral and supernatural unity. The
visible crucifixion of the incarnate Word thus has a
particular appropriateness because it manifests that all
things participate in the invisible cross.

In addition to the natural revelation of the Father
by the Son, Irenaeus details the theophanic appearances
of the Son to individuals of the Old Testament: Adam,
Cain, Noah, Abraham, Jacob, Moses, and others. From

the beginning, therefore, the Word had a certain visibility
and was "seen" even by people of the Old Testament. He
also spoke through the prophets, both in their preaching
and in their writings. The Word was thus implanted or
inseminated in the prophetic announcements of the Old
Testament, and the Church reaps the fruit of that
sowing. The great value of the Old Testament Scriptures
in evangelism of the Jews is therefore obvious. The
experiences of Peter, Cornelius and the Ethiopian eunuch
all evidence the benefit of this knowledge of the Word
through the Old Testament Scriptures, which fairly easily
grew into recognition of Jesus as the fulfillment of those
Old Testament prophecies. Evangelization of the Gentiles
was more difficult precisely because of the lack of evan-
gelistic preparation. The visit of Christ to the subterranean regions, after his death, was also a form of
reaping the fruit which had been sown in his various
modes of revelation in the Old Testament. There, He
appeared to those who had anticipated his coming, and
declared to them the good news of his coming, namely,
the remission of sins for those who had believed in him.

The coming of the Word in the flesh brought an
even more privileged revelation of the same Word who
had been revealing himself and the Father from the
beginning. This was an important stage in the economy
of salvation, because by means of the Incarnation, the
flesh is accustomed to see God and God is accustomed to
live with human beings. Thus progress is made toward
the eventual vision of God by humankind. The significance of the Incarnation is also demonstrated by means
of the concept of recapitulation. Christ recapitulated the
history of humanity in himself and thus procured salvation for humankind. Passing through all the ages of life,
he restored "all people" to communion with God. He
recapitulated in himself all the nations dispersed from

Adam onwards, and all the languages and generations of humankind. The salvific importance of the Incarnation is thus immense. Notice was taken earlier of the tendency to universalism in Irenaeus's doctrine of recapitulation, a tendency which was followed to that conclusion by Origen. However, Irenaeus does not pursue the concept to that conclusion. It would appear that in the recapitulatory work of Christ, involving both the Incarnation and the Passion, the objective salvation of humankind is accomplished, but individuals' personal participation in the saving fruit of that work depends upon their own response to divine revelation. No one could be saved without the recapitulatory work of Christ, but it does not automatically ensure the salvation of anyone.

The final stage of the Son's preparation of humanity for vision of the Father will be his millennial reign, following his second coming. This period is an important stage in the Irenaean scheme. During that time, the resurrected righteous of both Testaments will reign on earth with Christ and prepare themselves, through the contemplation of the Son, for the immediate vision of the Father in heaven. Both those who lived before the Incarnation and desired to see Christ and those who have believed in Christ since he ascended to the Father will have the opportunity to know Christ in the flesh, and will be made ready to see the Father. Following the millennium, the saved will enter into an eternity with the Father, during which time they will continue to grow in their love and knowledge, even in its direct vision, through the mediation of the Son. Those who were called early in the economy of salvation will receive the same reward (incorruptibility) as those who were called later.

4. The ministry of the Holy Spirit

Attention has been given to the role of the Spirit in preparing humanity for the knowledge of the Father through the Son. He was active with the Word in creation and providence, as Wisdom, one of the two hands of the Father. He spoke through the prophets as they declared the Son to their generation, empowered the Son for his ministry, and was later sent by the Son to empower the disciples for the evangelization of the nations. It is the work of the Spirit to lead people to the Son, who presents them to the Father. Thus, just as it is impossible to approach the Father apart from the Word, it is likewise impossible to see the Son without the Spirit. The Spirit continues to speak through the New Testament Scriptures, but especially works in and through the Church. Indeed, his saving work is restricted to the Church, so that where the Spirit is the Church is found, and where the Church exists the Spirit is present and active.[3]

5. The faithful proclamation of divine revelation in the Church

Faced with the threat of Gnostic heresy and its claim to a "living voice," Irenaeus took refuge in the Church as recipient of the apostolic tradition. The revelation that the Father has made of himself by means of the Son is now to be found in the Church, where the Holy Spirit has placed gifted people, whom he enables to understand the revelation and to faithfully proclaim it.

---

[3]The work of the Holy Spirit is given much attention in recent discussion of the state of the unevangelized. For this reason, the paucity of material in Irenaeus is somewhat disappointing. However, it is not surprising when one considers the time in which he wrote and the Gnostic context which he addressed.

The apostles had had a privileged position, being instructed personally by Christ and then inspired by the Holy Spirit for the recording of divine revelation, as well as empowered for its proclamation. They were instrumental in starting churches made up of those who believed in Christ and were baptized in the name of the Father, Son and Holy Spirit, and they handed those churches on to other people of their choosing. It was Irenaeus's conviction that these successors of the apostles—the presbyters or bishops of the churches—were the ones whose testimony to divine revelation was to be believed. When there was a question regarding the truth, it was to these people that one ought to listen, since they are the ones to whom the apostles handed on the truth. This objective truth that was handed down (*tradere*) was therefore designated the "tradition" or the "rule of truth." Its authenticity was recognizable by the consensus of the testimony of the churches all over the world to this core of truth. A particularly significant witness was to be found in the church at Rome, which had a normative role for Irenaeus, as a church whose presbyters could be traced back to Peter and Paul, and one which was a meeting point of Christians traveling from all over the world.

For those who lived in Irenaeus's day and afterwards, the divine revelation is therefore to be found in the Church. Not only is the testimony to truth clearly found there, but it is in and through the Church alone that the Holy Spirit carries out his saving operations. To be outside of the Church, as an institution led by the successors of the apostles, would be to be outside of the Holy Spirit and therefore separated from all his life-giving work. *Since no one knows the Father except by means of revelation by the Son, and no one sees the Son except by the ministry of the Holy Spirit, and no one has the Holy Spirit except those who are a part of the Church, participation in the institutional Church (that is, the*

visible Church led by the apostolic successors) becomes the
sine qua non for knowledge of the Father.

6. The necessity of human response to divine revelation

Irenaeus foresaw two possible destinies for
people: the vision of God, which is life, or separation from
God's light, which is darkness and death. The choice
between these destinies rests squarely with the individual. God has manifested himself to all people, and given
to all the capacity to believe in him. Those who believe in
the Father and the Son and who follow God, as Abraham
(the father of the faithful) had done, will be saved. They
receive the adoption as children and, provided they stead-
fastly maintain their faith, they will progress toward the
vision of the Father. Those who respond to the revelation
of God are given an increasing capacity to see the light of
God. Those who do not respond, however, blind themselves and are eventually abandoned by God to the
darkness which they have chosen for themselves. The
justice of God in their judgment is therefore evident
because it is the implementation of their freely chosen
self-condemnation. There is no deficiency in divine
revelation that causes the condemnation of any person.
The fault lies in the individual.

7. The non-Christian

Irenaeus never uses the term "non-Christian." He
speaks of the unbeliever, the Gentile, the pagan, the
ungodly, sinners, the unbelieving, and those who are
outside the Church. The existence of non-Christians,
designated by a variety of names, is thus perfectly clear.
They are those who neither acknowledge the Creator nor
recognize the providence of God from which they benefit;

those who serve the creature and worship "idols of demons"; those who know God's commandments but do not do them; those who do not believe in the Father and the Son; those who not only personally reject the truth concerning the one God (Father, Son and Holy Spirit), but who lead others astray with them.

Irenaeus had a very negative view of other religions. The gods they served were idols of demons. However, he recognized that not all people are equally privileged in regard to divine revelation. The Gentiles or pagans did not have the words of God. However, God's punishment of the unbeliever is appropriate to the grace that he had experienced and is graded according to the opportunity of divine revelation that he had received. This is a conclusion drawn from the statement of Jesus concerning the more severe judgment of those who rejected the incarnate Christ, as compared to the people of Sodom, who had less revelation. The justice of God is evident in that distinction.

This study has concluded that Irenaeus viewed the world as evangelized to such an extent that no one was without specific revelation of Christ. This is a very important aspect of his view of the non-Christian. He therefore views non-Christians as those who had deliberately rejected Christ and preferred the darkness of their own way. He says nothing of unbelievers before Christ, who were without sufficient revelation to believe and be saved. He does not speculate about those who had neither Christophanies nor typical anticipations of Christ because of being out of contact with Israel. Although the ungodly of Psalm 1:1 are people who do not "know God," nothing is said to imply that their lack of knowledge was due to insufficiency of revelation. Irenaeus's focus is on those who have the Scriptures and have heard the proclamation of the faith by the Church, but who have chosen not to believe.

8. The thesis of Irenaeus

In summary, the position of Irenaeus might be stated as follows:

1) God the Father has revealed himself to all people, from the beginning, by his two hands—the Word(Son) and Wisdom (Spirit)—in various modes. These included creation and providence, theophanic appearances of the pre-incarnate Logos; the preaching and writings of Moses and the prophets; the incarnate Word; the preaching and writings of the apostles, who handed on to their successors in the Church the truth taught by Christ, which they recollected and recorded with the help of the Holy Spirit; and the preaching of the Church all over the world, united in its testimony to the apostolic faith.

2) Jesus Christ, by his incarnation, obedient life, death and resurrection, has recapitulated the whole history of humankind and has, thereby, accomplished an objective reconciliation of all things to the Father. He will return to raise the righteous dead of all ages and will reign on earth with the resurrected righteous, who will become accustomed to the vision of God through their contact with the incarnate Word. At the close of that reign, the wicked will be judged, and the righteous will enter an eternity of ever-expanding knowledge of the Father.

3) Only those who believe in the Father and the Son, and do God's will, can be included among the righteous who will see the Father and live with him for eternity. People of all periods of history are saved on the same basis, and all will be prepared for eternity by the rule of Christ on earth, following his return.

4) The judgment of those who do not believe in order to be saved is a just act on God's part because of the universality of his self-revelation and because of the

freedom which all people had either to believe and to obey or to disbelieve and disobey.

5) An unbeliever or "non-Christian" would therefore be someone who had known of Christ, but who had not believed in him or "desired to see him," as the case might be. The non-Christian religions are a false worship, their gods being idols of demons. Therefore, non-Christians are not saved, and non-Christian religions are not means of salvation. The same would be true of those outside of Israel, in the Old Testament, or those who lived before the patriarchs and who were outside of the one economy which was carried forward by the revelatory activity of the pre-incarnate Logos. "Unbelievers," in all stages of the economy, were not saved.

B. Irenaeus and "Anonymous Christianity"

1. "Anonymous Christianity" restated

In order to determine to what extent Irenaeus may validly be cited as an early proponent of concepts that "anticipated" the theology of "anonymous Christianity," it will be helpful to summarize the main points of the theory as Karl Rahner has developed it.

Rahner's definition of the "anonymous Christian" is clear. He is "the pagan after the beginning of the Christian mission, who lives in the state of Christ's grace through faith, hope and love, yet who has no explicit knowledge of the fact that his life is oriented in grace-given salvation to Jesus Christ."[4] Basic to Rahner's theory are the following theses:

1) It is God's will that all people should be saved,

---

[4]"Observations on the Problem of the 'Anonymous Christian,'" in *TI*, (1979), 14:283.

a fact often described as the "universal salvific will of God."[5]

   2) In spite of original and personal sin, God therefore offers all people a "genuine possibility of attaining to their own salvation." This offer of salvation exists before the practical proclamation of it and makes possible both the proclamation and the acceptance of it.

   3) By the grace of God, all people have been given a "supernaturally elevated transcendence," a "transcendental experience of the absolute merciful closeness of God." Although people may not be distinctly conscious of this, it is a reality in the inmost core of their persons. In the "depth of his concrete nature," a human is a being who "looks for the presence of God himself." This is one side of the event of revelation.

   4) One can say that people have faith if they "freely accept their own unlimited transcendence," which is graciously directed toward God. When people accept themselves in freedom as they are, in faithfulness to their own moral conscience, they are said to accept divine revelation (i.e., the *a priori* awareness of humanity) in faith.

   5) The incarnation of the Word constituted a call to the human race to "share the life of God supernaturally." Because of the Incarnation, humanity has already "become ontologically the real sanctification of individual men by grace and also the people of the children of God." By virtue of this "consecration," they are already a "people of God which extends as far as humanity itself."

   6) Because of this ontological reality brought into being by the Incarnation, the Church is a twofold reality. In addition to the established juridical organization, one

---

   [5]A fuller exposition of this summary, with source documentation, is found in Chapter 1.

can also describe the Church as "humanity consecrated by Incarnation." The institutional Church is thus the "concrete historical manifestation of the salvation which is achieved by the grace of God throughout humanity." It is the explicit expression of what is present as a hidden reality outside the visible Church.

7) Hence, people who "accept the concrete reality of their nature totally, in a free act of a supernatural justification by faith and love," are to be considered members of the Church. They have personally accepted (albeit unconsciously) the membership of the people of God which is already a fact on the historical plane. This is not merely membership in an "invisible" Church. It is an "invisible" belonging to the "visible" Church by grace, and it has a "visible relation" to that Church even when it is not constituted by baptism, or by an "externally verifiable profession of the faith."

8) Non-Christian religions before Christ were, in principle, willed by God as legitimate ways of salvation. The coming of Christ, and his death and resurrection, made these religions obsolete. However, non-Christian religions may maintain some validity after the Incarnation, for individuals who have not been presented with the message of Christ so clearly that rejection of that message as the way of salvation offered by God would be a grave fault. Therefore, prior to that point at which the claims of Christ are clearly presented and understood, the non-Christian religion, as a way of salvation accepted from the genuine motives of conscience, does lead one to God.

2. Anticipations in Irenaeus?

To what extent is it valid to speak of Irenaeus as anticipating the theology of "anonymous Christianity"?

a. Misleading statement

It is clear from the careful study that has been made of Irenaeus's doctrine of revelation that such a statement could be very misleading. The reader of previously cited authors who point to Irenaeus as anticipating "anonymous Christianity" is likely to assume a much closer affinity between Irenaeus and the theology of "anonymous Christianity" than is actually the case. From the analysis that has been made of Irenaeus's position, as summarized above, it is clear that the conclusions which Irenaeus himself reached closely resemble the motivations that have traditionally stimulated missionary activity.[6] To cite as an antecedent of "anonymous Christianity" a man who believed that only those are saved who are members of the institutional Church, and who expressly confess its rule of truth, would seem a highly questionable appeal to history. In short, any reference to Irenaeus as an "antecedent," a "forerunner," or an "anticipator" of modern optimism concerning the state of the non-Christian (such as one finds in the theory of "anonymous Christianity") will have to be very cautiously worded.

There are, perhaps, two lines of approach which might be taken to the theology of Irenaeus in order to find legitimate "antecedence." Both of these will be examined.

1) Irenaeus did not address the situation which is addressed by the theology of "anonymous Christianity," because he was not conscious of significant groups of

---

[6]Cf. Walbert Bühlmann's description of the missionary seal which grew out of the motivation to save the souls of pagans who were going to hell unless they heard and believed the Gospel (*God's Chosen Peoples*, trans. Robert R. Barr [Maryknoll, New York: Orbis Books, 1982], 106-7).

people without knowledge of Christ through the Church's witness. However, if the existence of unevangelized peoples is assumed, *inferences* could be drawn from the theological framework of Irenaeus which would point toward an optimism regarding the salvation of the "non-Christian."

2) Irenaeus was not himself a theologian of "anonymous Christianity." However, there are *aspects* of his theology which could be *developed in a different direction* from the one in which Irenaeus himself developed them, and which would then lead to different conclusions from the ones Irenaeus himself reached.

b. Inferences drawn from Irenaeus's system

It has been the contention of this study that Irenaeus described divine revelation and the non-Christian in the context of the assumption that the world had been evangelized. Those who were unbelievers had chosen to be so, in explicit rejection of the Christ whom the Church had proclaimed as Savior of the world. There is always some danger in speculation about "what would have happened if . . . ?" However, the question still has some validity, provided that the answers reached are recognized as tentative. The question which the modern student of Irenaeus may ask is: "What would Irenaeus have concluded about the salvation or judgment of the unbeliever, if he had started from the recognition that there are large groups of people who have never had the message of Christ presented to them in an intelligible fashion?"

Irenaeus argued that God's judgment of the unbeliever (the "non-Christian") was just, because the unbeliever had had the revelation concerning Christ and had rejected it. But what if there were unbelievers who had not had the revelation of the incarnate Word as proclaimed by the Church?

1) A Reformed direction? Might Irenaeus have followed the direction taken by a large part of the Reformed tradition, with its focus on Romans 1, 2, and 5? This view proposes that, by virtue of the solidarity of the human race in Adam (because of a federal headship or because of corporate solidarity, not because of "substantial" or "realistic" unity), all human beings sinned in Adam (Romans 5). That original sin included original guilt, and not only a tendency to personal sin and guilt. God has revealed himself to all, in creation (Romans 1:19-20), and has written his law on their hearts, and given them an inner witness to it, in conscience (Romans 2:15). However, because of the natural depravity of fallen humanity, which affects every aspect of their being, they suppress God's revelation, and worship the creature rather than the Creator, and they disobey God's law written on their hearts. The revelation in nature results only in condemnation because 1) sinful people always distort it idolatrously, and 2) it does not reveal Christ, faith in whom is necessary for salvation. Consequently, the non-Christian who does not hear of Christ is justly judged. The justice of that judgment, however, is not based on an assumption that non-Christians had adequate revelation to believe unto salvation, but on the ground of their unbelief and disobedience at the level of natural revelation, for which they are culpable because of a self-incurred inability in Adam.[7]

This direction appears unlikely. Although it has been demonstrated that Irenaeus had an understanding

---

[7]Cf. Bruce Demarest's review of the positions of Luther, Calvin and the Puritans on general revelation and its value for salvation. *General Revelation: Historical Views and Contemporary Issues* (Grand Rapids: Zondervan, 1982), 43-73.

of original sin, that was certainly not a major consideration for him, and would not likely be a starting point in defending the justice of divine judgment of the non-Christian. Irenaeus did not emphasize the insufficiency of natural revelation, as Reformed theology has done. Assuming that all people had more than natural revelation, he nonetheless gave it a positive importance, and spoke of the necessity of faith with regard to it. Furthermore, Irenaeus's emphasis on free will, and his reaction to Gnostic determinism, made him an unlikely "antecedent" of Reformed (predestinarian) theology.

An interesting attempt has been made to develop a more hopeful view of the salvation of "non-Christians" within the framework of traditional Reformed theology.[8] Neal Punt has suggested that the traditional Reformed manner of approaching the doctrine of election has been incorrect. The usual assumption has been that everyone is lost except those whom Scripture declares to be elect, namely, those who believe in Christ. Punt suggests that we ought rather to assume the election of everyone, unless Scripture specifically states otherwise. Rejection of Christ would thus be a clear sign of lostness (non-election or reprobation), but the position of those who do not know of Christ would be more hopeful than in the traditional formula as summarized above.

Faith in Christ is seen as the response of the elect who hear of Christ. It has, therefore, a conditional necessity (not unlike Rahner's conditional necessity of Church membership). The elect who do not hear the Gospel respond positively in regard to the revelation that they have received. The outcome is therefore similar to that discussed below, under B,2,b,2), but it begins from a Reformed concept of sovereign, divine election. Most of

---

[8]Neal Punt, *Unconditional Good News: Toward an Understanding of Biblical Universalism* (Grand Rapids: Eerdmans, 1980).

those who adopt the position described below would not work within the framework of unconditional election. They would be more likely to speak of an election based on God's foreknowledge. Irenaeus himself speaks of God's relationship to the unbelief of the non-Christian in terms of foreknowledge, and not of reprobation. A similarity to the work of Karl Barth is evident in regard to the concept of corporate, universal election in Christ.

Punt's work reminds one of the position of Ulrich Zwingli, in the sixteenth century. Zwingli also started with a strong doctrine of election and predestination as the cause of salvation. It is manifested in outward signs, and those signs differ according to one's situation. The pagans of antiquity, and those who have not had opportunity to hear the Gospel, may also be among the elect, because they will be judged on a different basis from those who have had Gospel revelation. Zwingli spoke hopefully, for instance, of the situation of Seneca or Socrates.[9] It is interesting to find this kind of optimism regarding the salvation of the non-Christian in a key Reformation figure.

2) Salvation on the basis of response to revelation at whatever level it is received? Irenaeus would not have surrendered his conviction of the justice of God's judgment of the unbeliever. The justice of God was too fundamental an aspect of the nature of God to be surrendered, and was viewed in coordination with his goodness. Irenaeus believed that people were judged according to their privilege or opportunity. This was a recognition that there are gradations within the modes of divine revelation. However, the assumption was that no

---

[9]Cf. Justo L. González, *A History of Christian Thought,* vol. 3: *From the Protestant Reformation to the Twentieth Century* (New York: Abingdon, 1975), 69, citing G. W. Locher, "Die Praëdestinations-lehre Huldrych Zwinglis," *TZ* 12 [1956]:526-48).

one was below the level of salvific revelation. If Irenaeus had recognized people who have no more than natural revelation, would he have accepted that natural revelation as sufficient to the salvation of those who receive no more? We can only speculate. It is significant, however, that Irenaeus viewed the natural revelation as mediated by the Son. Although it was possible to come to knowledge of God as Creator by reason alone, it was only by a special illumination of the Word that faith was possible, in response to that revelation. Is it possible to conceive that (given a different context) Irenaeus might have accepted the possibility of salvation by a Word-illumined response to natural revelation? If one considers only Irenaeus's discussion of natural revelation, such a direction is not conceivable. He did regard the revelation in creation, at least germinally, as salvific, and he paralleled it to the greater privilege of revelation in the incarnate Word. Within the Irenaean framework, a person saved in such a case would no doubt be resurrected at the return of Christ and would have the millennium to become accustomed to the knowledge of the Son, and to be prepared thereby for the vision of the Father. However, this view would have called for considerable change in other areas of Irenaeus's theology. He would have had to modify considerably his concept of the Spirit's work in salvation, and of the role of the institutional Church. However, Irenaeus developed his strong emphasis on saving revelation within the scope of the institutional Church in response to the threat of Gnostic schismatics. In a different context, he might have taken a different turn.

This perspective has a theological simplicity that is still far from "anonymous Christianity." It sees no need to classify the saved as "anonymous Christians," accepting these people as saved on the ground of Christ's work, through a believing response to the light that they had.

It does not describe this as a form of "implicit faith," or define it as an invisible form of membership in the visible Church. The assumption is simply made that explicit faith in Christ and membership in the Church are the means of salvation for those who know Christ and the Church, but that those who do not have that privilege are accepted on the basis of the response they make to the revelation that they do have. Among Protestant laypeople, this is a common view,[10] but it would call for considerable dislocation in Irenaeus's system to attribute the "seeds" of such a view to him.

3) Toward "anonymous Christianity"? Irenaeus did view God as willing the salvation of all people, and as offering to all people a possibility of salvation. From there on, Irenaeus and "anonymous Christianity" move in different directions, because of a difference in assumptions regarding the state of the evangelization of the world. Faith, for Irenaeus, has nothing to do with accepting one's own transcendence. It is recognition of the Creatorship of God, gratitude for his

---

[10]Quite commonly, however, those who place a positive value on the response of the pagan to natural revelation deny the sufficiency of that response and contend that God will send them the Gospel in some way, to enable an explicit faith. Cf. Thomas Aquinas, who suggested that God could send an angel to those who have no contact with Gospel messengers (cited by Henry van Straelen, *Ouverture à l'autre laquelle? L'apostolat missionnaire et le monde non chrétien* [Paris: Beauchesne, 1982], 215). Stanley Ellisen has argued for the theory that God sends the light of the Gospel to those who follow the light of creation, providence and conscience. He cites the case of the Ethiopian eunuch, Saul of Tarsus, and Cornelius of Caesarea as examples of this principle, representing the three streams of humanity from Ham, Shem, and Japheth ("Are Pagans Without Christ Really Lost?" *ConBapt* Spring 1983]:6-9). Likewise, Bruce Demarest argues for "the possibility that in exceptional circumstances God might choose to reveal himself in some extraordinary way, independently of Gospel proclamation" (*General Revelation*, 260-61).

providence, confession of the one God and Father of all, the one Son who is Lord and Savior of all, the one Holy Spirit, and the one economy of salvation. There is no need for a twofold reality of the Church, because all people have contact with the visible, institutional form. Membership is therefore defined in terms of that visibility. Non-Christian religions are not legitimate ways of salvation, because they all exist in conscious opposition to the Christian Church. If Irenaeus had known of non-Christian religions still without a hearing of the Gospel, he would more likely have postulated the salvation of individuals on account of a Word-illumined response to natural revelation, as under B,2,b,2) above, than because of revelational and salvific elements within the pagan religion. Irenaeus would not have called "Christian" any people who had no explicit knowledge of the fact that their life is "oriented in grace-given salvation to Jesus Christ."

In short, the differences of perspective are considerable, because of the difference of starting point. The "what if?" question is not, after all, a means by which one can demonstrate "antecedence" of "anonymous Christianity" with any degree of certainty.

4) Toward the even greater optimism of pluralistic soteriologies? Among those who have spoken approvingly of the Patristic period, for its perspective on revelation and salvation, is Raimundo Panikkar. He suggests that Christian theology has generally tried to "accentuate the differences between Christianity and the 'non-Christian' religions" but that "in the Patristic period things were different."[11] Panikkar himself goes beyond "anonymous Christianity" with regard to the

---

[11]*The Unknown Christ of Hinduism: Towards an Ecumenical Christophany*, revised and enlarged edition (Maryknoll, New York: Orbis Books, 1981), 164.

salvific role that he attributes to Hinduism and, by
extension, to other non-Christian religions. He makes
occasional use of Rahner's theology in forming his own
perspective, but his approach is not just an Asian model
of "anonymous Christianity." Panikkar contends that "it
is acceptable to Hindus to be 'anonymous Christians,'
provided one also admits that Christians are 'anonymous
Hindus.'"[12] Interestingly, Rahner himself was once
asked by a well-known Japanese philosopher: "What
would you say to my treating you as an anonymous Zen
Buddhist?" Rahner replied:

> You may and should do so from your point of view; I feel myself
> honored by such an interpretation, even if I am obliged to regard
> you as being in error if I assume that, correctly understood, to be
> a genuine Zen Buddhist is identical with being a genuine Chris-
> tian, in the sense directly and properly intended by such state-
> ments.[13]

The "proper sense" which Rahner intends is
different from the sense in which Panikkar would use the
term. For Rahner, there can come a point when the
knowledge which non-Christians have of the message of
Christ is such that it would be a "grave fault" for them to
reject it any longer "as the way of salvation offered by
God and as the fulfillment that goes beyond anything
that" was offered by their former religion.[14] Rahner thus
reserves an absoluteness to Christianity that transcends
the relative value of non-Christian religions which may
nonetheless lead an individual to God, in the period prior
to the coming of the message of Christ to that individual.
For Panikkar, on the other hand, Christianity and

---

[12]*The Unknown Christ*, 13.

[13]"The One Christ and the Universality of Salvation," *TI*, vol. 16
(1979), 219.

[14]"Church, Churches and Religions," *TI*, vol. 10 (1973), 48.

Hinduism are both transcended by something absolute. Both are therefore of relative value.

From Hebrews 1:1-2, Panikkar surmises that "not only the prophets of Israel but also the sages of Hinduism" are inspired by the Son, who has been present "in all human endeavours."[15] The Logos himself is thus speaking in Hinduism. Furthermore, "there is in Hinduism a living Presence of that Mystery which Christians call Christ."[16] From the point of view of the Christian, Christ's grace is the force which is impelling Hinduism and he is its ontological goal.[17] However, that is only true from the point of view of the Christian. In fact, the Mystery which Christians call Christ cannot be completely identified with him. He is the Mystery in the sense that "to see Christ is to reach that Mystery,"[18] but "he is only one aspect of the Mystery as a whole."[19] "Even though he is *the* Way when we are on that way," when Christians actually reach the summit, they discover Christ "in all those who have reached the Mystery, even if their ways have not been the Christian one."[20] It is only for the Christian that the Mystery is indissolubly connected with Christ. What Christians need to realize therefore, is that "in believing and loving Christ as the central symbol of life and Ultimate Truth," they are being drawn towards the selfsame Mystery that attracts all other human beings who are seeking to overcome their own present condition.[21]

Panikkar grants that apart from Christ there is

---

[15]*The Unknown Christ*, 1.
[16]Ibid., 2; cf. 169.
[17]Ibid., 3.
[18]Ibid., 24.
[19]Ibid., 25; cf. 168.
[20]Ibid., 25.
[21]Ibid., 23.

no redemption (Ephesians 1:3-14ff; Colossians 1:13-22). Therefore, anyone who is saved is saved by Christ, the only redeemer. Since "we know by reason and faith that God provides everybody with the necessary means of salvation," we must accept that "Christ is present in one form or another in every human being as he journeys towards God."[22] In some way, therefore, "Hinduism is incorporated into the universal economy of salvation by God through Christ."[23] Since there is no salvation outside the Church, the "'Church' should not be identified with a concrete organization, or even with adherence to Christianity."[24] The normal and ordinary means of salvation within the Christian Church are the sacraments. "Yet it remains true that Christ may be active and at work in the human being who receives any sacrament, whether Christian or any other."[25] Thus, the "good and *bona fide* Hindu" is saved by Christ, "not by Hinduism or Christianity *per se*, but through their sacraments, and ultimately, through the *Mysterion* active within the two religions."[26]

In this approach of Panikkar one can see clearly three of the aspects of Irenaeus's theology which might have developed in an optimistic direction. 1) God wills all people to be saved, 2) Christ is the Savior of all people, and 3) God provides everyone with the necessary means to salvation. However, Panikkar has moved on from those starting points to a position that is more distant from Irenaeus than is that of Rahner. It does not seem possible to stretch Irenaeus to the point at which Hindus could be confronted with the revelation of God in Christ,

---

[22]Ibid., 67-68.
[23]Ibid., 69.
[24]Ibid., 82.
[25]Ibid., 85.
[26]Ibid., 85-86.

could reject Christ as the way of salvation, and the triune God as the one true God, and yet be saved (through Christ) by the sacraments and worship of their Hindu religion.

In comparing Irenaeus with "anonymous Christianity," we encountered a situation that Irenaeus did not specifically address. Panikkar, on the other hand, has described a situation that Irenaeus did confront. There seems to be no reason to assume that Irenaeus would have felt different about Hindu gods and idols from how he felt about the gods of the Gentile religions of his day, which he called "idols of demons." There is no reason to believe that he would treat the Hindu's rejection of Christ in a manner different from his treatment of the rejection by the Gnostic or the pagan of his own day. There is no reason to suggest that he would consider the "visible" Church dispensable for Hindus who have their own concrete manifestation of the Mystery, in Hinduism.

Irenaeus had no inclination to suggest that the Mystery toward which Valentinus moved by means of his doctrine of the Aeons was none other than the Mystery toward vision of whom Irenaeus was progressing. Nor was Irenaeus ready to accept that when he and Valentinus reached the summit they would find that they had arrived by different but equally valid ways. Even if Valentinus had been a very sincere Gnostic, with a clear conscience, unless he had given up his erroneous beliefs concerning the Aeons, had believed in Christ as the one Son of God, and had participated in the visible Church, he would have been doomed. In short, while we may discern some carefully qualified "antecedence" of "anonymous Christianity" in the theology of Irenaeus, there is a clear contrast between his thought and that of the pluralism represented in Panikkar's work.

c. Development of aspects of Irenaeus's theology

James Dupuis, Gerald O'Collins, and Eugene Hillman all indicated Logos-Christology as the point of greatest hopefulness in the second- and third-century Fathers, vis-à-vis the salvation of "non-Christians." Particularly the activity of the pre-incarnate Logos was cited. It appears that those statements have generally assumed too great a similarity between Irenaeus and Justin or Clement of Alexandria. This study has demonstrated that the pre-incarnate revelatory activity of the Logos was seen more in terms of theophanies, prophecies and types which were specifically Christological than in terms of an activity of the Logos outside of God's working within his covenant people. However, we have noticed the significance of the activity of the pre-incarnate Logos in creation and providence, and the universal cohesiveness provided by the immanence of the Word, as symbolized in the cosmic cross. The parallel which Irenaeus draws between revelation in creation and revelation in the Incarnation is very important, seen also in the relationship between the cosmic cross and the visible cross, even though Irenaeus himself did not conceive of people who were limited to natural revelation. At that most basic level of revelation, faith or unbelief is critical. The economy of salvation moves in a straight line from Adam through Enoch, Noah, Abraham, his heirs, Moses and the Hebrew prophets, toward Jesus the Christ. From the beginning, this economy was characterized by a spirit of anticipation of his coming in the flesh.

Irenaeus does not speak of an activity of the Logos through pagan philosophers, as Justin does. The "seed of the Word" was not found in pagan philosophers, but in the Old Testament prophecies, whose fruit the Church reaped. Dupuis' comment that Irenaeus "made room for a salvific value of pre-biblical religions" is very doubtful, in view of this study.[27] Likewise, O'Collins' statement that Irenaeus saw the "Greek philosophers as 'Christians before Christ'" is incorrect, or at least greatly overstated (if one takes a maximally positive reading of Irenaeus's comment on Plato).[28] The statement is made out of a failure to distinguish adequately between the theologies of Justin and Irenaeus, and out of a conceptualization of the pre-incarnate saving activity of the Word that is different from Irenaeus's perspective. In view of the struggle that Irenaeus was having with the Gnostics, and the stress that he was forced to place on the Old Testament and apostolic Scriptures, it is very unlikely that he is the guide Vempeny is looking for with regard to the inspiration of non-biblical scriptures.[29]

The aspect of Irenaeus's theology which seems most likely to lead to an optimism regarding salvation is his doctrine of the Incarnation, including particularly the concept of recapitulation. Here one finds a fundamental and objective work of God in Christ that makes the salvation of all people possible. It is here that one finds some similarity to Rahner's concept of an ontologically real sanctification of humanity by the Incarnation. Irenaeus spoke of Christ's recapitulating the whole of humanity in order to sanctify it.

Mention was made in the previous chapter of the parallel drawn by Wingren between Irenaeus's doctrine of recapitulation and a Barthian doctrine of universal, corporate election in Christ, the elect One. Dai Sil Kim has compared this doctrine to Teilhard de Chardin's

[27]James Dupuis, "The Cosmic Christ in the Early Fathers," *IJT* 15 (July-September 1966):111.

[28]Gerald O'Collins, *Fundamental Theology* (New York: Paulist Press, 1981), 125.

[29]Ishanand Vempeny, *Inspiration in Non-Biblical Scriptures* (Bangalore: Theological Publications in India, n.d.), 61.

concept of "Omega."[30]   Origen developed recapitulation
into explicit universalism. It seems to this writer that
this is a place from which one could begin, in Irenaeus's
theology, to work toward an optimism concerning the
salvation of the non-Christian. However, the system one
would develop from this starting point would necessarily
be very different from that of Irenaeus. It would hardly
seem justified to call Irenaeus an "antecedent" of such a
system. Even to say that the seed of such a system is
found in Irenaeus would be somewhat misleading. One
might say that this "seed" was not allowed to grow to
maturity in Irenaeus, but that, too, is misleading. This
was an integral part of Irenaeus's whole theological
system. He grew the "seed" into fruit, within his own
system. Others may feel, however, that this is a seed
with different possibilities from those Irenaeus reaped
from it.

C. A Final Statement

Irenaeus presents a theology of revelation and
salvation that has an inner consistency. Beginning with
his presuppositions, the system is coherent. Although
unique in certain aspects, its overall perspective represents the view that has traditionally motivated Christian
missions: the view that salvation requires explicit faith
in Christ and that without the Church's missionary
outreach, people in other religions are going to be lost.
By changing the presuppositions of Irenaeus's system, we
can speculate concerning other directions which he might

---

[30]"Irenaeus of Lyons and Teilhard de Chardin: A Comparative
Study of 'Recapitulation' and 'Omega,'" *JEcSt* 13 (1976):69-93. José
González-Faus makes a similar comparison (*Carne de Dios: significado
salvador de la Encarnación en la teología de san Ireneo* [Barcelona:
Herder, 1969], 52).

have taken. By ignoring his own conclusions, but taking certain aspects of his theology as starting points, we can develop a position that reaches different conclusions. All of that, however, is modern speculation, and the conclusions reached by these means must be tentative. One would have to speak in very precise and carefully qualified terms in order to claim Irenaeus as an "antecedent" of such modern developments. However, taking all of these factors into account, one might make a statement such as this:

> *Irenaeus believed that those who were saved, who lived before the Incarnation of the Word, had responded in faith to the various modes of revelation by the pre-incarnate Logos. He believed that, after the ascension of Christ, only those are saved who are members of the institutional Church and who believe the "rule of truth" that capsulizes the apostolic faith of the Church. However, Irenaeus was not conscious of large groups of unevangelized people. If he had known of such groups, and if he had responded to the Gnostic challenge with less emphasis on the institutional Church, he might have allowed of the salvation of individuals outside of the institutional Church.*

This statement, and its supposition, could be based on the following factors in Irenaeus's theology:

1) God wills the salvation of humankind.

2) The Word's immanence in creation, symbolized by a cosmic cross, has a cohesive and reconciliatory effect upon all of creation which is not only physical but also moral and supernatural. It is this invisible cosmic cross that stands behind the saving work of Jesus on the visible cross.

3) The revelation by the Word in creation is life-giving and necessitates a human response of faith, which

is made possible by an illumination by the Word.

4) In Christ's incarnation, obedient life, death and resurrection, a recapitulation of the history of fallen humanity was made which objectively accomplished the salvation of humankind.

5) Within the economy of salvation, the same reward (knowledge of the Son of God, or immortality) is eventually given to all whom God calls, regardless of the particular stage of the economy in which they lived and in which they were called.

6) The just judgment of sinful people, by God, assumes their voluntary rejection of divine saving revelation to *all* people.

7) Those who believe and follow God are given a greater illumination of the mind.

8) People will be judged according to the privilege of revelation that they have received.

9) During the millennium, those who have not known the incarnate Word, but who have had some form of "anticipation" of him, will become accustomed to living with him and will be prepared for the vision of the Father.

The tentativeness of the summary statement is markedly different from those that have been cited from other authors. However, it more accurately represents the limits placed upon such a statement by our ignorance of what Irenaeus himself would have said in a different context from the one in which he actually wrote.

In formulating a position that addresses our own context, we would do well to give careful attention to the witness that Irenaeus bears to the apostolic tradition, although we recognize the "time-boundness" of his own theological formation. We must proclaim divine truth in our own age, in the power of the Spirit, that the divine economy of salvation may progress yet closer to that day when all things shall finally be summed up in Christ.

BIBLIOGRAPHY

A. Christianity and Non-Christians

In the past twenty-five years, there has been widespread interest in the theology of religions and the operations of divine grace outside of the bounds of the institutional Christian Church. Items included here are selected for their reference to the particular focus of this study on Irenaeus.

1. Books

Anderson, Norman. *Christianity and World Religions: The Challenge of Religious Pluralism.* Downer's Grove, Ill.: Inter-Varsity Press, 1984.

Balchand, Asanda D. *The Salvific Value of Non-Christian Religions According to Asian Christian Theologians, Writing in Asian-Published Theological Journals, 1965-70.* Manila: East Asian Pastoral Institute, 1973.

Bühlmann, Walbert. *God's Chosen Peoples.* Translated by Robert R. Barr. Maryknoll, N.Y.: Orbis Books, 1982.

Congar, Yves. *The Wide World My Parish; Salvation and Its Problems.* Baltimore: Helicon Press, 1961.

Daniélou, Jean. *Holy Pagans of the Old Testament.* Translated by Felix Faber. Baltimore: Helicon Press, 1956.

Demarest, Bruce. *General Revelation: Historical Views and Contemporary Issues.* Grand Rapids: Zondervan, 1982.

Dictionnaire de Théologie Catholique, 1923 ed. S.v. "Infidèles," by S. Harent.

Dupuis, James. *Jesus Christ and His Spirit: Theological Approaches.* Bangalore: Theological Publications in India, 1977.

Eliade, Mircea, and David Tracy, eds. *What Is Religion? An Inquiry for Christian Theology.* Concilium, no. 136. New York: Seabury Press, 1980.

Encyclopedia of Theology. The Concise "Sacramentum Mundi," s.v. "Revelation. I,B. Theological Interpretation," by Karl Rahner. New York: Seabury Press, 1975.

Geffré, Claude, and Jean Pierre Jossua, eds. *True and False Universality of Christianity.* New York: Seabury Press, 1980.

Hacker, Paul. *Theological Foundations of Evangelization.* St. Augustin: Steyler Verlag, 1980.

Hillman, Eugene. *Many Paths: A Catholic Approach to Religious Pluralism.* Faith Meets Faith Series. Maryknoll, N.Y.: Orbis Books, 1989.

―――. *The Wider Ecumenism.* New York: Herder & Herder, 1968.

Knitter, Paul F. *No Other Name? A Critical Survey of Christian Attitudes Toward the World Religions.* American Society of Missiology Series, No. 7. Maryknoll, N.Y.: Orbis Books, 1985.

Kraemer, Hendrik. *La foi chrétienne et les religions non chrétiennes.* Traduit de l'anglais par Simone Mathil. Paris: Delachaux et Niestlé, 1956.

Küng, Hans. *The Church.* Translated by Ray and Rosaleen Ockenden. London: Burns & Oates, 1967.

―――. *Freedom Today.* Translated by Cecily Hastings. New York: Sheed & Ward, 1966.

Küng, Hans, and Jürgen Moltmann. eds. *Christianity Among World Religions.* Concilium, vol. 183. Edinburgh: T. & T. Clark, 1986.

Kunnumpuram, Kurien. *Ways of Salvation: The Salvific Meaning of Non-Christian Religions According to the Teaching of Vatican II.* Poona: Pontifical Athenaeum, 1971.

Lindbeck, George. *"Fides ex auditu* and the Salvation of Non-Christians: Contemporary Catholic and Protestant Positions." In *The Gospel and the Ambiguity of the Church,* 92-123. Edited by Vilmos Vashta. Philadelphia: Fortress Press, 1974.

de Lubac, Henri. *Catholicism: A Study of Dogma in Relation to the Corporate Destiny of Mankind.* Translated by Lancelot C. Sheppard. New York: Sheed & Ward, 1958.

————. *The Church: Paradox and Mystery.* Translated by James R. Dunne. Staten Island, N.Y.: Alba House, 1969.

Martelet, G. *Les idées maîtresses de Vatican II. Introduction à l'esprit du Concile.* Paris: Desclée de Brouwer, 1966.

Maurier, Henri. *The Other Covenant; A Theology of Paganism.* Translated by Charles McGrath. Glen Rock, N.J.: Newman Press, 1968.

Neuner, Josef, ed. *Christian Revelation and World Religions.* London: Burns & Oates, 1967.

O'Collins, Gerald. *Fundamental Theology.* New York: Paulist Press, 1981.

Pannikar, Raimundo. *The Unknown Christ of Hinduism: Towards an Ecumenical Christophany.* Revised and enlarged edition. Maryknoll, N.Y.: Orbis Books, 1981.

Pathrapankal, Joseph, ed. *Service and Salvation: Nagpur Theological Conference on Evangelization.* Bangalore: Theological Publications in India, 1973.

Punt, Neal. *Unconditional Good News: Toward an Understanding of Biblical Universalism.* Grand Rapids: Eerdmans, 1980.

Rahner, Karl. "Anonymous Christianity and the Missionary Task of the Church." In *Theological Investigations*, vol. 12, 161-78. Translated by David Bourke. London: Darton, Longman & Todd, 1974.

———. "Anonymous Christians." In *Theological Investigations*, vol. 6, 390-98. Translated by Karl-H. and Boniface Kruger. London: Darton, Longman & Todd, 1969.

———. "Anonymous Explicit Faith." In *Theological Investigations*, vol. 16, 52-59. Translated by David Morland. London: Darton, Longman & Todd, 1979.

———. "Atheism and Implicit Christianity." In *Theological Investigations*, vol. 9, 145-64. Translated by Graham Harrison. London: Darton, Longman & Todd, 1972.

———. "Christianity and Non-Christian Religions." In *Theological Investigations*, vol. 5, 115-34. Translated by Karl-H. Kruger. London: Darton, Longman & Todd, 1966.

———. "Church, Churches and Religions." In *Theological Investigations*, vol. 10, 30-49. Translated by David Bourke. New York: Herder & Herder, 1973.

———. "Current Problems in Christology." In *Theological Investigations*, vol. 1, 149-200. Translated by Cornelius Ernst. London: Darton, Longman & Todd, 1961.

———. *Foundations of Christian Faith. An Introduction to the Idea of Christianity*. Translated by William V. Dych. New York: Seabury Press, 1978.

———. "Jesus Christ in Non-Christian Religions." In *Theological Investigations*, vol. 17, 39-50. Translated by Margaret Kohl. New York: Crossroad Publishing Co., 1981.

Rahner, Karl. "Membership of the Church According to the Teaching of Pius XII's Encyclical 'Mystici Corporis Christi.'" In *Theological Investigations*, vol. 2, 1-88. Translated by Karl-H. Kruger. London: Darton, Longman & Todd, 1963.

—. "The New Image of the Church." In *Theological Investigations*, vol. 10, 3-29. Translated by David Bourke. New York: Herder & Herder, 1973.

—. "Observations on the Problem of the 'Anonymous Christian.'" In *Theological Investigations*, vol. 14, 280-94. Translated by David Bourke. London: Darton, Longman & Todd, 1976.

—. *On the Theology of Death.* Translated by Charles H. Henkey. London: Nelson, 1961.

—. "The One Christ and the Universality of Salvation." In *Theological Investigations*, vol. 16, 199-224. Translated by David Morland. London: Darton, Longman & Todd, 1979.

—. "Religious Feeling Inside and Outside the Church." In *Theological Investigations*, vol. 17, 228-42. Translated by Margaret Kohl. New York: Crossroad Publishing Co., 1981.

Rahner, Karl, and Joseph Ratzinger. *Revelation and Tradition*. Translated by W. J. O'Hara. New York: Herder & Herder, 1966.

Rahner, Karl, and Herbert Vorgrimler. "Revelation." In *Concise Theological Dictionary*, 409-13. Edited by Cornelius Ernst and translated by Richard Strachan. London: Burns & Oates, 1965.

Roper, Anita. *The Anonymous Christian*. Translated by Joseph Donceel, S.J., with an afterword, "The Anonymous Christian According to Karl Rahner," by Klaus Riesenhuber, S.J. New York: Sheed & Ward, 1966.

Rossano, Pietro. "Theology and Religions." In *Problems and Perspectives of Fundamental Theology*, 292-308. Edited by René Latourelle and Gerald O'Collins. Translated by Matthew J. O'Connell. New York: Paulist Press, 1982.

Santos Hernández, Angel. *Salvación y paganismo; el problema teológico de la salvación de los infideles*. Santander: Sal Terrae, 1960.

Schlette, Heinz Robert. *Towards a Theology of Religions*. Translated by W. J. O'Hara. Freiburg: Herder, 1966.

van Straelen, Henry. *The Catholic Encounter with World Religions*. Westminster, Md.: Newman Press, 1966.

————. *Ouverture à l'autre laquelle? L'apostolat missionnaire et le monde non chrétien*. Paris: Beauchesne, 1982.

Thils, Gustave. *Propos et problèmes de la théologie des religions non chrétiennes*. Paris: Casterman, 1966.

Thomas, Owen Clark, ed. *Attitudes Toward Other Religions: Some Christian Interpretations*. New York: Harper & Row, 1969.

Tillich, Paul Johannes. *Christianity and the Encounter of World Religions*. New York: Columbia University Press, 1963.

Vempeny, Ishanand. *Inspiration in the Non-Biblical Scriptures*. Bangalore: Theological Publications in India, n.d.

Wainwright, Geoffrey ed. *Keeping the Faith: Essays to Mark the Centenary of Lux Mundi*. London: SPCK, 1989.

Wang, Joseph Tch'ang-Tche. *Saint Augustin et les vertus des païens*. Avec préface de Jules Lebreton. Paris: Beauchesne, 1938.

Weger, Karl-Heinz. *Karl Rahner: An Introduction to His Theology*. Translated by David Smith. New York: Seabury Press, 1980.

2. Articles

Blanchard, M. "Christianity as Fulfilment and Antithesis." *IJT* 17 (1968): 5-20

Blue, J. Ronald. "Untold Billions: Are They Really Lost?" *BSac* 138 (October-December 1981): 338-50.

Borland, James. "A Theologian Looks at the Gospel and World Religions." *JETS* 33 (March 1990): 3-11.

Boutin, Maurice. "Anonymous Christianity: A Paradigm for Interreligious Encounter?" *JEcSt* 20 (Fall 1983): 602-29.

Brow, Robert. Review of *The World Religions*, by Norman Anderson. In *CT* 75 (July 2, 1971): 25-26.

Burns, J. Patout. "The Economy of Salvation: Two Patristic Traditions." *TS* 37 (1976): 598-619.

Buschmann, A. "Theology and the Non-Christian Religions." *TT* 16 (June 1960): 459-70.

Clasper, P. D. "Christianity and Other Religions." *SEAJT* 1 (April 1960): 22-26.

Coffey, David. "The Salvation of the Unbeliever in St. Thomas Aquinas and Jacques Maritain." *Australasian Catholic Record* 41 (1964): 179-98, 265-82.

Congar, Yves M.-J. "Au sujet du salut des non-catholiques." *RScRel* 32 (January 1958): 53-65.

D'Costa, Gavin. "Karl Rahner's Anonymous Christian: A Reappraisal." *ModTh* 2 (January 1985): 131-48.

DiNoia, J. A. "Implicit Faith, General Revelation and the State of Non-Christians." *Thom* 47 (April 1983): 209-41.

Dupuis, J. "The Cosmic Christ in the Early Fathers." *IJT* 15 (July-September 1966): 106-20.

Ellisen, Stanley. "Are Pagans Without Christ Really Lost?" *ConBapt* (Spring 1983): 6-9.

Goerner, H. C. "Christianity and Non-Christian Religions." *RevExp* 51 (April 1954): 217-29.

Greenwood, R. P. "Extra ecclesiam nulla salus; Its Treatment in Recent Roman Catholic Theology." *Th* 76 (August 1973): 416-25.

Hacker, Paul. "The Christian Attitude Toward Non-Christian Religions: Some Critical and Positive Reflections." *ZMR* 55 (1971): 81-97.

————. "The Religions of the Gentiles as Viewed by the Fathers of the Church." *ZMR* 54 (1970): 253-78.

Hick, John H. "Learning from Other Faiths. IX. The Christian View of Other Faiths." *ExpTim* 84 (November 1972): 36-39.

Hillman, Eugene. "Evangelization in a Wider Ecumenism: Theological Grounds for Dialog with Other Religions." *JEcSt* 12 (Winter 1975): 1-12.

————. "Is the Church Still Necessary?" *Con* 6 (Spring 1968): 24-30.

Johnson, W. O. "Non-Christian Salvation." *JBR* 31 (July 1963): 216-24.

Klug, Eugene F., and Randall W. Shields. "Extra Ecclesiam Nulla Salus: A Statement of the Department of Systematic Theology [Concordia Theological Seminary, Fort Wayne] *ConTQ* 50 (July-October 1986): 161-63.

Knitter, Paul. "European Protestant and Catholic Approaches to the World Religions: Complements and Contrast." *JEcSt* 12 (Winter 1975): 13-28.

————. "Roman Catholic Approaches to Other Religions: Developments and Tensions." *IBMR* 8 (April 1984): 50-54.

————. "World Religions and the Finality of Christ: A Critique of Hans Kung's *On Being a Christian*." *Hor* 5 (Fall 1978): 151-64.

de Letter, P. "Revelation in Non-Christian Religions." *ClerM* 29 (December 1965): 466-68.

Luneau, Auguste. "Pour aider au dialogue: les Pères et les religions non-chrétiennes." *NRT* 89 (September-October 1967): 821-41; 89 (November 1967): 914-39.

Macquarrie, J. "Christianity and Other Faiths." *USQR* 20 (November 1964): 39-48.

Maddox, Randy. "Karl Rahner's Supernatural Existential: A Wesleyan Parallel?" *EvJ* 5 (Spring 1987): 3-14.

McVeigh, Malcolm J. "The Fate of Those Who've Never Heard: It Depends [Four Evangelical Positions]." *EMQ* 21 (October 1985): 370-79.

Méhat, André. "La philosophie troisième testament? La pensée grecque et la foi selon Clément d'Alexandrie." *LV* 32 (January-March 1983): 15-23.

Nicholls, Bruce J. "The Salvation and Lostness of Mankind." *EvRT* 15 (January 1991): 4-21.

Osburn, Evert D. "Those Who Have Never Heard: Have They No Hope?" *JETS* 32 (September 1989): 367-72.

Packer, James I. "Are Non-Christian Faiths Ways of Salvation?" *BSac* 130 (April-June 1973): 110-16.

Pelagia, Robert M. "The Theory of the Moment of Full Vision at Death." *CTTW* 28 (January-April 1983): 79-81.

Pinnock, Clark H. "Toward an Evangelical Theology of Religions." *JETS* 33 (September 1990): 359-68.

Race, Alan. "Christianity and Other Religions: Is Inclusivism Enough?" *TH* 89 (May 1986): 178-86.

Riesenhuber, K. "Der Anonyme Christ nach K. Rahner." *ZKT* 86 (1964): 286-303.

———. "Rahner's 'Anonymous Christian.'" *TD* 13 (Autumn 1965): 163-71.

Schineller, J. Peter. "Christ and Church: A Spectrum of Views." *TS* 37 (December 1976): 545-66.

Schreiter, Robert J. "The Anonymous Christian and Christology." *Miss* 6 (January 1978): 29-52.

Segers, Joseph. "The True Religion and Religions." *CTTW* 28 (January-April 1983): 76-78.

Sequeira, Andrew Anil. "A Christian Approach to Non-Christian Religions." *NZM* 39 (1983): 132-34.

Sharpe, Eric J. "Christian Attitudes to Non-Christian Religions: A Bibliographical Survey." *ExpTim* 86 (March 1975): 168-71.

Slater, R. H. L. "Christian Attitudes to Other Religions." *CanJT* 2 (October 1956): 215-24.

Stransky, Thomas F. "The Church and Other Religions." *IBMR* 9 (October 1985): 154-58.

Thomas, O. C. "Barth on Non-Christian Knowledge of God." *ATR* 46 (July 1964): 261-85.

Tillich, Paul et al. "Discussion: Christianity and Other Faiths [Replies to J. Macquarrie, and rejoinder]." *USQR* 20 (January 1965): 177-89.

Vandervelde, George. "The Grammar of Grace: Karl Rahner as a Watershed in Contemporary Theology." *TS* 49 (September 1988): 445-59.

Wiles, Maurice. "Christianity and Other Faiths: Some Theological Reflections." *TH* 91 (July 1988): 302-8.

B. Irenaeus and the Gnostics

The literature dealing with second-century Gnosticism is continually growing, particularly as a result of the Nag Hammadi discoveries. The major concern of this thesis has been Gnosticism as Irenaeus defined it. However, the following works have been of help in explicating the context in which Irenaeus developed his theology of revelation.

1. Books

Cross, Frank Leslie, ed. *The Jung Codex, a Newly Recovered Gnostic Papyrus; Three Studies.* London: Mowbray, 1955.

Foerster, Werner, ed. *Gnosis: A Selection of Gnostic Texts.* Vol. 2: *Coptic and Mandean Sources.* Translated and edited by R. L. McL. Wilson. Oxford: Clarendon Press, 1974.

Grant, Robert McQueen, ed. *Gnosticism: A Source Book of Heretical Writings from the Early Christian Period.* New York: Harper, 1961.

————. *Gnosticism and Early Christianity.* Revised edition. New York: Harper & Row, 1966.

Groningen, G. van. *First Century Gnosticism: Its Origin and Motifs.* Leiden: E. J. Brill, 1967.

Hedrick, Charles W., and Robert Hodgson Jr., eds. *Nag Hammadi, Gnosticism, and Early Christianity.* Peabody, Mass.: Hendrickson, 1986.

Helmbold, Andrew. *The Nag Hammadi Gnostic Texts and the Bible.* Grand Rapids: Baker, 1967.

Jonas, Hans. *The Gnostic Religion; the Message of the Alien God and the Beginnings of Christianity.* Revised edition. Boston: Beacon Press, 1963.

MacRae, George W. *Studies in New Testament and Gnosticism.* Selected and edited by Daniel J. Harrington, S.J., and Stanley B. Marrow, S.J. Good News Studies, vol. 26. Wilmington, Del.: M. Glazier, 1988.

Orbe, Antonio. *Cristología gnóstica; introducción a la soteriología de los siglos II y III.* Biblioteca de Autores Cristianos, nos. 385, 385. Madrid: La Editorial Católica, 1976.

————. *Hacía la primera teología de la procesión del Verbo.* Estudios Valentinianos, vols. 2 & 3. Rome: Apud Aedes Universitatis Gregorianae, 1958.

————. *Los Primeros herejes ante la persecución.* Estudios Valentinianos, vol. 5. Rome: Apud Aedes Universitatis Gregorianae, 1956.

————. *La Unción del Verbo.* Estudios Valentinianos, vol. 3. Rome: Libreria Editrice dell' Università Gregoriana, 1961.

Perkins, Pheme. *The Gnostic Dialogue: The Early Church and the Crisis of Gnosticism*. New York: Paulist Press, 1980.

Pétrement, Simone. *Le Dieu séparé: les origines du gnosticisme*. Paris: Cerf, 1984.

Quispel, Gilles. *Gnostic Studies*. Vol. 1. Istanbul: Nederlands Historisch-Archaeologisch Instituut in het Nabije Oosten, 1974.

Robinson, James M., ed. *The Nag Hammadi Library in English; Translated and Introduced by Members of the Coptic Gnostic Library Project of the Institute for Antiquity and Christianity*. Rev. ed. San Francisco: Harper, 1988.

Sagnard, F.-M. *La gnose valentinienne et le témoignage de Saint Irénée*. Paris: Vrin, 1947.

Sanders, E. P. *Jewish and Christian Self-Definition*. Vol. 1: *The Shaping of Christianity in the Second and Third Centuries*. Philadelphia: Fortress Press, 1980.

Timothy, Hamilton Baird. *The Early Christian Apologists and Greek Philosophy. Exemplified by Irenaeus, Tertullian and Clement of Alexandria*. Assen: Van Gorcum, 1973.

Vallée, Gérard. *A Study in Anti-Gnostic Polemics: Irenaeus, Hippolytus and Epiphanius*. Studies in Christianity and Judaism: 1. Waterloo, Ont.: Wilfrid Laurier University Press, 1981.

Yamauchi, Edwin M. *Pre-Christian Gnosticism: A Survey of the Proposed Evidences*. Grand Rapids: Baker, 1983.

2. Articles

Edwards, M. J. "Gnostics and Valentinians in the Church Fathers." *JTS* ns 40 (April 1989): 26-47.

Grant, Robert M. "Carpocratians and Curriculum: Irenaeus's Reply." *HTR* 79 (June-July 1986): 127-36.

Green, Henry Alan. "Suggested Sociological Themes in the Study of Gnosticism." *VigChr* 31 (1977): 169-80.

McGuire, Anne M. "Valentinus and the *Gnōstikē Hairesis*: Iren, Haer I,xi,1 and the Evidence of Nag Hammadi." *StudPat* 18, vol. 1; edited by E. A. Livingstone. Kalamazoo, Mich.: Cistercian Publications, 1985, 247-52.

Ménard, Jacques E. "Le Repos, salut de Gnostique." *RScRel* 51 (January 1977): 71-88.

Norris, Richard A. "Irenaeus and Plotinus Answer the Gnostics: A Note on the Relation Between Christian Thought and Platonism." *USQR* 36 (Fall 1980): 13-24.

Orbe, Antonio. "Los Hombres y el creador según una homilía de Valentin (Clem., Strom. IV,13,89-91,3)." *Greg* 55 (1974): 5-48; 339-68.

———. "San Ireneo y el conocimiento natural de Dios. Part I." *Greg* 47 (1966): 441-71.

Pearson, Birger A. "Early Christianity and Gnosticism: A Review Essay." *RSR* 13 (January 1987): 1-8.

Perkins, Pheme. "Irenaeus and the Gnostics: Rhetoric and Composition in Irenaeus's Treatise vs. the Excerpts from Theodotus." *HTR* 67 (1974): 35-53.

Reimherr, O. "Irenaeus and the Valentinians." *LQ* 12 (February 1960): 55-59.

Thomassen, Einar. Review of Layton, Bentley, ed. *The Rediscovery of Gnosticism (Proceedings of the International Conference on Gnosticism at Yale, March 28-31, 1978). Vol. 1: The School of Valentinus*. Studies in the History of Religions, Supplements to Numen, 41. Leiden: E. J. Brill, 1980, in *JAAR* 50 (June 1982): 298-99.

Tugwell, Simon. "Irenaeus and the Gnostic Challenge." *ClerR* 66 (April 1981): 127-30; 135-37.

Wilson, R. McL. "Slippery Words II. Gnosis, Gnostic, Gnosticism." *ExpTim* 89 (July 1978): 296-301.

Winling, Raymond. "Le Christ-Didascale et les didascales gnostiques et chrétiennes d'après l'oeuvre d'Irénée." *RScRel* 57 (October 1983): 261-72.

C. The Missiological Context

Bailey, Cyril et al. *The History of Christianity in the Light of Modern Knowledge. A Collective Work.* London: Blackie & Son, 1929.

Bruce, Frederick Fyvie. *The Spreading Flame: The Rise and Progress of Christianity from Its Beginnings to the Conversion of the English.* London: Paternoster Press, 1958.

Carrington, Philip. *The Early Christian Church.* Vol. 2: *The Second Christian Century.* Cambridge: University Press, 1957.

Cave, William. *Lives of the Most Eminent Fathers of the Church That Flourished in the First Four Centuries with an Historical Account of the State of Paganism Under the First Christian Emperors.* Vol. 1. Oxford: Thomas Tegg, 1840.

Chadwick, Henry. *The Early Church.* Baltimore: Penguin Books, 1967.

Eusebius. *The History of the Church from Christ to Constantine.* Translated with an introduction by G. A. Williamson. New York: New York University Press, 1966.

Farrar, Frederic W. *Lives of the Fathers. Sketches of Church History in Biography.* Vol. 1. London: Adam & Charles Black, 1907.

Fisher, George Park. *History of the Christian Church.* New York: Charles Scribner's Sons, 1897.

Gouilloud, André. *Saint Irénée et son temps; deuxième siècle de l'Eglise.* Lyon: Briday, 1876.

Harnack, Adolf. *The Expansion of Christianity in the First Three Centuries.* Translated and edited by James Moffat. London: Williams & Norgate, 1904.

Jedin, Hebert, and John Dolan, eds. *Handbook of Church History.* 7 vols. New York: Herder & Herder, 1965-81. Vol. 1: *From the Apostolic Community to Constantine,* by Karl Baus.

Justin Martyr. *Writings of St. Justin Martyr.* Translated and edited by Thomas B. Falls. The Fathers of the Church. A New Translation. Vol. 6. New York: Christian Heritage, 1948.

Kane, J. Herbert. *A Concise History of the Christian World Mission: A Panoramic View of Missions from Pentecost to the Present.* Grand Rapids: Baker, 1978.

———. *A Global View of Christian Missions From Pentecost to the Present.* Grand Rapids: Baker, 1971.

Knudsen, Johannes. "Celtic Christianity." *Dialog* (Minnesota) 22 (Winter 1983): 56-59.

Latourette, Kenneth Scott. *A History of the Expansion of Christianity.* Vol. 1: *The First Five Centuries.* Grand Rapids: Zondervan, 1970.

Schaff, Philip. *History of the Christian Church.* Vol. 2: *Ante-Nicene Christianity, A.D. 100-325.* New York: Charles Scribner's Sons, 1888.

Tertullian. *Apologetical Works.* Translated by Emily Joseph Daly. The Fathers of the Church. A New Translation. Vol. 10. New York: Fathers of the Church, 1950.

Unnik, Willem Cornelis van. *Newly Discovered Gnostic Writings: A Preliminary Survey of the Nag Hammadi Field.* Studies in Biblical Theology. Napierville, Ill.: Allenson, 1960.

Ward, Maisie. *Early Church Portrait Gallery.* London: Sheed & Ward, 1959.

D. Irenaeus

1. Primary Sources

Froidevaux, L. M. Translator. *Irénée de Lyon. Démonstration del Prédication apostolique.* Sources Chrétiennes, no. 62. Paris: Editions du Cerf, 1959.

Migne, J. P., ed. *Patrologiae Cursus Completus. Patrologiae Graecae.* Tomus VII. Lutetiae Pariscorum, 1857.

Reynders, Bruno. *Lexique comparé du texte Grec et des versions latine Arménienne et Syriaque de "l'Adversus Haereses" de Saint Irénée.* 2 vols. Corpus Scriptorum Christianorum Orientalium, nos. 141, 142. Louvain: L. Durbecq, 1954.

Roberts, Alexander, and W. H. Rambaut. Translators. "Irenaeus. Against Heresies." In *The Ante-Nicene Fathers. Translations of the Writings of the Fathers down to A.D. 325.* Vol. 1. Edited by Alexander Roberts and James Donaldson. American Reprint. New York: Charles Scribner's Sons, 1925.

Rousseau, Adelin, Louis Doutrelaeu, Bertran Hemmerdinger, and Charles Mercier. *Contre les Hérésies.* Sources Chrétiennes, nos. 99, 100, 152, 153, 210, 211, 263, 264, 293, 294, Paris: Editions de Cerf, 1965-82.

Smith, Joseph P. Translator. *Proof of the Apostolic Preaching.* Ancient Christian Writers, no. 16. Westminster, Md.: Newman Press, 1952.

2. Secondary Sources

a. Books

Armstrong, Arthur Hilary, ed. *The Cambridge History of Later Greek and Early Medieval Philosophy.* Cambridge: University Press, 1967.

Armstrong, Arthur Hilary, and R. A. Markus. *Christian Faith and Greek Philosophy.* London: Darton, Longman & Todd, 1960.

Aubin, Paul. *Le Problème de la "conversion." Etude sur un terme commun a l'Hellénisme et au Christianisme des trois premiers siècles.* Théologie historique, no. 1. Paris: Beauchesne et ses fils, 1962.

Aulén, Gustaf. *Christus Victor: An Historical Study of the Three Main Types of the Idea of the Atonement.* Translated by A. G. Hebert. London: SPCK, 1953.

von Balthasar, Hans Urs. *Herrlichkeit. Eine theologische Ästhetik.* Einseideln: Johannes Verlag, 1962.

Bardy, Gustave. *La théologie de l'Eglise de saint Clément de Rome à saint Irénée.* Paris: Editions du Cerf, 1945.

Benoit, André. *Saint Irénée; introduction à l'étude de sa théologie.* Etudes d'histoire et de philosophie religieuses, no. 52. Paris: Presses Universitaires de France, 1960.

Bethouzoz, Roger. *Liberté et grâce suivant la théologie d'Irénée de Lyon: le débat avec la gnose aux origines de la théologie chrétienne.* Étude d'éthique chrétienne 8. Paris: Cerf, 1980.

Bethune-Baker, James Franklin. *An Introduction to the Early History of Christian Doctrine to the Time of the Council of Chalcedon.* London: Methuen & Co., 1903.

Brox, N. *Offenbarung, Gnosis und gnostischer Mythos bei Irenäus von Lyon.* Salzburger Patristiche Studien des Internationalen Forschungszentrums für Grundfragen der Wissenschaften Salzburg. Vol. 1. Salzburg: Anton Pustet, 1966.

Brunner, Emil. *Man in Revolt: A Christian Anthropology.* Translated by Olive Wyon. London: Lutterworth Press, 1939.

———. *The Mediator: A Study of the Central Doctrine of the Christian Faith.* Translated by Olive Wyon. London: Lutterworth Press, 1934.

Cairns, David. *The Image of God in Man.* With an introduction by David E. Jenkins. London: Collins, 1973.

Capéran, Louis. *Le Problème du salut des infidèles; essai historique.* Toulouse: Grand Séminaire, 1934.

Congar, Yves M. J. *Je crois en l'Esprit Saint.* Vol. 2. Paris: Cerf, 1979.

———. *Tradition and Traditions: An Historical and Theological Essay.* New York: Macmillan Co., 1967.

Daley, Brian E. *The Hope of the Early Church. A Handbook of Patristic Eschatology.* Cambridge: University Press, 1991.

Daniélou, Jean. *Advent.* Translated by Rosemary Sheed. London: Sheed & Ward, 1950.

———. *Christ and Us.* New York: Sheed & Ward, 1961.

———. *A History of Early Christian Doctrine Before the Council of Nicaea.* Vol. 2: *Gospel Message and Hellenistic Culture.* Translated, edited and with a postscript by John Austin Baker. Philadelphia: Westminster Press, 1973.

Dewar, Lindsay. *The Holy Spirit and Modern Thought: An Inquiry into the Historical, Theological and Psychological Aspects of the Christian Doctrine of the Holy Spirit.* London: A. P. Mowbray & Co., 1959.

Downing, Francis Gerald. *Has Christianity a Revelation?* London: SCM Press, 1964.

Dufourcqu, Albert. *Saint Irénée.* Paris: Libraire Bloud et Cie, 1905.

Fallon, Timothy P., S.J., and Philip Boo Riley, eds. *Religion and Culture: Essays in Honor of Bernard Lonergan, S.J.* Albany: State University of New York Press, 1987.

González, Justo L. *A History of Christian Thought.* Vol. 1: *From the Beginnings to the Council of Chalcedon.* Nashville: Abingdon Press, 1970.

González-Faus, José Ignacio. *Carne de Dios: significado salvador de la Encarnación en la teología de san Ireneo.* Barcelona: Herder, 1969.

Harnack, Adolf. *History of Dogma.* Vol. 2. Translated from the third German edition by Neil Buchanan. New York: Russell & Russell, 1958.

Hick, John. *Evil and the God of Love.* London: Macmillan, 1966.

Houssiau, Albert. *La Christologie de saint Irénée.* Louvain: Publications Universitaires de Louvain, 1955.

Jossua, Jean Pierre. *Le Salut, incarnation ou mystère pascal chez les Pères de l'Eglise de saint Irénée à saint Léon le Grand.* Paris: Cerf, 1968.

Kelly, J. N. D. *Early Christian Doctrines.* Second edition. New York: Harper & Row, 1960.

Kopas, Jane, ed. *Interpreting Tradition: The Art of Theological Reflection.* The Annual Publication of the College Theology Society, 1983, vol. 29. Chico, Calif.: Scholar's Press, 1984.

Latourelle, René. *Theology of Revelation, Including a Commentary on the Constitution 'Dei Verbum' of Vatican II.* Staten Island, N.Y.: Alba House, 1966.

Lawson, John. *The Biblical Theology of Saint Irenaeus.* London: Epworth Press, 1948.

Lebeau, Paul. "Koinonia. La signification du salut selon saint Irénée." In *Epektasis. Mélanges patristiques offerts au Cardinal Jean Daniélou*, 121-27. Edited by Jacques Fontaine and Charles Kannengiesser. Paris: Gabriel Beauchesne, 1972.

Lebreton, Jules. *Histoire de dogme de la Trinité des origines au Concile de Nicée*. Vol. 2. Paris: Gabriel Beauchesne, 1928.

de Lubac, Henri. *The Church: Paradox and Mystery*. Translated by James R. Dunne. Staten Island, N.Y.: Alba House, 1969.

Luneau, Auguste. *L'Histoire du salut chez les Pères de l'Eglise: la doctrine des âges du monde*. Théologie historique, no. 2. Paris: Beauchesne et ses fils, 1964.

Maloney, George A. *The Cosmic Christ from Paul to Teilhard*. New York: Sheed & Ward, 1968.

Mersch, Emile. *The Whole Christ. The Historical Development of the Doctrine of the Mystical Body in Scripture and Tradition*. Translated by John R. Kelly. London: Dennis Dobson, 1938.

Ochagavía, Juan. *Visibile Patris Filius; A Study of Irenaeus's Teaching on Revelation and Tradition*. Orientalia Christiana Analecta, no. 171. Rome: Pont. Institutum Orientalium Studiorum, 1964.

Orbe, Antonio. *Antropología de san Ireneo*. Madrid: Biblioteca de Autores Cristianos, 1969.

Pelikan, Jaroslav. *The Christian Tradition. A History of the Development of Doctrine*. Vol. 1: *The Emergence of the Catholic Tradition (100-600)*. Chicago: University of Chicago Press, 1971.

Prestige, George Leonard. *God in Patristic Thought*. London: SPCK, 1964.

Quasten, Johannes. *Patrology*. Vol. 1: *The Beginnings of Patristic Literature*. Westminster, Md.: Newman Press, 1950.

Rondet, Henri. *Original Sin: The Patristic and Theological Background.* Translated by Cajetan Finnegan. Shannon, Ireland: Ecclesia Press, 1972.

Schoedel, William R., and Robert L. Wilken, eds. *Early Christian Literature and the Classical Tradition, In Honorem Robert M. Grant.* Théologie historique, 54. Paris: Beauchesne, 1979.

Swete, Henry Barclay. *The Holy Spirit in the Ancient Church: A Study of Christian Teaching in the Age of the Fathers.* London: Macmillan & Co., 1912.

Tavard, George. *Holy Writ or Holy Church: The Crisis of the Protestant Reformation.* New York: Harper & Bros., 1959.

Thornton, L. S. *Revelation and the Modern World, Being the First Part of a Treatise on the Form of the Servant.* London: Dacre Press, 1950.

Turner, H. E. W. *The Patristic Doctrine of Redemption. A Study of the Development of Doctrine During the First Five Centuries.* London: A. R. Mowbray, 1952.

Vernet, F. "Irénée," in *Dictionnaire de théologie catholique.* Edited by A. Vacant, E. Mangenot and E. Amann. Vol. 7, part 2. Paris: Librairie Letouzey et Ané, 1923.

Wingren, Gustaf. *Man and the Incarnation: A Study in the Biblical Theology of Irenaeus.* Translated by Ross Mackenzie. London: Oliver & Boyd, 1959.

Wolfson, Harry Austryn. *The Philosophy of the Church Fathers.* Vol. 1: *Faith, Trinity, Incarnation.* Third edition revised. Cambridge, Mass.: Harvard University Press, 1970.

b. Articles

Abramowski, Luise. "Irenaeus, *Adv. Haer.* III,3,2: Ecclesia Romana and Omnis Ecclesia; and Ibid, 3,3: Anacletus of Rome." *JTS* 28 (April 1977): 101-4.

d'Ales, Adhémar. "La doctrine de la récapitulation en saint Irénée." *RechSR* 6-7 (1916): 185-211.

Bandstra, A. J. "Paul and an Ancient Interpreter: A Comparison of the Teachings of Redemption in Paul and Irenaeus." *CTJ* 5 (April 1970): 43-63.

Bouyer, L. "Gnosis: le sens orthodoxe de l'expression jusqu'aux Pères Alexandrins." *JTS* 4 (October 1953): 188-203.

Daniélou, Jean. "Saint Irénée et les origines de la théologie de l'histoire." *RechSR* 34 (1947): 227-31.

Donovan, Mary Ann. "Alive to the Glory of God: A Key Insight into St. Irenaeus." *TS* 49 (June 1988): 283-97.

———. "Irenaeus in Recent Scholarship." *SecCent* 4 (Winter 1984): 219-41.

Downing, Victor K. "The Doctrine of Regeneration in the Second Century." *EvRT* 14 (April 1990): 99-112.

Enslin, M. S. "Irenaeus: Mostly Prolegomena." *HTR* 40 (1947): 137-65.

Escoula, Louis. "Le verbe sauveur et illuminateur chez saint Irénée." *NRT* (1939): 385-400; 551-67.

———. "Saint Irénée et la connaissance naturelle de Dieu." *RScRel* 20 (May-October 1940): 252-70.

Gualtieri, Antonio. "Descriptive and Evaluative Formulae for Comparative Religion." *TS* 29 (1968): 52-71.

Hefner, Philip. "Theological Methodology and St. Irenaeus." *JR* 44 (1964): 525-57.

Holstein, Henri. "La tradition des Apôtres chez saint Irénée." *RechSR* 36 (1949): 229-70.

Houssiau, A. "L'exégèse de Matthieu 11,27b selon saint Irénée." *ETL* 29 (1953): 328-54.

Kereszty, Roch. "The Unity of the Church in the Theology of Irenaeus." *SecCent* 4 (Winter 1984): 202-18.

Kim, Dai Sil. "Irenaeus of Lyons and Teilhard de Chardin: A Comparative Study of 'Recapitulation' and 'Omega.'" *JEcSt* 13 (Winter 1976): 69-93.

Lebreton, Jules. "La connaissance de Dieu chez saint Irénée." *RechSR* 16 (1926): 385-406.

Loewe, William P. "Irenaeus's Soteriology: *Christus Victor* Revisited." *ATR* 67 (January 1985): 1-15.

Luckhart, Robert. "Matthew 11,27 in the *Contra Haereses* of St. Irenaeus." *RUO* 23 (April-June 1953): 65-79.

Mambrino, Jean. "'Les Deux Mains de Dieu' dans l'oeuvre de saint Irénée." *NRT* 79 (April 1957): 355-70.

McCue, James F. "The Roman Primacy in the Second Century and the Problem of the Development of Dogma." *TS* 25 (1964): 161-96.

Meijering, E. P. "God, Cosmos, History; Christian and Neo-Platonic Views on Divine Revelation." *VigChr* 28 (1974): 248-76.

de Moor, Leonard. "The Idea of Revelation in the Early Church. Part 2." *EvQ* 50 (1978): 230-38.

Orbe, Antonio. "La definición del hombre en la teología del S. II°." *Greg* 48 (1967): 522-76.

―――. "La revelación del Hijo por el Padre según san Ireneo (Adv. haer. IV,6). Para la exégesis prenicena de Mt. 11,17." *Greg* 51 (1970): 5-83. (English summary, 83-86.)

―――. "San Ireneo y el conocimiento natural de Dios. Part II." *Greg* 47 (1966): 710-47.

―――. "San Ireneo y el régimen del milenio." *StudMiss* 32 (1983): 345-72.

―――. "Visión del Padre e incorruptela según san Ireneo [Gen 1:26; Isa 6:5; 2 Cor 12:3]" *Greg* 64 (1983): 199-241.

Potter, P. "St. Irenaeus and 'Recapitulation.'" *DomSt* 4 (1951): 192-200.

Pycke, Nestor. "Connaissance rationelle et connaissance de grâce chez saint Justin." *ETL* 37 (1961): 52-85.

Quinn, Jerome D. "'Charisma Veritatis Certum': Irenaeus, *Adversus Haereses* 4,26,2." *TS* 39 (1978): 520-25.

Reist, Irwin W. "The Christology of Irenaeus." *JETS* 13 (Fall 1970): 241-51.

Robinson, Charles K. "St. Irenaeus on General Revelation as Preparation for Special Revelation." *DDR* 43 (Fall 1978): 169-80.

Torrance, T. F. "The Deposit of Faith." *SJT* 36 (1983): 1-28.

Unger, D. "Christ's Role in the Universe According to St. Irenaeus." *FranSt* NS 5 (March 1945): 3-20; (June 1945): 114-37.

Vandermarck, William. "Natural Knowledge of God in Romans: Patristic and Medieval Interpretation." *TS* 34 (March 1973): 36-52.

van Unnick, Willem C. "An Interesting Document of Second-century Theological Discussion (Irenaeus, Adv. Haer. 1.10.3)." *VigChr* 31 (1977): 196-228.

Walker, A. "The Recapitulation Theme in St. Irenaeus." *Diak* 12 (1977): 244-56.

Wilken, Robert L. "The Homeric Cento in Irenaeus, *Adversus Haereses* I,9,4." *VigChr* 21 (1967): 25-53.

Wingren, Gustaf. "The Doctrine of Creation: Not an Appendix but the First Article." Translated by E. M. Carlson. *WW* 4 (Fall 1984): 353-71.

INDEX OF REFERENCES TO IRENAEUS'S WORKS

Adversus Haereses

I Preface 1 35
I Preface 2 39, 42
I,1,1 44, 48
I,1,2 44
I,1,3 44
I,1,4 44
I,1,5 44
I,1,6 44
I,1,7 44
I,1,8 44
I,2,1 48, 49
I,2,2 48, 49
I,2,3 48, 49
I,2,4 49
I,2,5 50
I,2,6 50
I,3,6 229
I,4,1 138
I,5,3 109
I,5,6 106
I,6,1 50, 55, 119, 213
I,6,2 54, 214
I,6,3 200n20, 207
I,6,4 55, 213
I,7,1 168n87
I,7,2 54, 119
I,7,4 106
I,7,5 54, 213, 234, 235
I,8,1 50, 203
I,8,2 138
I,8,3 168n87
I,9,1 50, 203

I,9,2 203
I,9,3 158, 203
I,9,4 202, 203
I,9,5 202n25
I,10,1 83, 161, 178, 229
I,10,2 52, 70, 80, 191, 206,
  209n35, 229
I,11,1 46
I,11,2 46
I,11,3 46, 84
I,11,4 46
I,11,5 48
I,13,5 200n20, 207
I,14,1 48, 83
I,14,6 119
I,15,3 119
I,15,5 83
I,19,1 48
I,20,3 49, 129, 130n5
I,21,2 55
I,21,4 55, 56
I,22,1 133n9, 202n22,
  202,n23
I,23,2 39, 201
I,23,5 39
I,24,1 39, 201
I,24,4 54
I,25,1 39, 201
I,26,1 39, 54
I,27,2 191n8
I,27,3 234
I,29 39, 43
I,30 39
I,30,13 54

I,30,14 51

II,6 89
II,6,1 92, 104, 105, 107, 112,
    116, 124, 129, 131
II,6,2 104, 107, 114
II,6,4 128n3
II,7,6 152n55
II,7,7 152n55
II,9,1 105n69, 109, 192n9
II,9,2 38, 223
II,10,1 105n69
II,12,7 149
II,13,2 108n76
II,13,4 83, 110n84
II,13,8 110n84, 129n3
II,13,9 110n84
II,14,2 65
II,14,7 129
II,14,9 38
II,18,2 83
II,19,1 90
II,22,4 160, 216
II,22,6 216
II,24,2 84
II,25,4 83
II,27,1 202n23
II,27,2 91
II,28,1 202n23, 203n27
II,28,2 118n105, 148
II,28,3 165, 167
II,28,5 110n84, 129n3
II,28,6 110n84, 129n3
II,30,2 91n22
II,30,3 91n22
II,30,7 119
II,30,9 130, 143n40
II,31,1 41
II,34,2 83
II,35,4 188

III, Preface 188, 191
III,1,1 79, 188, 190, 202

III,1,2 202, 244
III,2 192
III,2,1 51, 19, 202n23
III,2,2 51, 189, 192, 193
III,3 192
III,3,1 193, 194n13, 195,n13
III,3,2 192, 196, 199n18, 200
III,3,3 192, 196, 199n18
III,3,4 200, 201, 207
III,4 192
III,4,1 192, 193, 194, 206
III,4,2 184, 193, 229, 242,
    244
III,4,3 40, 201
III,5 192
III,5,1 192
III,5,2 229
III,5,3 145, 225, 238
III,6,1 144, 181, 228n16, 240
III,6,1 122-23, 145
III,6,3 225
III,6,5 182n18, 225
III,7,1 220
III,9,2 123
III,9,3 41, 181
III,10,2 150
III,10,3 154, 227
III,10,5 157n64
III,11,1 41, 202n23
III,11,3 119, 150
III,11,5 83, 151
III,11,6 80, 121, 139n26,
    144, 188n1, 206, 237
III,11,9 44, 58
III,12,1 43, 51
III,12,2 43, 51
III,12,3 43, 51
III,12,4 43, 51
III,12,5 43, 51, 229
III,12,6 43, 51, 62, 202n23,
    225, 226
III,12,7 43, 51, 130, 147, 191
III,12,8 130, 147

III,12,12 19
III,12,13 133n10, 225, 226
III,13,1 157n64
III,13,2 43
III,14,2 191n8
III,15,1 202n23, 228
III,16,1 41
III,16,2 123
III,16,3 157n64
III,16,6 161, 162
III,16,8 41, 166, 208
III,17,1 181, 197n16, 216
III,17,2 182
III,17,3 181, 183
III,17,4 41, 157n64, 244
III,18,1 133, 156n63, 160
III,18,3 158, 181
III,18,7 156n63, 160
III,19,1 154, 156n63, 244
III,19,2 110n84
III,19,3 156n63
III,20,2 87, 158
III,21,9 244
III,21,10 160, 217
III,22,1 54, 152n53
III,22,3 161
III,23,1 156n63
III,23,7 156n63
III,24,1 183, 184, 191, 192,
  206, 229
III,24,2 82, 84, 85, 90, 93,
  100n49, 207
III,25,1 90, 96n37, 103n60,
  110, 115, 116, 124, 131,
  135n16, 243
III,25,3 41, 214
III,25,4 243
III,25,5 91, 110, 223, 243
III,25,7 208, 229

IV, Preface 3 41
IV, Preface 4 157n64, 175,
  244

IV,1,1 228
IV,2,3 146
IV,2,4 41
IV,2,7 156, 227
IV,4,3 176, 218
IV,5 156
IV,5,1 88
IV,5,2 145
IV,5,3 144, 227, 229
IV,5,4 144, 158n66, 227, 229
IV,5,5 144, 227, 231n22
IV,6,1 49, 91, 111, 112, 127,
  129
IV,6,3 111, 127, 128, 129
IV,6,5 101, 111, 113, 134,
  227, 230, 242
IV,6,6 91, 101, 113, 113n93,
  114, 132, 134, 146, 151,
  152, 220, 227, 233, 242
IV,6,7 96, 101, 111, 129, 130,
  132, 134, 164, 226
IV,7,1 144
IV,7,2 147, 229
IV,7,4 129, 144, 175n4
IV,8,1 182, 231n22
IV,8,2 157n63, 231n22
IV,9,1 145, 151, 158n66
IV,9,2 150, 151, 165
IV,10,1 123n126, 143, 144,
  145, 147, 237, 240
IV,11,2 165n82
IV,12,2 165
IV,12,4 145, 145n42, 150
IV,13,1 108, 230, 231
IV,14,2 158n66
IV,15,1 231
IV,15,2 230
IV,16,1 237
IV,16,2 149, 152, 227, 232,
  236
IV,16,3 83, 148, 232
IV,16,4 146, 150
IV,17,4 230

IV,18,3 143, 231n23, 235
IV,19,2 82
IV,19,3 93, 100n49
IV,20 94n32
IV,20,1 82, 85, 149n48, 175
IV,20,2 166n84
IV,20,3 175
IV,20,4 85, 91, 93, 100n49,
  147n44
IV,20,5 82, 83, 85, 86, 87, 88,
  121, 165, 178, 180n15, 184
IV,20,6 85, 87, 153n58, 175,
  178, 184
IV,20,7 133, 134, 151,
  153n58, 233
IV,20,8 157n64, 177
IV,20,9 145, 152
IV,20,10 157n64
IV,20,11 145
IV,21,1 229
IV,22,1 217n7
IV,22,2 135, 168-69, 173,
  228, 230n20, 231n22, 234
IV,23,1 147, 150
IV,23,2 147, 149, 150
IV,24,1 147, 156n63
IV,24,2 95, 147, 225, 228,
  229, 242
IV,25,1 227
IV,25,2 235
IV,25,3 123, 147
IV,26,1 147
IV,26,2 41, 194, 209n34, 244
IV,26,4 194
IV,26,5 194n13, 204
IV,26,6 243
IV,27,2 163, 164, 173, 228,
  234
IV,28,1 242
IV,28,2 165, 242
IV,28,3 215, 216
IV,29,1 220, 244, 246
IV,29,2 145, 219, 244

IV,31,1 240
IV,31,2 240
IV,31,3 240
IV,32,1 195, 204
IV,32,2 229n17
IV,33,1 177, 178
IV,33,4 152n53
IV,33,7 41, 209, 229
IV,33,8 191, 195n14
IV,33,9 240
IV,33,10 241
IV,34,1 146
IV,34,2 209
IV,34,3 157n64
IV,34,4, 235
IV,35,4 202n23
IV,36,3 144, 237, 240
IV,36,4 150, 222, 240
IV,36,5 78
IV,36,6 230n19
IV,36,7 152n53, 166
IV,37,1 78, 88, 89, 219,
  220n12
IV,37,2 41, 219, 220n12
IV,37,3 220n12
IV,37,4 220n12
IV,37,5 219, 220, 226
IV,37,6 220n12
IV,37,7 191n8, 220n12
IV,38,1 84
IV,38,2 216
IV,38,3 84, 87, 91
IV,39,1 230n17
IV,39,3 78, 220
IV,39,4 219, 220
IV,41,2 228, 230

V, Preface 156, 191, 192
V,1,1 181
V,1,2 54, 178
V,1,3 176
V,2,2 157n63
V,5,1 175, 236

V,5,2 133n10
V,6,1 54, 175, 176
V,8,1 183
V,8,3 108, 224
V,9,3 183, 230, 231
V,12,2 54
V,14,1 143, 144, 160, 235, 237
V,15,4, 143
V,16,1 133n10
V,16,2 83, 152n53, 176
V,16,3 156-57n63, 191n7, 217
V,17,1 143, 157n63, 157n64
V,17,2 143, 157n63
V,17,3 157n63
V,17,4 142
V,18,2 157n64, 180n15
V,18,3 136, 137, 139, 142
V,19,2 157n64
V,20,1 185, 191, 202n22, 209n35
V,20,2 161, 182n18, 185, 195, 204, 210
V,21,1 156n63, 216
V,21,3 156n63
V,27,1 228, 230, 242, 244
V,27,2 217n8, 220
V,29,2 162n79
V,32,1 169
V,32,2 169, 229
V,33,7 157n64
V,33,15 177n9
V,34,1 169
V,35,1 169
V,36,1 165, 167
V,36,2 167, 180n15
V,36,3 83

Proof of the Apostolic Preaching

2 145, 182n18, 224, 230
3 202, 202n25, 228, 229, 230
4 228
5 152n55, 156n63, 175, 176, 179-80
6 156n63, 178, 181, 202n22
7 156n63, 179, 180
8 83, 156n63, 182, 243, 245
9 181n17
11 152n55, 175
17 181n17, 235
21 238
22 152n53, 152n55, 176, 237
24 144, 182n18, 238
25 144
30 161
31 156n63, 217
32 157n64, 160
33 160
34 137, 139, 140, 141, 142, 160, 161
37 156n63, 217n7
38 156n63
40 145
41 79, 197n16
42 238
44 144, 240
45 144
46 145
47 83, 127, 151
49 178, 179
51 227
52 227
53 227
55 220n12
67 178
69 157n63
70 83
73 182
86 79
87 227,230
94 209
97 152n55
98 228

INDEX OF NAMES AND SUBJECTS

Abel 53, 143, 160, 234-36, 239, 241

Abraham 86, 121, 144, 145, 148, 149, 151, 169, 182, 227, 229-31, 234, 236-40, 255, 260, 278

Adam 109, 112, 121, 125, 143, 155, 159-61, 176, 215-17, 221, 232, 238, 255, 268, 278

Ambrose 27

Anaxagoras 65

Anonymous Christianity 4-9, 11-14, 26, 30, 31, 33, 62, 65, 77, 81, 123, 124, 147, 169, 172, 173, 186, 232, 234, 236, 237, 239, 241, 246, 250, 251, 263, 265-67, 271, 272, 273, 274, 277

Atheism 12, 18, 65

Augustine 8, 9, 27, 70, 217, 222

Aulén, Gustaf 155-157, 217

Barth, Karl 131, 220-22, 224, 270, 279

Benoit, André 32, 69, 70, 119, 130, 158, 174, 204, 209, 214, 215

Blanchard, M. 4

Boutin, Maurice 8

Brunner, Emil 155, 156, 176, 217

Church
extent of, in second century 67-81, 253-54
salvation outside of, 1, 2, 27-28, 64-67, 276-78
salvation through the, 4n9, 13, 19-26, 26-28, 30, 182-87, 188-212, 243, 245, 247, 248n33, 258-63, 264-69, 271-74, 280, 281

Clement of Alexandria 4, 6-10, 31, 58, 65, 98, 100, 120, 128, 164, 196, 209, 223, 224, 250, 278

Congar, Yves M.-J. 65-67, 194, 195, 206

Cornelius 27, 130, 147, 149, 256, 272

Cosmic cross 136, 140-42, 171, 255, 278, 281

Creation
knowledge of the Father through 84-118, 123-26, 131-42, 170-71, 220, 233-34, 242-46, 254, 262, 268, 271, 281-82
revelatory role of the Spirit in, 175-77, 186, 258, 262
revelatory role of the Word in, 7, 85-86, 89, 91-105, 109-15, 123-26, 131-42, 170-71, 220, 233-34, 242-46, 254, 255, 262, 268, 278, 281-82

Cyprian 1, 27, 70, 211

Daley, Brian 167

Daniélou, Jean 43, 47, 48, 51,
    80, 99, 120, 145, 150, 153,
    158, 159, 162, 165, 191,
    192, 202, 253, 254
de Chardin, Teilhard 118,
    156, 279, 280
de Letter, P. 29, 30
de Lubac, Henri 5, 9, 12,
    186, 210
de Moor, Leonard 31
DiNoia, J. A. 17
Dualism 41, 47, 54, 62, 110,
    252
Dufourcqu, M. A. 93, 100
Dupuis, James 5, 6, 278,
    279

Edwards, M. J. 36, 43
Enoch 227, 234, 236, 239,
    241, 278
Escoula, Louis 93-95, 97,
    116
Ethiopian eunuch 147, 149,
    150, 256, 272
Eusebius 70-72, 76, 196

Faith (*see also* Unbelief)
    implicit (*see also* Anony-
        mous Christianity) 17,
        62, 63, 172, 228, 248, 272
    insufficiency of, according
        to Gnostic teaching 55,
        252
    necessity of, for salvation
        1-3, 9, 13, 16, 17, 19, 21,
        22, 27, 28, 78, 113, 114,
        116, 117, 155, 156, 164,
        185-86, 209-12, 220, 222,
        226-49, 260-66, 268-72,
        276-78, 281
Freedom of the will 17, 78,
    89, 176n8, 214, 218-21,
    242, 243, 245, 263, 264,

269

Gnosticism 33-48, 51-63, 65,
    71, 89, 103, 106, 110, 122,
    129, 138, 143, 162, 175,
    188-91, 207, 209, 211, 213,
    214, 218, 224, 230, 251,
    252, 258, 269, 271, 277,
    281
González-Faus, José 88, 113,
    117, 134, 138, 153, 157,
    161, 176, 233, 236, 280
Goodness of God as self-revel-
    ation 78, 84, 86, 87, 91,
    223, 245, 254, 270
Gospel, necessity of, for sal-
    vation 1, 3, 12, 25, 28, 33,
    64, 81, 88, 115, 192, 234,
    248, 250, 253, 254, 266,
    269, 270, 272, 273
Gospel of Truth 57-60
Green, Henry 36, 40, 207
Gregory of Nazianzus 27
Gregory of Nyssa 8, 27, 161

Hacker, Paul 5, 10, 13, 66
Harnack, Adolf 143, 155-57,
    159, 217
Heathen 3, 18, 19, 38, 61,
    102, 103, 110, 225, 243
Heaven 23, 51, 76, 87, 122,
    137, 145, 161, 165-68, 175,
    178, 183, 228, 244, 257
Heretics 42, 127, 149, 154,
    162, 184, 188, 194, 200,
    201, 203, 207, 208, 210,
    224, 225, 245, 251
Hillman, Eugene 7, 278
Hochban, John 231
Holy Spirit (*see also under*
    Creation, Providence)
    174-87
Houssiau, Albert 96-98, 100,

Houssiau, Albert (*continued*) 101, 120, 123, 130, 133, 136, 152, 153, 168

Illumination by God 84, 99n45, 104, 108, 112, 114, 115, 118, 124, 125, 141, 170, 206, 246, 247, 271, 273 282
Image of God 54, 114, 152, 160, 176, 183, 237
Immanence of God 108, 140, 255, 278, 281
Immortality 39, 87, 154-56, 161, 166, 170, 206, 230, 244, 254, 282
Incomprehensibility of God 52, 86, 88
Infant salvation 216
Innocent XI 17

Jacob 86, 145, 255
Jerome 9, 194
Jesus Christ (*see* Word)
Jews (and Judaism) 37, 58, 61, 62, 105, 108, 114, 116, 117, 120, 121, 129, 130, 147, 207, 209, 224-27, 256
Jonas, Hans 41, 43, 44, 53, 56
Justin Martyr 4, 6-10, 31, 65, 74, 75, 97-100, 119, 128, 136, 138, 153, 175, 179, 250, 278, 279

Kelly, J. N. D. 175, 176, 192, 202, 205, 206
Knitter, Paul 29
Knowledge of God (*see* Creation, Faith, General revelation, Goodness of God, Illumination, Incomprehensibility, Providence, Reason, Special revelation, Vision of God)
Küng, Hans 2, 3, 80

Lawson, John 68, 156-59, 181, 196, 197, 199, 204, 207, 214, 215, 219
Lebreton, Jules 93, 94, 100, 120, 179
Libertinism 41
Liberty, human (*see* Freedom of the will)
Loewe, William P. 149
Logos spermatikos (*see* under Word)
Lot 227, 236, 239-41, 245
Luckhart, Robert 129, 130
Lumen gentium 18, 22
Luneau, Auguste 9, 121, 122, 238, 248

Marcion 40, 58, 120, 122, 146, 168, 172, 189, 200, 201, 214, 223, 234
Marcus 40, 69, 70
Millennium 165, 168, 171, 173, 257, 271, 282
Missions 1, 3, 33, 69, 72, 73, 146, 225, 250, 280
Moses 98, 121, 138, 145, 146, 148, 151, 182, 231, 232, 236, 255, 262, 278

Natural revelation (*see* General revelation)
Noah 29, 30, 121, 144, 164, 227, 234, 236-39, 255, 278
Non-Christian religions (*see* Religions, non-Christian)
Non-Christians, the status of (*see also* Pagans) 1-5, 9-12, 14, 16, 17, 22-25, 28-34, 61, 64, 66, 67, 88, 120,

Non-Christians (*continued*)
131, 169, 186, 222, 223,
247, 248, 250, 251, 254,
260, 261, 263, 265-70, 273,
274, 278, 280

Ochagavía, Juan 82, 83, 95,
96, 99, 102, 115, 127, 145,
146, 151-53, 166, 179, 180,
197, 202, 205, 210
O'Collins, Gerald 6, 7, 8,
278, 279
Orbe, Antonio 56, 58, 98, 99,
101, 102, 104-17, 122, 123,
130, 138-42, 152, 153, 171,
176, 218
Origen 7, 8, 52, 70, 128, 161,
189, 257, 280
Original sin 14, 25, 214, 216,
218, 268, 269

Paganism 33, 61, 69, 99, 252
Pagans (*see also* Non-Christians) 10, 12, 26, 28, 47,
61, 69, 89, 90, 100, 103,
109, 110, 112, 115-17, 120,
121, 124-26, 135, 169, 170,
173, 211, 223-25, 232, 234,
239, 241, 246-49, 252, 260,
261, 263, 266, 270, 272,
273, 277, 278
Pagels, Elaine H. 42, 45, 46,
54
Panikkar, Raimundo 10,
273-77
Patriarchs 109, 111, 123,
125, 135, 144, 146, 148,
163, 164, 178, 228, 232,
238, 263
Perkins, Pheme 37, 38, 43,
44, 46, 47, 51, 52, 54, 56,
61-63, 189
Pinnock, Clark 3

Pius XII 17, 20, 81
Plato 90, 98, 99, 110, 126,
138, 223, 243, 244, 279
Polycarp 68, 69, 200
Providence (*see also* Goodness of God)
knowledge of the Father
through 48, 50, 84, 89-
106, 108-18, 124-26, 131-
42, 164, 167, 169-72, 177,
183n20, 186, 223, 233,
243-46, 249, 254, 255,
258, 260, 262, 272, 273,
278
role of the Spirit in 177,
183n20, 186, 258, 262
role of the Word in 91, 92-
106, 108-18, 124-26, 131-
42, 164, 167, 169-72, 233,
255, 262, 278
Ptolemaeus 40, 42, 48, 59,
104, 168
Puech, H. C. 43, 58
Punishment, eternal 3, 33,
262-63, 269, 280
Punt, Neal 269, 270

Quispel, G. 58, 59

Rahner, Karl 5, 6, 9, 11-27,
30, 66, 67, 81, 172, 173,
243, 247, 248, 250, 251,
263, 269, 274, 276, 279
Reason, role of in salvation
93-118, 124-26, 177, 218,
252, 271, 276, 277
Recapitulation 41, 118, 119,
137, 142, 156-62, 171, 178,
210, 216, 221, 235, 256,
257, 279, 280, 282
Religions, non-Christian (*see
also* Non-Christians,
Paganism) 3, 4, 5, 6, 9,

Religions (*continued*) 10, 11, 14, 22-25, 28-32, 33, 37, 66, 131, 250, 263, 265, 273, 274

Repentance 1, 245

Revelation (*see also* Goodness of God, Theophanies, Wisdom, Word)

general (*see also* Creation, Providence) 2, 3, 14, 16-19, 25, 29, 91-99, 101-18, 121, 124, 130, 135, 173, 183, 231-34, 245, 246, 254, 255, 268, 269, 271-73, 278

special 29, 92, 96, 107, 109, 115, 124, 125, 148

universality of 89-91, 94, 96, 101, 118, 124, 136-42, 237, 242, 245, 262, 274

Rossano, Pietro 8

Rousseau, Adelin 82, 86, 92, 100, 101, 107, 133, 136-38, 165, 169, 185, 190, 191, 195, 197-99, 201, 202, 215, 216

Rule of truth 201, 202, 204, 208, 211, 228, 244, 245, 259, 266, 281

Salvation (*see* Church, Creation, Faith, Gospel, Providence, Reason, Repentance, Revelation, Universal salvific will)

Schlette, Heinz 11

Schmidt, Carl 43

Smith, Morton 35

Tertullian 70, 75, 76, 110, 203, 223, 231

Theophanies 112, 135, 143, 148, 232, 246, 255, 262, 278

Thornton, L. S. 31, 151

Tillich, Paul 10

Tradition of the Church (*see also* Rule of Truth) 37, 51, 52, 68, 72, 79, 80, 82, 89, 90, 109-12, 116, 125, 127, 128, 144, 169, 171, 179, 184, 188-202, 204-6, 208, 209, 211, 226, 229, 245, 258, 259, 268, 282

Unbelief 3, 65, 77, 108, 113, 114, 116, 215, 220, 221, 228, 234, 244, 260, 268, 270, 278

Universal salvific will 13, 30, 77, 89, 124, 264

Universalism 62, 157, 161, 171, 212, 244, 257, 269, 280

Valentinus 27, 36, 39, 40, 42-46, 53, 54, 56, 58, 59, 77, 102-4, 109, 110, 115, 138, 153, 200, 201, 234, 277

Vallée, Gérard 40, 41, 207, 223

van Unnik, Willem Cornelis 37, 40, 43, 44, 58, 65

Vatican II 9, 12, 17, 203, 248

Vempeny 7, 279

Vernet 93, 159

Vision of God 85-88, 105, 120, 121, 125, 134, 150, 158, 169, 171, 184, 233, 245, 254, 256, 260, 262

Wingren, Gustav 38, 157, 220-22n12, 229n17, 279

Wisdom of God 8, 49, 85, 91, 105, 109, 175, 177, 185,

Wisdom of God (*continued*)
  254, 258, 262
Word (*see also* Cosmic cross,
  Creation, Illumination,
  Providence, Wisdom)
  descent into Hell 163-
    64,172, 228
  incarnate 20, 23, 225,
    264, 271, 282
  Logos spermatikos 7, 8,
    123
  mediator of revelation
    111-118, 121-26, 127-73,
    177, 179-81, 192, 226,
    227, 230, 232, 233, 239-
    46, 255-57, 262, 271, 273,
    281, 282
  pre-incarnate 23, 27, 28,
    91-100, 135, 152, 153,
    229, 232, 233, 236, 237,
    239-46, 262, 263, 271,
    278, 281

Zwingli, Ulrich 270

ABOUT THE AUTHOR

TERRANCE L. TIESSEN is currently Professor of Theology and Ethics at Providence Theological Seminary in Manitoba, Canada. For 13 years, he taught theology at Asian Theological Seminary in the Philippines. With an M.A. from Wheaton College Graduate School and a Th.M. from Westminster Theological Seminary, he completed his Ph.D. at the Loyola School of Theology of Ateneo de Manila University. It was during his time as a missionary that he developed an interest in the subject of the salvation of the unevangelized. Years of teaching theology in another culture gave him a great appreciation for the theologians of the early centuries of the Church's history. He has authored a number of scholarly articles, including "Gnosticism as Heresy: The Response of Irenaeus," forthcoming in a collection of papers from the Conference on Christianity in the Context of Early Hellenistic Judaism and Gnosticism (Toronto, June, 1991).